The Magistrates' Court

An Introduction

Putting justice into words

The Pocket A-Z
of Criminal Justice

~ **Bryan Gibson**

A quickly absorbed jargon-busting
introduction to the language of criminal
justice and its unique and fascinating usages.

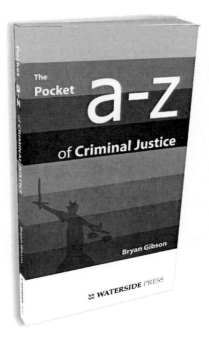

- **Get up to speed** with the
  language of criminal justice
- **Touchstones** aid
  understanding and memory
- **Handy reference guide** for
  students and practitioners

The Pocket A-Z draws together words
and phrases commonly encountered by
practitioners and researchers - connecting
key terms, concepts, processes, laws, people
and events.

2,000 plus entries and cross-references provide insight and
perspective, making it invaluable to anyone involved in criminal
justice work or study.

It also includes extensive sections on **Touchstones and
Curiosities**, commonly encountered **Acronyms and
Abbreviations** and a **Timeline**.

April 2009 | P/back | ISBN 978-1-904380-50-4

View sample entries and order at **WatersidePress.co.uk**

☙ **WATERSIDE** PRESS

The Magistrates' Court

An Introduction

FIFTH EDITION

Bryan Gibson

Consultant Mike Watkins

≋ WATERSIDE PRESS

THE MAGISTRATES' COURT: AN INTRODUCTION

Fifth Edition

Bryan Gibson
Consultant **Mike Watkins**

Published 2009 by
Waterside Press
Sherfield Gables
Sherfield on Loddon
Hook
Hampshire
United Kingdom RG27 0JG

Telephone +44(0)1256 882250 Low cost UK landline calls 0845 2300 733
E-mail enquiries@watersidepress.co.uk
Online catalogue www.WatersidePress.co.uk

ISBN 1904380 522 (Paperback)
ISBN-13 9781904380528 (Paperback)

Cataloguing-In-Publication Data A catalogue record for this pocketbook can be obtained from the British Library.

Cover design © 2009 Waterside Press.

North American distributor International Specialised Book Services (ISBS), 920 NE 58th Ave, Suite 300, Portland, Oregon, 97213-3786, USA
Tel: 1 800 944 6190 Fax 1 503 280 8832 orders@isbs.com www.isbs.com

Printed by the MPG Books Group in the UK

e-book *The Magistrates' Court: An Introduction* is available as an e-book and also for subscribers at myilibrary.com (eBook ISBN 9781906534806)

Previous editions were published in 1989, 1995, 1999 and 2001 (data available on request)

Contents

Preface

The first edition of this book was written 20 years ago. Its purpose then, as now, was to fill a gap in the literature. There was no comparable guide for anyone coming 'cold' to the topic (which is still the case, so far as I am aware).

It immediately struck a cord and has been continuously in print ever since through four editions, enabling newcomers to quickly get to grips with the subject.

The time has now come not just for updating, but a radical rethink, so that this new edition is a completely fresh one, re-written so as to incorporate the best of the old but also to take account of the way in which the magistracy and the way in which the magistrates' courts are administered have evolved towards the end of the first decade of the twenty-first century. Naturally, it also takes account of many changes of law, practice, procedure and sentencing.

But the book remains true to its roots. It was never intended as a 'clever' tome, rather as a straightforward account for a range of potential readers, whether coming to the topic for the first time or seeking to widen their understanding.

What struck me when I first ventured into a magistrates' court was how bewildering things can seem to an outsider. Everything invited questions: 'Why did they do that' or 'So whatever does that mean'. Written at a basic, but informative, level this book is for people who want answers to these kinds of question. I hope that it will also help them to place the work of magistrates' courts within a wider social and justice-related context. After all, magistrates are part of the community, local and national: a key component in helping to keep liberal democracy alive and well.

Past editions appealed in particular to newly and recently appointed magistrates as well as more seasoned participants in the work of the courts (who seemed to appreciate a work focusing on key points so as to reduce what can be a complex world into what I hope is easy reading and manageable 'chunks').

The current edition has also been re-focused so as to emphasise the kind of training which now exists, related materials and the national competences which magistrates must acquire and continually hone through appraisal and other mechanisms (see, in particular, *Chapters 3* and *4*). It also tries to bring out the importance of judicial independence, and the unique nature of a magistracy not schooled in law but supported in its task by legal advisers who themselves are nowadays subject to similarly rigorous and ongoing training, development and progression.

Magistrates' courts are one of our oldest public institutions, with a considerable heritage (see *Chapter 1*). In their modern guise they are perhaps unrecognizable compared with what went before, including due to a high level of 'on the job' training for both magistrates and staff (see mainly *Chapters 3, 4* and *6*). There is also nowadays greater clarity with regard to fairness and due process in relation to those people coming into contact with the courts - whether as defendants, victims, witnesses or practitioners - and integrity in general (see in particular *Chapter 5*).

I hope that some of this filters through in the pages which follow. The text returns repeatedly to the nature and content of judicial decision-making, the need for impartiality, equality of treatment, even-handedness and structured decision-making.

Magistrates are for the largest part ordinary citizens,[1] drawn from a broad spectrum of society, selected against set criteria and trained for the role which they perform as an unpaid public service. Nowhere else in the world has anything like it existed or withstood the test of time.

It is in many ways remarkable that a way of 'doing justice' (or 'delivering' it as some people prefer to say) based on a working relationship between ordinary citizens making their voluntary contribution to public service and qualified professionals has survived. If anything it seems to to be growing stronger.

The arrangements for training and development have undergone a sea change since the first edition of this book was published. This has led to greater clarity concerning each and all of magistrates' many functions, duties and responsibilities. A good sense of the wide range of magistrates' work can be gained from *Chapters 7* to *10*.

Ultimately, magistrates uphold those values for which they were appointed (*Chapter 3*) and so long as this continues no one is likely to seriously challenge or wish to change the way in which local justice is delivered. Recent national developments have concentrated not so much on altering the existing arrangements, but making sure that they work well and effectively. That is why the system described in this edition reflects an enhanced 'professionalism' in all matters.

If magistrates are publicly criticised on occasions it is perhaps largely due to the fact that they are having to react to the requirements of rapidly changing and sometimes poorly thought out or partly implemented legislation, or to other external factors or uncertainties beyond their control, rather than due to any fundamental flaw in what is now called 'Criminal Justice: Simple, Speedy, Summary' (CJSSS) (*Chapter 2*).

---

1. See the note on district judges (magistrates' courts) in *Chapter 1*.

I hope that the *Glossary* at the end of the book will help readers to understand many everyday terms. There is sometimes a tendency across the Criminal Justice System (CJS) to 'speak in code' and anything that helps people to understand the everyday (and sometimes hidden) language of the courts serves to alleviate this. It has been extended and refined in this edition to take account of some of the many new abbreviations and terms (no doubt there are already new ones waiting in the wings!).

A short *Timeline* has been added in order to give a sense of the rich heritage of the magistracy and its key stages of development over the centuries.

Throughout the book the intention has been to explain things in a straightforward and accessible way. The aim was to provide an overview free from superfluous chapter and verse (which the more advanced reader can supplement by further reading in specialist areas, or by finding an experienced 'helping hand').

Court staff and senior magistrates can be a mine of information for newer colleagues, other CJS practitioners or students. The internet is also now a ready source of information (although care must be taken to ensure that it is accurate and up-to-date). The addresses of a number of useful websites are incorporated within the text.

Acknowledgements

It would be impossible to thank all of the people who have in some way contributed to the sum of knowledge that went into writing this book. My especial thanks are due to Mike Watkins who is closer to the everyday action than I am and who kindly agreed to act as a consultant and contribute some of the text. Winston Gordon and Andy Wesson also assisted with earlier editions and must be thanked for helping to create the emerging foundations on which this edition builds.

I am indebted to the Magistrates' Association and Justices' Clerks' Society whose materials and publications contain so much that is of use to someone trying to piece together trends and developments; and the Judicial Studies Board for giving permission for me to to reproduce examples from their Sentencing Guidelines - and whose website has also been particularly useful in keeping up-to-date.

Some of the authors I have worked with such as John Hostettler (on whose recent *History of Criminal Justice in England and Wales* I was involved in the editing), Peter Villiers (who similarly allowed me to learn more about *Police and Policing*), Paul Cavadino (with whom I recently wrote a third edition of *The Criminal Justice System*) and David Faulkner of the Centre for Criminological Research, Oxford University who helped with books on *The New Ministry of Justice* and *The New Home Office*.

This book could not have been written but for the 25 years that I spent working in the magistrates' courts and so it is to many ex-colleagues that I also owe a debt of gratitude. Preparedness to share and discuss information and views, especially where these impact on core values, is an indelible feature of life in the magistrates' court.

This edition follows a new format. It is also available to institutions and others as an e-book, including through a growing number of *ilibraries* (not an error as my proof reader and spell check thought, but another addition to the burgeoning world of the 'iword'). I have Alex Gibson to thank for this. He has revamped all Waterside Press publications for the modern age and made them available anywhere, as if by magic. (I doubt whether I ever imagined, when writing the first edition that one day the book might be opened anywhere in the world at the flick of a mouse).

Finally, Jane Green has worked tirelessly on the house-editing.

Bryan Gibson
April 2009

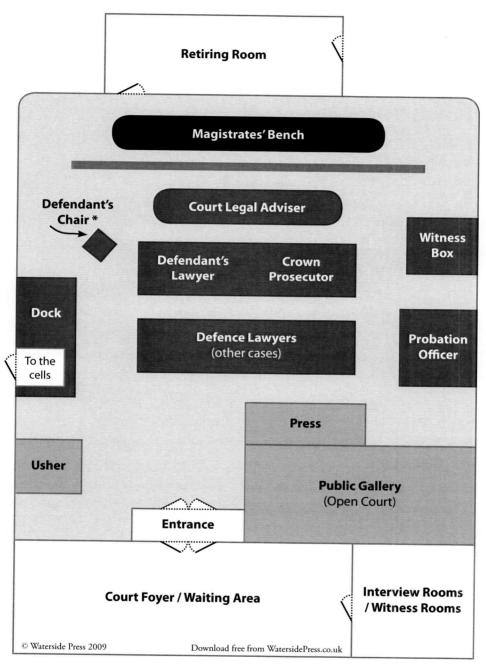

Example of a courtroom layout

* Use of the dock or a chair for the defendant can vary: see *Dock* in the *Glossary*
A less formal arrangement is likely re youth or family work, *Chapters 8* and *9*

About the author

Bryan Gibson is a barrister, former co-editor of *Justice of the Peace* and a regular contributor to specialist journals. He has also written for *The Times, Guardian, Sunday Express,* BBC TV and *The Stage.* He founded Waterside Press in 1989 where as director and editor-in-chief he has been engaged in 'putting justice into words' through a range of books about the courts, sentencing, prisons, policing, human rights, diversity, restorative justice, legal history and penal reform.

He was for 25 years a justices' clerk and during much of that time an elected member of the Council of the Justices' Clerks' Society (and chair of its influential Criminal Law Committee and National Criminal Law Network) when he also served as legal adviser to the Magistrates' Association's Sentencing of Offenders Committee.

In the 1990s he was one of several pioneers who succeeded in getting a system of Unit Fines onto the Statute Book (briefly since it was abolished 18 months later!). Whilst working in Basingstoke, Hampshire he helped to develop the country's first 'Custody-free Zone' for juvenile offenders which was sustained for over three years.

He is the author of *The Criminal Justice System* (2008) (with Paul Cavadino); The *New Ministry of Justice* and *The New Home Office* (both 2007; 2nd editions 2008); *Law, Justice and Mediation: The Legend of St Yves* (2007) which introduced the patron saint of lawyers to an English audience; and the Waterside Press *Pocket A-Z of Criminal Justice* (2009) on which the entries in the *Glossary* in this work are based.

Consultant

Mike Watkins is a freelance training consultant. A solicitor (now non-practising), he worked for over 33 years in the Magistrates' Courts Service, 22 of these as a justices' clerk (and latterly) Director of Legal Services for Warwickshire where he also had lead responsibility for the training of all of the magistrates in that county.

He has written national training materials for the Judicial Studies Board, the Magistrates' Association and the Universities of Birmingham and Cambridge.

His other publications with Waterside Press include the former *Magistrates' Bench Handbook, An Introduction to the Youth Court* and *The Sentence of the Court* (four editions: both with other co-authors). He also acted as consultant on Bryan Gibson's *Criminal Justice Act 2003: A Guide to the New Procedures and Sentencing.*

CHAPTER ONE

Introduction

A 25 year-old man will appear before magistrates charged with the murder of ....

IMAGES OF THE MAGISTRACY

Members of the public may well have seen or heard reports such as this in the newspapers or on the radio and TV. They will often have seen press reports (or even just lists) of 'court results' setting out the decisions of magistrates following court hearings in local magistrates' courts. They may then have wondered:

- Why the magistrates' court: isn't it a jury that deals with murder cases?
- What part do magistrates play when it comes to a charge of murder?
- Who and what are these magistrates anyway?
- What sorts of things do they do?
- Aren't they 'middle aged, middle class and middle-minded: all greengrocers, farmers and retired colonels?
- They're all white: why aren't there any black magistrates?
- So-and-so in the Packing Department at work is a magistrate and she always strikes me as sensible and down to earth: she's an ordinary sort of person so what's she doing being a magistrate?
- Why can't I be a magistrate?

This book provides answers to all these questions and many more. It will also be seen how great are the misperceptions contained in some of the comments above.

'Justice of the Peace' or 'Magistrate'?
These two descriptions tend to be used interchangeably. People are appointed to the office of justice of the peace (JP) and can then after undergoing training as described in *Chapter 3* sit as magistrates in a magistrates' court to hear cases brought before that court. As is also explained in that chapter such people usually keep the title of JP after they retire from that role (though their powers then effectively cease).

So, in this sense, JP is a generic title whilst 'magistrate' describes those JPs who sit in court to make judicial decisions, or to 'adjudicate' on cases as it is called. In other words, all magistrates will be JPs, but not all JPs will be serving magistrates.

District judges

Other people sit 'as magistrates'. Most strikingly there are a number of district judges who do so. Their full title is 'district judge (magistrates' courts).[1] They are professional lawyers who have been appointed to that position as a full-time (or in some cases part-time) occupation. They have all the powers of a magistrates' court described in later chapters but sit alone in court to make the same kinds of decisions. Possibly, they sit to hear more complex, locally sensitive or lengthy cases, but also to help deal with long lists of more ordinary cases in times of pressure.

The work of ordinary everyday magistrates

The chapters which follow concentrate on the work of ordinary magistrates. They explore in much greater detail issues such as who magistrates are, how they are appointed, what sort of work they do and the skills, values and safeguards to justice they bring to their duties. However, much of what is said about what happens in court will apply equally to district judges. They are part of the same system of justice described in *Chapter 2*.

Magistrates of the kind already described earlier are not qualified lawyers (except possibly purely coincidentally). They are 'lay' people who voluntarily serve in that capacity as a form of public service. How this works and how they manage to understand the law is described in *Chapter 6, Magistrates and the Law*.

It is sufficient for now to note the lay nature of the vast majority of JPs (although the longstanding term 'lay magistrate' tends no longer to be used as detracting from the training and skills for the role which are explained in *Chapters 3* and *4*).

The appointments system for magistrates, which is also explained in *Chapter 3*, should dispel some of the casual observations noted at the start of this chapter.

A SHORT HISTORICAL NOTE

The concept of justices of the peace has roots going back to at least the eleventh century although it is usually the Justices of the Peace Act 1361 which is credited with marking the start of what has become the magistracy of today.

Events of that decade, including in particular the Black Death and the wars with France, prompted the king, Edward III, to take measures to ensure good order and to maintain his authority in difficult times via the 1361 Act. He did so in the following terms (and in the typically never-ending sentences of the times):

First, That in every County of England shall be assigned for the keeping of the Peace, one Lord, and with him three or four of the most worthy in the County, with some learned in the Law, and they shall have Power to restrain the Offenders, Rioters, and all other Barators,

---

1. Once called 'stipendiary magistrates', i.e. paid a stipend. There are atypical situations in which someone may act 'as a magistrate' when not a JP involving certain holders of high judicial office.

and to pursue, arrest, take, and chastise them according their Trespass or Offence; and to cause them to be imprisoned and duly punished according to the Law and Customs of the Realm, and according to that which to them shall seem best to do by their Discretions and good Advisement . . . and to take and arrest all those that they may find by Indictment, or by Suspicion, and to put them in Prison; and to take of all them that be [not][2] of good Fame, where they shall be found, sufficient Surety and Mainprise of their good Behaviour towards the King and his People, and the other duly to punish; to the Intent that the People be not by such Rioters or Rebels troubled nor endamaged, nor the Peace blemished, nor Merchants nor other passing by the Highways of the Realm disturbed, nor [put in the Peril which may happen] of such Offenders: . . .

The 1361 Act remains in force[3] and quite apart from the fact that it still contains the power to bind people over (*Chapter 10*) other things can be noted:

- the role was not restricted to just a 'lord' but included 'four of the most worthy in the county': this is still very exclusive and hierarchical but by the standards of those times it represented the start of a process that would eventually, hundreds of years on, open up the magistracy to ordinary members of the public from diverse backgrounds: see *Chapter 3*
- magistrates at that time appeared to be investigators, prosecutors and sentencers (and even possibly gaolers) all rolled into one, whereas today these functions are clearly separated out: *Chapter 2*
- magistrates (or at least 'some of them') were required to be 'learned in the law'. That requirement no longer applies, although again as will be seen later (particularly in *Chapters 3 and 4*) magistrates do now undertake considerable training for that role. They receive their formal and technical legal advice from legally qualified justices' clerks and their legal teams (*Chapter 6*)
- at that time (and until as late as 2005) the jurisdiction of magistrates was largely based on local commission areas (mainly county based). Individual magistrates are now appointed to a single, national commission and exercise a jurisdiction over the whole of England and Wales.

The role and heritage of justices of the peace have continued and developed for nearly six and half centuries and although unique have been adapted for use in many parts of the world although rarely with so great an input by ordinary members of the public.

---

2. Possibly an early 'typo': clearly the aim was to penalise people who were 'not of good fame'. Apparently the clerics who later translated the Act from its original Norman-French inserted the '[not]' which does not appear in the original version. It is nothing new in the law: in 1990 a Home office document said that offenders should get their 'just desserts' (or puddings!) rather than 'deserts' (what is deserved).
3. Still with the '[not]' intact.

Other landmarks and events

The *Timeline* at the end of the book identifies a number of other landmarks. These include such events as 'reading the Riot Act' before calling on the local militia to keep order (1660), the Bill of Rights which set judges and magistrates on the road to judicial independence (1689), the 'police courts' of the mid-1700s onwards (magistrates are emphatically not police or any other kind of courts, other than their own), the Vagrancy Act 1837 and a host of juvenile and Criminal Justice Acts across the years. Legislation as recent as the Constitutional Reform Act 2005 finally entrenched magistrates' judicial independence (see particularly *Chapters 2* and *5*).

CREATURES OF STATUTE

It is sometimes pointed out that magistrates' courts are 'creatures of statute'. By this is meant that they exist solely as a legal entity under Parliamentary legislation and that their powers and jurisdiction stem from (and are defined and limited by) various Acts of Parliament and 'Statutory Instruments' (or SIs: see the *Glossary*). Some of the principal Summary Jurisdiction Acts, Magistrates' Courts Acts, Courts Acts and Criminal Justice Acts are noted in the *Timeline* at the end of the book.

But magistrates' courts are also creatures of the Common Law which they follow and apply, as all courts must. They also apply their judicial discretion to the facts and merits of individual cases. They swear or affirm that they will act according to both the law *and* 'the usages of the Realm' (*Chapter 3*).

Many other things affect their 'existence'. They follow Practice Directions from the Lord Chief Justice and other senior members of the judiciary. They are part of a hierarchy of courts and work within a larger network of services known as the Criminal Justice System (even if they must act 'at a distance' to preserve their judicial integrity) (see especially *Chapters 2* and *5*). They use skills and 'competences' acquired through training, development and experience on the bench (*Chapters 3* and *4*); and their inherent powers and jurisdiction allow them to deal with residual matters. Laws cannot always anticipate every minute twist and turn, even if, importantly, there is now a Criminal Procedure Rule Committee (CPRC) which is seeking to codify procedures and integrate these across the criminal courts. They follow guidelines issued by the independent Sentencing Guidelines Council (SGC) (*Chapter 7*), pursue good practice, engage in case management, apply human rights law, give reasons and explanations. They employ structured decision-making so as to deal fairly, effectively and consistently with the cases coming before them.

So magistrates and their courts are creatures of statute 'of a kind'. But they are much more than that as the chapters which follow will show.

THE MODERN MAGISTRACY

The involvement of ordinary members of the public in the delivery of justice is at the heart of our judicial and social system. There are around 30,000 magistrates and many members of the public are called for jury service, itself democratised since 2003 by being opened up to a wider range of people (including to magistrates).

The earlier administrative functions of magistrates (at one stage they were also the local authority) have all but disappeared and their current role is almost wholly a judicial one. Another distinction can be drawn between the administrative (in the sense of 'appertaining to management' or 'administration') and the judicial. As will be seen in *Chapter 2* there are key mechanisms separating out the management role of HM Court Service (HMCS) and decision-making by magistrates.

For practical purposes all criminal proceedings, ranging from parking to murder, start out in the magistrates' courts. Over 95 per cent of these cases are finalised by acquittal or conviction and sentence by magistrates. In fact magistrates pass sentences in relation to some 1.3 million offences each year, or 5,000 every working day nationally.

Although unpaid, magistrates do receive certain travel, subsistence and loss of earnings allowances (but not an attendance allowance) (*Chapter 3*). Their make-up is widely varied in terms of social, ethnic, occupation, age and other backgrounds, so that perceptions of magistrates as 'middle-class, middle-minded' people (above) are increasingly resonant of a bygone age and less inclusive times.

TIMES PAST

The image of magistrates contained in historical novels such as *Mist Over Pendle* or Thomas Hardy's *Mayor of Casterbridge* (Hardy was himself a magistrate[4] in Dorset) riding from town to town on horseback to deal with offenders may have a touch of romance but such scenes are now decidedly very long gone.

Pictured in the nineteenth century, the character George in Julian Barnes' 2005 novel *Arthur and George* says of magistrates:

> But then, what were magistrates anyway? They scarcely qualified as members of the legal profession. Most were just self-important amateurs dressed in a little brief authority.

If only George were around today ...

---

4.   As was of course Henry Fielding at Bow Street, perhaps England's most famous magistrates' court which closed its doors in 2007. Many well-known people have served quietly on the bench.

CHAPTER TWO

Magistrates and the Justice System

Most citizens will have a broad idea of what is meant by 'Justice System'. Yet even some regular practitioners might find it hard to describe every part of it. People tend to work in and train for a particular specialism or area of the system. They may know something of its adjacent parts, but there will be other parts, more remote from their everyday work, where their knowledge and understanding will be less well rounded. What *is* important is to quickly acquire a view of the bigger picture: of how the various departments, organizations and 'building blocks' fit together. This chapter gives an overview, placing magistrates and their courts at its centre.

Three main parts to the system

Magistrates' courts are part of three distinct 'sub-systems' of justice:

- the Criminal Justice System (or CJS)
- the Civil Justice System; and
- the arrangements for Family Courts and related matters.

It may be helpful to visualise different networks of courts, processes and inter-agency arrangements. There are common aspects: a witness is a witness and taking an oath (or making an affirmation) follows the same pattern wherever it occurs. But, as will be explained, rules, procedures, practice and e.g. matters of evidence may differ.

Magistrates also carry out tasks which are not quite so readily compartmentalised as explained in *Chapter 10, A Diverse Mix of 'Other' Responsibilities*.

THE CRIMINAL JUSTICE SYSTEM (CJS)

It is perhaps criminal cases with which most people associate magistrates' courts. They are a mainstay of 'the adult magistrates' court' (a term explained in *Chapter 7*). Criminal cases tend to be the most visible. They can hit the headlines (even if tens of thousands of them never feature in the media). They are talked about. Some have become landmarks such as the Stephen Lawrence case which is mentioned later in this chapter. The main stages of a criminal case are:

- the reporting of or detection of crime
- criminal investigation
- prosecution

- a plea of guilty or failing this a trial
- conviction or acquittal
- sentence (when and if someone is convicted)
- the carrying out of sentences (sometimes styled 'offender management')
- release on parole (with regard to longer custodial sentences) or on licence
- work with offenders in prison or in the community; and
- work with victims of crime.

Many readers will have visited a magistrates' court (see 'Open Court' below), seen offenders doing unpaid work in the community (sometimes nowadays wearing distinctive, brightly coloured 'tabbards') and will be familiar with popular (if not always precise) representations of the CJS from books, films and TV. The term 'law enforcement' extends to matters such as crime prevention, crime reduction, arrest, detention and making sure that offenders comply with orders of the court. Fines must be paid or the defaulter will be pursued. If someone does not keep to the terms of his or her community sentence or prison release licence then the 'breach' will be followed up and that person may find himself or herself back in court or being recalled to prison.

Key components of criminal justice
The main components of the CJS are:

- the police
- the Crown Prosecution Service (CPS) or other public prosecutors such as local authorities, HM Revenue & Customs (HMR&C), the Department for Work and Pensions and with regard to cases inevitably bound for trial and sentence in the Crown Court, the Serious Fraud Office (SFO)[1]
- judges and magistrates (also known as 'the judiciary'), and jurors[2]
- HM Court Service (HMCS)
- the National Probation Service (NPS)
- HM Prison Service (HMPS); and
- the Parole Board (with regard to longer term offenders).

These are supplemented by a range of agencies or services whose aims, purposes and roles are noted at various points in this or other chapters of the book.

---

1. The CPS is entitled to take over many public or other prosecutions (but not, e.g. those of the Attorney-General or SFO)
2. Jurors would not normally be considered as 'judiciary'. They are ordinary, untrained members of the public.

Crime prevention and crime reduction

The shared priorities of practitioners across the CJS include the twin aims of crime prevention and crime reduction. Unlike the situation in many countries, there is no national police force for England and Wales. The 'thin blue line' is maintained by local police forces and police authorities.[3] Policing does fall within the remit of the Home Office (see later in this chapter), but the police, like magistrates, are locally or area-based, the former under a chief constable.[4] Each chief constable decides how his or her force will operate, within any nationwide guidelines, duties or legitimate directives.[5]

By 'police officer' is usually meant a constable from one of the 43 ordinary or 'civil' police forces, whose boundaries, broadly speaking, coincide with the arrangements to provide other CJS services. There are some specialist (or 'non-geographic') forces such as the British Transport Police (BTP) or Ministry of Defence Police (MODP). Some policing bodies are geared to the age of the internet and the international nature of some modern-day crime, such as Interpol, Europol and the Child Exploitation and Online Protection Centre (CEOP).

The Crown Prosecution Service (CPS) prosecutes offences (once they are referred to it by the police[6]) after reviewing each case to see whether it meets various tests and criteria, including whether there is enough evidence and whether prosecution is in the public interest. A striking example of where it might not be in the public interest is provided by decisions of the CPS in a number of cases in which those involved in helping terminally-ill people to attend clinics abroad to commit 'assisted suicide' have not been prosecuted. Like the police officer on the street, the Crown prosecutor exercises discretion. Equally, like the police, the CPS has targeted pressing problems such as domestic violence and hate crime (offences aimed at minority groups: see *Chapter 7* and the *Glossary*). There is a Code for Crown Prosecutors and specialist prosecutors, e.g. for rape cases, fraud and juveniles. Some lesser matters can be conducted in the magistrates' court by designated CPS case workers who, unlike Crown prosecutors, need not be fully qualified as solicitors or barristers.

There are some agencies with both an investigating and prosecuting function, such as the Serious Fraud Office (SFO) and HM Revenue & Customs (HMR&C). There are in fact several hundred types of public prosecutor who may be able to use far-reaching investigatory powers.[7] Alongside the police, they bring cases to court where magistrates regularly make decisions concerning the liberty of the subject,

---

3. Police boards in Scotland and Northern Ireland.
4. Or in the case of the Metropolitan Police Service (MPS) a commissioner.
5. For an overview, see *Police and Policing: An Introduction* (2009), Villiers P, Waterside Press.
6. The term 'police' is widely defined for this purpose: see the Prosecution of Offences Act 1985.
7. Readers may be aware of criticisms levelled at local authorities which used legislation intended for terrorism cases in order to deploy surveillance techniques with regard to benefit fraud. The heightened context for law enforcement cannot be ignored. There has been a sea-change in methods, techniques and approaches. Powers have been greatly enhanced post-September 11.

including whether a suspect or accused person should:

- be held in police detention whilst an investigation continues
- be given bail or kept in custody pending their trial; or
- where magistrates have jurisdiction (see 'Summary Powers' below) be sentenced to imprisonment or some other sentence.

How cases come before magistrates, bail-related matters, the trial of a criminal case and sentencing are outlined in *Chapter 7*.

The CPS has wide powers to take over cases from most other public prosecutors (but not, e.g. the Attorney General). It can also do so when a private citizen brings a prosecution. In the Stephen Lawrence Case (1993) which involved the racist murder of a black youth by white young men, Stephen's parents relied on this ancient right of a private individual to launch their own prosecution after the CPS declined to proceed with the case. Notoriously, the defendants were acquitted, but the case became a rallying-point in relation to the proper treatment of minorities by the police and other CJS services after the former were deemed to be 'institutionally racist'. It also triggered a change to the double jeopardy law: the fundamental rule of English criminal law under which no one can be tried twice for the self-same matter. They can now so far as certain scheduled, mostly serious, offences are concerned.

Once a Case Reaches Court

The arrangements for access to justice (including legal aid), the work of the courts, for carrying out sentences and parole are all Ministry of Justice (MOJ)-related responsibilities. The administration of the courts apart, two key MOJ-related CJS services are the NPS and HMPS, which jointly make up the National Offender Management Service (NOMS). The duties of the NPS include producing pre-sentence reports for the courts and managing offenders in the community as described in *Chapter 7*. HMPS carries out custodial orders of the courts by holding prisoners in secure and humane conditions, whether they are:

- on remand, i.e. awaiting their trial or sentence; or
- serving sentences of imprisonment or detention in a young offender institution (YOI) after being convicted of offences.[8]

HMPS operates different prison regimes according to the type and length of the prisoner's sentence and the requirements of individual prisoners such as their need to participate in courses, education, training or pre-release rehabilitation and reset-

---

8. Other forms of detention may also be involved or managed by HMPS, such as immigration detention centres or 'holding centres'. These do not involve magistrates and are beyond the scope of this work.

tlement schemes in readiness for their return to and 'reintegration' into the community. The security and control of prisons and the safety of prisoners and staff within a prison and the protection of members of the community from the escape of dangerous or 'high-risk' prisoners are primary considerations for HMPS. The NPS organizes and facilitates a wide variety of community sentences in the guise of 'generic community sentences' (*Chapter 7*) and cooperates with HMPS concerning release from prison and the continuation of preventive work with offenders within the community, sometimes dubbed 'seamless', 'end-to-end' or 'integrated' sentences.

All these processes have undergone a great deal of refinement in modern times. Many are still evolving and it is important for judges, magistrates and all other CJS practitioners to keep up-to-date with local as well as national developments: one reason for a range of training and liaison arrangements.

CJS Online

CJS Online is a government web-site (cjsonline.gov.uk) where it is declared that the purpose of the CJS is:

> to deliver justice for all, by convicting and punishing the guilty and helping them to stop offending, while protecting the innocent.

CJS Online notes that key goals of the CJS are (paraphrased) to:

- improve effectiveness and efficiency in bringing offenders[9] to justice
- increase public confidence in the fairness and effectiveness of the CJS
- increase victim satisfaction and witness satisfaction
- consistently collect, analyse and use good quality ethnicity data to identify and address 'race disproportionality'; and
- increase the recovery of criminal assets.

The last of these aims refers to proceeds of crime which for many years remained largely untouched by conviction alone, leaving open the question whether 'crime pays'. Since the Proceeds of Crime Act 2002, many ill-gotten criminal gains can be recovered via the Crown Court and traced by the Serious Organized Crime Agency (SOCA) whose role also includes the targeting of organized crime and money laundering.[10] Magistrates cannot order people to give up their assets, but they do have important powers to order compensation to victims of crime, restitution of property and (in the youth court) reparation (*Chapters 7* and *8*). The possibility of large scale

---

9. The original says 'offences': readers can make up their own mind if 'offenders' is more appropriate.
10. Many readers will have experienced the money laundering and identification procedures that now occur whenever a substantial financial transaction occurs. There have been 15 money laundering statutes since 1993. Banks, solicitors, accountants and businesses must make suspicious activity reports (SARs).

criminally obtained assets being involved may be one reason, at the mode of trial stage described in *Chapter 7*, to send a case to the Crown Court.

The 'wider criminal justice family'

The CJS can be viewed as a network of agencies and services of which those already mentioned form the core. Each agency has its own role, responsibilities, duties, areas of expertise, discretion and historical background.[11] But there are many other people involved in CJS work, such as forensic examiners, scientists, technicians, inspection teams, review bodies, medical practitioners and those specialising in aspects of treatment, therapy or recovery from addiction or misuse of drugs or alcohol.

Beyond the formal CJS lie what is sometimes styled 'the wider criminal justice family' which encompasses myriad less well-known or visible roles. They include those of individuals who befriend or act as mentors to offenders, engage in crime prevention schemes, are members of Independent Monitoring Boards (IMBs) (in prisons) or Independent Custody Visitors (ICVs) (visitors to police cells). The voluntary or 'non-statutory' sector includes nationwide undertakings such as Victim Support (see also the note on 'Compensation' in *Chapter 7*),[12] Witness Service and charitable bodies such as Nacro[13] and Rainer Crime Concern (RCC).[14]

Research, experts and referral schemes

Some people might include here organizations involved in gathering evidence-based research to discover, e.g. 'what works' with offenders. There are in fact many CJS scenarios in which an expert, analyst, medical practitioner, drug specialist or researcher may be called upon. The public tend to hear of the 'interesting' ones, such as offender profilers, psychologists who advise the police on the kind of offender who may have been responsible for a spate of offences. Many CJS processes involve 'referrals' to such people for their opinions or assessments. The term referral is also used to describe the process whereby an offender is referred to a facility, project or scheme involved in crime prevention or crime reduction objectives.

'Partners in Crime'

Under the heading 'Working Together to Cut Crime and Deliver Justice' CJS Online refers to the Criminal Justice Strategic Plan 2008-2011 against which all CJS developments occur. It sets out how the CJS agencies or services will work together to deliver a justice system which (paraphrased):

---

11. See *A History of Criminal Justice in England and Wales* (2009), Hostettler J, Waterside Press.
12. The website addresses of many of these CJS bodies appear in the list at the back of the book. A considerable amount of specialist information is readily available from those sources.
13. Formerly the National Association for the Care and Resettlement of Offenders.
14. For the work of several of these see the *Glossary* at the end of this work.

- is effective in bringing offenders to justice, especially serious offenders[15]
- engages the public and inspires confidence
- puts the needs of victims at its heart; and
- has simple and efficient processes.

These can only be achieved through the combined efforts of everyone involved in delivering criminal justice services and related decision-making.

Within the CJS, multi-agency 'partnerships' are a mechanism for maintaining a system of justice rather than a process of disconnected stages.[16] Multi-Agency Public Protection Arrangements (MAPPAs) bring together various practitioners alongside the police to monitor dangerous or high-risk offenders from whom members of the public need to be protected. Each partner brings something different to the table. Combined information and expertise are designed to enhance effectiveness and efficiency. Protocols or 'understandings' may flesh out such arrangements. Each member retains his or her operational independence, powers, duties and discretions. Linked to all forms of partnership is the need for sound liaison and communication.

As will be seen, special arrangements exist concerning the judiciary. Judges and magistrates are unlikely to see themselves as partners with other CJS practitioners in the ordinary sense, rather as taking part in appropriate inter-agency discussions (even when this involves HM Court Service): see 'Protecting the Judiciary', below.

Developments at Government level

A restructuring of government departments in 2007 led to a fresh context and impetus for partnership as between the MOJ, Home Office, Office of the Attorney General and (with regard to juveniles) Department for Children, Schools and Families (DCSF). There is a Cabinet Committee on Crime and the Criminal Justice System (CCCCJS). A similar approach occurs with Criminal Justice Boards (national and local) and this filters down to people on the ground, sometimes called frontline practitioners. It all contrasts markedly with former times when inter-departmental and inter-agency suspicion, mistrust, issues of jurisdiction, territory and a lack of shared aims and values was often a feature of criminal justice processes.

The Youth Justice System (YJS)

This is the name given to that part of the CJS which deals with juveniles (those below the age of 18) as outlined in *Chapter 8, The Youth Court*. People aged 18 or over are referred to as 'adults' and offenders who are aged 18-20 inclusive as young offenders (YOs); who normally appear in the adult magistrates' court or Crown Court, but are subject to some special considerations as noted in *Chapter 7, The*

---

15. Due to the presumption of innocence, the term 'offender' is only used *after* someone has been convicted.
16. A distinction emphasised by Lord Justice Auld in his 'Review of the Criminal Courts' (2002).

'Adult' Magistrates' Court. Those below the age of 18 are 'juveniles' or 'youths'. The former term has been used in this book, but this is simply a matter of choice.

THE CRIMINAL COURTS

Each of the courts of law belongs within a hierarchy of courts as represented in *Figure 1* overleaf and further described re criminal proceedings in what follows.

Magistrates' courts

At the base of the system are the magistrates' courts. This is where over 95 per cent of criminal cases start and end by way of a conviction or acquittal; and (if there is a conviction) sentence. Magistrates deal with summary offences (relatively minor ones) and some either-way matters (see 'Touchstones of Summary Justice' below and *Chapter 7*). All criminal cases start out in the magistrates' court. The magistrates' court and Crown Court are known as 'lower courts'.

Crown Court and Jury Trial

Above the magistrates' court stands the Crown Court. Both courts deal with either-way offences, i.e. those which by statute can be tried in either the magistrates' court or Crown Court depending on the outcome of a procedure known as 'mode of trial' (currently in a state of transition: see *Chapter 7*). Examples are theft, lesser burglaries, most criminal damage matters and certain assaults.

The Crown Court also deals with 'indictable only' or 'purely indictable' offences. As the description implies these offences, such as murder, manslaughter, rape and aggravated burglary (e.g. where weapon is involved) cannot be dealt with by magistrates. But magistrates still receive such cases at the very outset, sending them to the Crown Court once basic matters concerning legal aid and bail (both *Chapter 7*) have been settled. Trial in the Crown Court, whether for an indictable only offence or an either way offence, is known as a 'trial on indictment'.

The Crown Court is where trial by judge and jury takes place; and that court has generally greater powers. The judge rules on law, directs the jury and sentences convicted offenders. The jury decides whether the accused person is guilty or not. In the magistrates' court, it is the magistrates' who decide upon the facts and merits of a case as well as directing themselves on the law as it applies to each case. But they are aided in this by their advisers, see 'Magistrates and the Law' below and *Chapter 6*.

Crown Court judges are known as circuit judges, recorders and assistant recorders (the last two being part-time circuit judges): see further the *Glossary*.

Appeal to the Crown Court

Someone convicted and/or sentenced by a magistrates' court can appeal to the Crown Court against the decision of a magistrates' court. It is necessary to distinguish an

SUPREME COURT
Supreme Court Justices
(from November 2009)

HOUSE OF LORDS (until November 2009)
Law Lords
Appeals from the Court of Appeal or High Court, the latter e.g. re judicial review, etc.

COURT OF APPEAL
Lords Justices

Criminal Division	Civil Division
Appeals from the Crown Court against conviction and/or sentence	*Appeals from the High Court (or other civil courts and tribunals) in civil cases*

HIGH COURT OF JUSTICE
High Court Judges (aka Justices)

Queen's Bench Division*	Chancery Division	Family Division
Appeals in civil matters	*Equity, trusts. tax, etc.*	*Family Matters*
Divisional Court of the QBD		**Divisional Court of the FD**
Case Stated /Judicial Review (JR) Usually from magistrates (and re JR also from public authorities)		*Appeals from the FPC (and other family jurisdictions)*

CROWN COURT
Circuit Judges, Recorders and Assistant Recorders (see *Glossary*)

Trial by Judge and Jury following committal by magistrates Sentencing (including after committal by JPs)	*Appeals from Magistrates' Courts / Youth Courts: Chapter 7 against conviction and/or sentence*

MAGISTRATES' COURTS

Adult Court *Chapter 7*	**Youth Court** *Chapter 8*	**Family Proceedings Court (FPC)** *Chapter 9*
Ordinary magistrates / JPs	**Youth panel JPs**	**Family panel JPs**

District judge (magistrates' courts) *Chapter 1*
Summary trial and sentence
Committals to the Crown Court for trial or sentence
Magistrates also have their own appellate jurisdiction: Chapter 10

Figure 1: The courts hierarchy in outline
*The QBD also has it's own 'first instance' jurisdiction (see *Glossary*) as well as a Commercial Court and Admiralty Court. There is also a local county court (including for civil and family cases). There is a freestanding right of appeal to the European Court of Human Rights: *Chapter 5*

appeal against conviction, which can be made within 21 days of being found guilty (or any extension of time allowed by the Crown Court: known as leave to appeal out of time) and appeal against sentence. The Crown Court can impose any sentence that the magistrates could have imposed, so that the offender risks an increase in his or her sentence (though, naturally, hoping for a decrease). Magistrates have a role at the Crown Court with regard to certain appeals as is explained in *Chapter 10*.

High Court of Justice

Above the Crown Court stand the 'higher courts', starting with the High Court of Justice. Its Queen's Bench Divisions (QBD) deals with appeals on matters of law from magistrates' courts by way of 'case stated', 'judicial review' or, more rarely, by making a 'declaration'. High Court judges are known as 'Justices'.[17]

Case stated

This is a means of appealing on a point of law from a magistrates' court to the High Court.[18] Appeal is open to either party. It is heard by a Divisional Court (DC) of the Queen's Bench Division (QBD). The magistrates set out in writing the facts which they found to exist and say what legal principles they applied to them. The DC either upholds their legal interpretation or makes some other decision, e.g. to quash the conviction or order a re-hearing. Magistrates can refuse what they believe to be a frivolous application to state a case or require the applicant to clarify the matter of law. Although perhaps unusual, they can ask someone to enter into a recognizance to 'prosecute' (continue with) the appeal.[19]

Judicial review

Judicial review (JR) is a process by which participants (either party and possibly other interested parties) who are 'aggrieved' by a decision of magistrates may, within six months (usually), ask the High Court to consider whether the magistrates in question acted judicially, fairly and reasonably, within their jurisdiction, powers and processes. If they did not do so, the High Court can quash their decision, order a re-hearing and make orders to prevent the error recurring. JR can also be sought against other public entities, officials and Ministers of State.

Declarations and declarations of incompatibility

Analogous to an appeal is a High Court declaration which can again be applied for by either party. Public authorities (e.g. courts, the police, the CPS or Criminal Defence Service) will act upon the law as declared. Note also that with regard to 'primary' legislation (Acts of Parliament), the higher courts can make a declaration

---

17. Contrast magistrates who may also be described as 'justices' (lower case 'j'), i.e. shorthand for justice of the peace (JP): *Chapter 1*.
18. It can be from the Crown Court but only in very limited situations.
19. For 'recognizance' see the *Glossary*.

of incompatibility with human rights law as further explained *Chapter 5*.[20]

Court of Appeal

Also above the Crown Court but exercising a different type of jurisdiction to the High Court is the Court of Appeal (CA). It has a Criminal Division and a Civil Division. Anyone convicted by a jury at the Crown Court can appeal to the Court of Appeal on questions of law. If the case turns on the facts (i.e. the verdict of a jury) that person may only appeal after obtaining a certificate from the Crown Court judge that the case is fit for appeal or, more usually, leave to appeal from the CA itself. The CA must allow an appeal against conviction on the (sole) ground that it is unsafe. There is also a right of appeal to the CA against a sentence imposed by the Crown Court, with the leave of the latter court. The CA may quash the sentence and substitute any which the Crown Court could have made if, taking the case as a whole, the appellant is not dealt with more severely overall.

The Criminal Justice Act 2003 introduced in-trial appeals against evidentiary and other rulings by a trial judge (usually expedited to avoid delay re the trial itself); but not, e.g. extending to a ruling that a jury be discharged; or if an appeal can be made to the CA in the ordinary way. Judges of the CA are known as Lord Justices.

House of Lords and Supreme Court

The House of Lords is the upper chamber of the Houses of Parliament and, in a CJS context (pending the opening of the Supreme Court in its place), the highest court of appeal in the UK. The Appellate Committee of the House of Lords is presided over by a senior Law Lord. It consists of Law Lords (aka Lords of Appeal in Ordinary). It sits apart from the main business of the House in a committee room and its rulings carry great weight. From the Autumn of 2009 it will be replaced by a new Supreme Court.[21]

European Court of Human Rights

A further (or alternative form of) appeal is possible to the European Court of Human Rights (Eur. Ct. HR): see further *Chapter 5*.

Other mechanisms for correcting 'errors'

There are other ways in which something which is (or is perceived to be) incorrect, etc. can be challenged or put right. These include:

- an Attorney General's reference to the Court of Appeal against an 'unduly lenient sentence' (extending now to certain decisions by magistrates)
- the Criminal Cases Review Commission (CCRC) which investigates miscarriages

20. Note also the 'statutory declaration' under 'Other mechanisms for correcting errors' later in this section.
21. For details, see, e.g. justice.gov.uk/what we do/supreme court

of justice
- rectification: magistrates can rectify their own, limited, mistakes to avoid the need for an appeal as can the Crown Court; and
- a 'statutory declaration' which someone who has been convicted without knowledge of criminal proceedings can make in order to have them restarted.[22]

CIVIL AND FAMILY COURTS

The distinction between criminal and civil matters is fundamental. Civil cases involve proceedings between individuals, corporate bodies (or possibly the State in this capacity). They involve separate rules of procedure and evidence, generally less stringent than those for criminal cases. There is normally a lower standard of proof: see the note on the 'Burden and Standard of Proof' in *Chapter 5*. Civil courts deal with claims such as those for damages for negligence, nuisance or 'torts' (civil wrongs). Occasionally, due to the lower standard of proof, a civil claim may succeed where a criminal charge would fail. A civil claim may be based on the existence of a criminal conviction;[23] conversely a prosecution on matters arising in a civil case.[24]

The main civil courts are the local county court which deal with such matters as the recovery of personal, company or other debts, cases involving landlords and tenants and other, lesser civil cases; the High Court (Queen's Bench and Chancery Divisions) which has a wide-ranging jurisdiction as a court 'of first instance', e.g. in relation to major or complex civil claims; the Court of Appeal (Civil Division) and ultimately the House of Lords/Supreme Court. Magistrates also deal with certain civil matters and increasingly certain civil behaviour orders (CBOs): *Chapter 10*.

Family Courts
Separate to and distinct from the civil courts as such (but still civil in their broad nature rather than criminal) are those dealing with family matters, ranging from divorce to child protection and adoption. The county court and High Court (Family Division) also deal with such matters, whilst the magistrates' court plays an important part through its 'family proceedings court': *Chapter 9*.

---

22. Further qualification and explanation is beyond the scope of this introductory work.
23. e.g. so as to obtain recompense from a perpetrator in a civil court when compensation is not forthcoming in criminal proceedings or from the Criminal Cases Compensation Authority (CCCA).
24. As Lord Jeffrey Archer and Jonathan Aitken both found to their cost re perjury arising in civil matters. Oscar Wilde was also imprisoned after evidence in a quasi-civil case pointed to his affair with Alfred Lord Douglas: also a reminder of how the nature of crime may change over time.

TOUCHSTONES OF SUMMARY JUSTICE

As noted in *Chapter 1*, summary justice has a long pedigree. It is essentially 'local', uses 'summary' powers and aims to deliver 'simple, speedy, summary justice'.

A Tradition of Local Justice

Throughout their history magistrates have been locally-based, operating within their own communities and exposed to everyday life around them. Most readers of this book will know a magistrate who lives or works alongside them, but who gives up time each week or so to sit in court or be trained for this form of voluntary service.

Local justice areas

In 2005 the overall administration of the magistrates' courts passed from local committees[25] to HM Court Service (HMCS). But they are still organized in Local Justice Areas (LJAs), to which individual magistrates are assigned. There are other local features: Bench Training and Development Committees (BTDCs) (*Chapter 4*); and the fact that, even though magistrates' jurisdiction is now nationwide (see 'Summary Powers' below), each court deals mainly with cases arising in its own LJA. Liaison with other parts of the CJS is also partly a local function.

In certain parts of England and Wales the idea of local justice goes further. In 2005, the pioneering North Liverpool Community Justice Centre was established. Based on the Red Hook Center, New York, USA, it is a community resource providing a court function and crime prevention measures linked to social and welfare services. A judge is in overall charge.[26] The work focuses on low-level offending, anti-social behaviour (ASB) and the enforcement of court orders; but the judge can also deal with more serious criminal cases as appropriate. Co-ordination of CJS services locally and the involvement of the immediate community are key features. It was followed by similar schemes in other cities and towns from 2007 onwards.

Summary Powers

As this book goes to press magistrates jurisdiction remains in a state of flux due to certain provisions of the Criminal Justice Act 2003 remaining unimplemented. Others have been brought into force piecemeal or experimentally for limited periods. It is thus best first to describe the situation in the standard way that it has existed for many years. In broad terms, magistrates' maximum powers are as follows:

- up to six months per offence or 12 months in aggregate where consecutive sentences
  (those which are to run after one another rather than concurrently) are ordered but

---

25. Called Magistrates' Courts Committees (MCCs).
26. Who holds a joint appointment as district judge (magistrates' courts) and circuit judge.

only for either way offences: see *Chapter 7*;

- magistrates can also, at the same time, put into effect a sentence of imprisonment which was suspended on an earlier occasion (so that they can sometimes rise above the 12 month mark in total, but that is not the norm);[27]
- some summary offences do not attract imprisonment at all, so that the court will be limited to a fine or discharge (but since the Criminal Justice and Immigration Act 2008 no longer a community sentence since, as explained in *Chapter 7*, community sentences can now only be used if the offence is 'imprisonable' (see the *Glossary*)).

The main effect of the changes, if and when they occur, is that magistrates' powers would rise to 12 months per offence subject to an overall maximum of 18 months.

Again, as things exist now, they can commit to the Crown Court for sentence in respect of an either way offence that they themselves have agreed to deal with at the mode of trial stage: see *Chapter 7*. This power is set to disappear in due course, probably to tie in with the increase in summary powers to 12 months per offence once that happens.

An essential point is that there is a difference in powers between the magistrates' court and the Crown Court in respect of an identical either way offence. With regard, e.g. to theft, magistrates are limited to six months per offence (12 in future) whereas the Crown Court can send someone to prison for seven years. The Crown Court's powers are much greater for more serious offences, many of them of course 'indictable only' (above).

Questions of jurisdiction also extend to the use of other powers: see generally both of the sections on 'Sentencing' and 'Ancillary Orders' in *Chapter 7*.

Criminal Justice: Simple, Speedy, Summary

Criminal Justice: Simple, Speedy, Summary (CJSSS) is a modern-day way of working based on simpler processes and procedures. It was successfully piloted (tested) in magistrates' courts in four areas of the country. CJSSS seeks to improve the way cases are managed and dealt with, focusing 'on methods that make the justice system work well'. The success of pilot projects in Thames, Camberwell, Coventry and West Cumbria led to a national programme of implementation in 2007-2008. When he was Lord Chancellor, Lord Falconer remarked that CJSSS has:

> provided a clear demonstration of what can be achieved when all of the agencies involved in criminal justice work together in a simpler, faster, more focused way ... Simple things have made a real difference [such as] clear and constructive inter-agency communication, information being available in advance and greater familiarity with cases being brought before the court.

---

27. In defiance of simple explanations, sentences of under 12 months (known as 'custody plus' and 'intermittent custody') are also on the Statute Book but remain unimplemented since 2003.

The CJSSS results showed that, e.g. (paraphrased):

- the average time taken between someone being charged with an offence and the conclusion of the case had more than halved to 23 days
- there has been a 30 per cent increase in guilty pleas at first hearings with 59 per cent of guilty pleas being dealt with there and then
- first hearings had very often become final hearings
- with contested cases 70 per cent were concluded after just two hearings; and
- there were 'significant improvements' in the time taken to bring people to justice with trials being held on the date first fixed and in good time, between six to ten weeks after the case first reached court.

The CPS and the police work together to ensure all relevant details are included in the advance information files handed to accused people and their legal representatives, with a view to a reduction in the number of requests for adjournments, leading to quicker, simpler processes and less inconvenience to victims and witnesses.

MAGISTRATES AND THE LAW

Magistrates are not qualified lawyers[28] so that the system of summary justice rests on a unique relationship between them and their legal advisers if they are to comply with the particularly exacting and increasingly complex standards and rules demanded in a court of law.

Justices' Clerks and Court Legal Advisers
The justices' clerk is the chief legal adviser to a bench of magistrates as a whole. Justices' clerks must be barristers or solicitors of at least five years standing. In more everyday terms, legal advice is in practice provided within or outside of the courtroom by one of a team of court legal advisers under the overall management of the justices' clerk. The adviser is not party to decisions and must tread the delicate balance between remaining alert but not becoming involved unless and until required to act or invited or required to give advice as explained in *Chapter 6*.

The Justices' Clerk's Society
The Justices' Clerks' Society (JCS) founded in 1839 is the professional body representing JCs and assistant JCs. A main aim of the JCS is to keep under review the operation of the law, especially that administered by magistrates, draw attention to defects, and to promote improvements. See jc-society.co.uk

---

28. Except in so far as a district judge (magistrates' courts) can be so described: *Chapter 1*.

THE MINISTRY OF JUSTICE

The MOJ was established in 2007, largely by transferring to this new Department of State the functions of the former Department of Constitutional Affairs (DCA). To this were added other justice-related responsibilities which were being relinquished by an overburdened Home Office (see further below). It now works trilaterally alongside the Home Office and Department of the Attorney General and as already noted alongside the Department for Children, Schools and Families (DCSF) with regard to juveniles The MOJ remit includes responsibilities in relation to:

- HM Courts Service (HMCS)
- the judiciary (but via independent bodies such as the Judicial Office under the Lord Chief Justice; the Judicial Appointments Commission (JAC); Office for Judicial Complaints (OJC); and Judicial Communications Office (JCO))
- the National Offender Management Service (NOMS) comprising the National Probation Service (NPS) and HM Prison Service (HMPS)
- sponsorship of related HM Inspectorates
- other independent bodies such as Independent Monitoring Boards (IMBs) (in prisons); the Parole Board; Prisons and Probation Ombudsman
- legal aid and assistance via the Community Legal Service (CLS) and Legal Services Commission (LSC))
- sponsorship of the Sentencing Guidelines Council (SGC) and Sentencing Advisory Panel (SAP) (*Chapter 7*)
- sponsorship of the Law Commission (concerned with law reform)
- hosting the cross-departmental Office for Criminal Justice Reform (OCJR)
- the Privy Council and its Judicial Committee; and
- human rights.[29]

As noted at the start of this chapter it also has key constitutional responsibilities. Its management has been restructured under various Directors General.

The Justice Secretary and Lord Chancellor [30]

This is the dual title, since 2007, of the responsible Minister of State at the MOJ. He or she need not be a lawyer (the former convention was that he or she was). He or she is a politician appointed by the Prime Minister and a member of the Cabinet. Since 2005 he or she has had no direct involvement in the selection of judges or

29. See further *The New Ministry of Justice: An Introduction* (2nd edn. 2008), Gibson B, Waterside Press.
30. Since, re courts and judges, many responsibilities remain referable to 'the Lord Chancellor', the convention has been adopted of using that title within this book. The media tends to us 'Justice Secretary'.

magistrates, judicial discipline, etc. See also 'Protecting the Judiciary' below.

HER MAJESTY'S COURT SERVICE (HMCS)

HMCS is an executive agency of the MOJ whose remit is to 'deliver justice' effectively and efficiently. It is structured into 25 areas within 7 regions. Its role encompasses the administration of the magistrates' court, Crown Court, and (together with a Royal Courts of Justice group) the High Court and Court of Appeal (all noted above). For further detail, see hmcourts-service.gov.uk

Two mechanisms are of particular interest in relation to magistrates' courts. The first is the Justices' Issues Group (JIG) via which the interests and concerns of magistrates about HMCS matters are brought to the attention of management. This might cover such things as the closure of courthouses, staff transfers and general matters of 'housekeeping'. The Area Judicial Forum (AJF) in contrast is a purely judicial mechanism in which HMCS has only a passive observer role and where it may also 'act as a postbox'. The AJF discusses matters of a judicial nature as between magistrates, judges and their different levels of judicial responsibility and concern.

COURTS BOARDS

Courts Boards were established in 2005 as part of a major rearrangement in the way that HMCS functions and courts are managed within a unified administration. In relation to magistrates' courts, they also took over the 'watchdog' aspects of the role of the 42 former independent local Magistrates' Courts Committees (MCCs) which administered magistrates' courts, but with different functions because, under the Courts Act 2003, HMCS is responsible for the administration and funding of most of the courts in England and Wales. The boards were created to work in partnership with HMCS. They do not themselves manage, administer or make decisions about the running of the courts, but act as a kind of sounding board. Centrally, they consider what is happening in an area and give advice and make recommendations to foster improvements. Neither do they have any remit concerning judicial decisions, but must both respect and support judicial independence.

One intention is to combine a community focus and input with judicial expertise and experience. Their membership consists of at least one judge; two lay magistrates; two other members who 'appear to have knowledge or experience of the work of the courts' in the area; and two who 'appear to be representative of local people'. Regulations set out the procedures for appointment, selection of a chair from among board members and so on. They also cover board procedures and a range of technical matters.[31] Members must use their independent judgement to ensure that the perspective of the local community and people who use the courts is taken into account.

Each Courts Board works with its HMCS Area Director.[32] Its main focus is the Area Business Plan formulated by that director which sets out how it is intended that the resources available are intended to be used vis-à-vis HMCS's overall objectives for criminal (including youth), civil and family work. Directors take a corporate approach, considering the wider impact of local issues and working with other Area Directors and their Regional Director to ensure that the administration of the work of the courts is managed effectively and efficiently across administrative and agency boundaries. Likewise, there are arrangements for the chairs of different Courts Boards to meet and discuss matters of common interest.

HM INSPECTORATE OF COURT ADMINISTRATION

HMICA came into being in 2005 under the Courts Act 2003. Its responsibilities include: inspections and reports to the Lord Chancellor on the administrative support systems of the Crown Court and magistrates' courts (it also inspects the county court: see 'Civil and Family Courts' above). The work of anyone 'making judicial decisions or exercising any judicial discretion' is excluded from its remit. It acts independently of the MOJ and HMCS to provide 'assurance to Ministers of State and the public about the safe and proper delivery of court services'. Key areas of inspection include:

- diversity and its promotion/achievement
- public governance and accountability
- transparency, fairness, leadership and strategic management
- finance; buildings; information technology and equipment
- administrative processes and their effect on court users
- enforcement 'to ensure prompt and effective action re compliance with court orders'; and
- quality of service.

It also monitors HMCS targets, priorities, performance and improvement action.

---

31. For further information, see e.g. 'Courts Board Guidance' (2005), Cm 6461.
32. Special arrangements exist in London where 'area' and 'region' amount to the same thing and its Courts Board works with the Regional Director.

There are often themed, joint inspections by a number of criminal justice inspectorates across various criminal justice agencies

OTHER CJS-RELATED GOVERNMENT DEPARTMENTS

As already indicted the CJS is centrally a tripartite venture between the Ministry of Justice, Home Office and the Office of the Attorney General.

The Home Office

This most historic office of State dates from the late-1300s and in its 'modern' guise from 1782. Since 2007 it focuses primarily on law and order, public safety, the protection of the public, policing (via independent police authorities and police forces: see the start of this chapter), crime prevention and crime reduction, asylum and immigration (via the UK Border Agency (UKBA)) and terrorism (including in conjunction with an Office for Security and Counter-Terrorism (OSCT)). This amalgam of tasks is sometimes described as 'homeland security' (an Americanism), i.e. matters referable to the internal security of the UK re which the Metropolitan Police Service (MPS) also has a nationwide responsibility.[33] The HO is also responsible for safeguarding personal identity, CJS-related developments in science, technology and research and has links to MI5 (aka the Security Service) and GCHQ (the government 'listening station').

The Home Secretary

The responsible Minister of State is the Home Secretary. Home Secretaries have at times 'clashed' with the judiciary, but the convention is that politicians do not ordinarily openly criticise judges or magistrates. A systemic failure to deport foreign prisoners following their sentences as per the recommendations of judges led to the departure of Charles Clarke (Home Secretary 2004-2006). Dr. John Reid (2006-2007) famously declared that the Home Office was 'unfit for purpose';[34] leading to the transfer of certain HO responsibilities to the MOJ as described earlier.[35] The Home Secretary has certain inherent powers, including to deport or exclude foreigners from the UK where he or she deems them to be 'not conducive to the public good'. There are also, following the Police Reform Act 2002, extensive default powers in relation to police authorities, including to step in if a force is wholly failing.

---

33. External matters of security fall to the Foreign and Commonwealth Office (FCO).
34. A description Prime Minister Tony Blair had in 1997 made about the entire CJS.
35. See further *The New Home Office: An Introduction* (2nd. edn. 2009), Gibson B, Waterside Press.

PROTECTING THE JUDICIARY

Various mechanisms exist to ensure the protection of judges and magistrates from improper influences, consistent with adequate provision of administrative and support services to enable them to carry out their tasks, principally via HM Court Service (HMCS) (above) and various channels of liaison and communication. This is usually emphasised by saying that they enjoy judicial independence. 'The Nature of Judicial Decision-making' itself is described in *Chapter 5* and *6*.

Justices' Interest Groups (JIGs) and Area Judicial Forums (AJFs) have already been noted together with the fact that the responsibilities of HM Inspectorate of Courts Administration (HMICA) (also above) do not extend to forms of 'judicial inspection'. Rather, judicial accountability exists via the appeal system (see 'Criminal Courts of Law' above) or, in the event of misconduct, Advisory Committees (*Chapter 3*), an Office for Judicial Complaints (OJC), or the general law.[36]

Under the Constitutional Reform Act 2005, the Lord Chancellor has a duty to protect judicial independence. The first Justice Secretary and Lord Chancellor, Jack Straw asserted, on taking up office, that this was his first priority.

The Lord Chief Justice is the key point of reference for judges and magistrates rather than any Minister of State or public official. Except in those rare situations where discretion is removed by law in favour of 'mandatory sentences' judges and magistrates apply their own discretion, steered by guidelines, precedents and good practice and led by the judiciary itself which in turn is aided by consultation.

Judges and magistrates swear an oath of allegiance to the Sovereign but, since the Bill of Rights 1689 when 'royal justice' ceased, there has been increasing recognition of the importance of judicial independence. This is encapsulated in doctrines such as the Separation of Powers under which the Executive (Government), Legislature (Parliament) and Judiciary have separate roles. This is reinforced by the Rule of Law which among other things holds that everyone 'no matter how high' is subject to and falls under the same law as everyone else.[37]

OPEN JUSTICE

Openness and its stable mates visibility, transparency and accountability are key aims and values of all public services. The historic principle of 'open court' under

---

36. Such as the offence of perverting the course of justice. In general terms judges and magistrates cannot ordinarily be sued for damages in the civil courts at least so long as they are acting *bona fide.*

37. But not the Sovereign in whose name the law is made and enforced. Other anomalies include diplomatic immunity and public interest immunity (PII) (when the latter can be conferred, e.g. on an informer, even in some instances to the extent of allowing him or her to participate in criminal offences).

which anyone can enter a magistrates' court or Crown Court as an observer (subject to courtroom capacity and individual good behaviour) is now reinforced by Article 6 of the European Convention on Human Rights which states that:

> Judgement shall be pronounced publicly but the press and public may be excluded from all or part of the trial in the interests of morals, public order or national security in a democratic society, where the interests of juveniles or the protection of the private life of the parties so require, or to the extent strictly necessary in the opinion of the court in special circumstances where publicity would prejudice the interest of justice.

In exceptional circumstances, criminal courts can sit *in camera* (i.e. completely in private), in the interests of national security or when life and limb are at stake (a rare thing in practice). Another exception to the normal open court rule is when a magistrates' court is considering whether to issue a warrant of further detention (see *Chapter 7*). Youth courts are not open to the public; but the media may attend although they cannot take photographs in a courtroom (which is a criminal offence) and must not publish the names of juveniles unless a court allows these to be disclosed in the interests of justice; a similar rule extends to child participants in cases of all kinds but places the onus of actively making a restriction order on the court in individual cases. In relation to the initial proceedings in magistrates' courts in respect of indictable only and either way offences (*Chapter 7*), reports may only contain bare details of a case unless the accused person applies for this restriction to be lifted (he or she may want to attract publicity, e.g. in the hope that defence witnesses will come forward). There are various powers under which courts can restrict or delay publication in the interests of justice.[38]

THE MAGISTRATES' ASSOCIATION

The Magistrates' Association (MA) was established in 1920 and incorporated by Royal Charter in 1962. It enjoys the patronage of the Sovereign and publishes a monthly journal, *The Magistrate*. It acts as a sounding-board for the views, opinions and concerns of magistrates nationwide and, relying on this expertise, responds to Government and others as well as initiating projects and proposals of its own.

For many years it published its own sentencing guidelines (latterly in consultation with the Justices' Clerks' Society and others) which were a reference point for the Magistrates' Courts Sentencing Guidelines now produced by the Sentencing Guidelines Council (SGC) and issued in definitive form in 2008 (see *Chapter 7*).

The vast majority of JPs subscribe voluntarily to the MA and many actively attend branch meetings, conferences or social events. There is a National Council of around 100 members which is democratically elected by local branches, each

---

38. However, all such matters should be considered in the light of moves to further 'open up the courts'.

of which sends two or three representative to serve on this national body. Various standing committees cover a range of subjects, i.e. a:

- **Family Courts Committee** whose role it is to consider Family Panel issues, develop MA policy on family issues, liaise with relevant government departments and initiate guidance re matters of the kind noted in *Chapter 8*

- **Judicial Policy and Practice Committee** which considers the operation of the CJS and inter-agency issues of the kind mentioned earlier in this chapter, including the impact of new legislation. Its brief also includes case management, judicial independence (above) and the relationships with HMCS. This committee is usually chaired by the overall chair of the MA

- **Road Traffic Committee** to deal with items such as are noted in *Chapter 11.*

- **Sentencing Policy and Practice Committee** to monitor sentencing practice, contribute to MA policy on such matters and (subject to the work of the Sentencing Guidelines Council) provide guidance on sentencing

- **Support, Training and Development Committee** to monitor legal changes, assess training needs, promote quality (and appropriate) training, create and provide training materials, and support members on domestic issues such as court sittings, attendance rotas, appraisal, mentoring, financial allowances, conduct, employment issues, etc; and

- **Youth Courts Committee** which initiates and progresses 'beneficial changes' in the youth justice system (*Chapter 8*).

There is a national secretariat based in London. A good deal of information is available to the general public at the association's website: magistrates-association.org.uk (and other matters to MA members via a portal).

CHAPTER THREE

Becoming a Magistrate

Chapters 1 and *2* may have awakened your curiosity as to who magistrates are. The section on 'Open Court' may have spurred your interest enough for you to call in at your local magistrates' court and observe for an hour or so from the public gallery. For those readers who may have gone further and submitted an application to become a magistrate, or even been appointed to the bench, they may wish to take stock of the appointments process and what follows on from it.

It is still within living memory that magistrates were not openly recruited but approached via a sort of 'intelligence network' (often involving existing magistrates), a 'tap on the shoulder' and an invitation to 'let their names go forward'. There would be no truly probing interview and in due course successful 'applicants' would receive a letter confirming their appointment and a request to 'report for duty'. Similarly, the further back one goes, there were no structured training requirements, simply some advance reading. Anecdotes abound concerning women appointees being given helpful advice on their choice of hat for court sittings!

No matter how capable, responsible and dedicated such people might have been in themselves this form of appointment and 'training' process was clearly destined to change. Set out below is the typical process leading up to the modern-day appointment of new magistrates. Although practices and timings may vary locally to reflect home conditions, there is substantial nationwide consistency.

RECRUITMENT AND APPOINTMENT

Magistrates are appointed on behalf of the Crown by the Lord Chancellor[1] who acts in close consultation with the Lord Chief Justice in accordance with provisions of the Constitutional Reform Act 2005. The Lord Chancellor discharges this function through local Advisory Committees, often chaired by the Lord-Lieutenant for the area, representing the Crown.[2]

Although serving magistrates constitute the majority of the membership, to avoid suggestions of 'self-perpetuation' or 'cloning',[3] at least a third of the members of Advisory Committees are non-magistrates, themselves selected via an open public recruitment process. These non-magistrate members not only broaden the basis and skills of Advisory Committees but have the express role of providing independent

---

1. See the explanation of the use of this title in *Chapter 2*.
2. Advisory Committees are non-departmental public bodies or NDPBs.
3. As it is dubbed, i.e. whereby Advisory Committees (or for that matter any other appointing committees) simply appoint people 'like themselves', thus perpetuating narrowness rather than diversity.

assurance that proper procedures and criteria are being followed. All members of Advisory Committees receive training for their role.

Functions of Advisory Committees

The functions and responsibilities of Advisory Committees are contained in the Lord Chancellor and Secretary of State's 'Directions for Advisory Committees on Justices of the Peace' (2008). The duties are wide and varied and include:

- establishing the number of new magistrates required
- arranging what is (usually) an annual recruitment process
- undertaking appropriate publicity to bring the recruitment process to the widest possible public attention
- looking at applications and interviewing candidates
- recommending suitable candidates to the Lord Chancellor and Lord Chief Justice for appointment
- investigating allegations of misconduct by existing magistrates[4]
- making sure that magistrates maintain a minimum number of court sittings and also that they do not sit too frequently (see later in the chapter)
- recruiting its own membership as and when replacements are required
- submitting an annual report to the Lord Chancellor
- considering any draft case for the appointment of a district judge (magistrates' courts) in their area (see *Chapter 1*); and
- working within a national code of conduct.

Advisory Committees try to make sure that members of the public generally are made aware that applications are being sought and this is particularly directed towards those sectors of a local community that are currently not broadly reflected within the local bench of magistrates concerned. The aim is to ensure diversity and that all sectors of the local community have the opportunity to contribute to summary justice. Appointment is purely on merit. All eligible candidates usually receive at least a first interview (below) so that Advisory Committees can be busy at certain times of the annual appointments cycle.

Quite independently of the active recruitment process, any potential candidate can download an application form by visiting one of a number of official websites.[5]

---

4. But 'lack of competence' (see later in the chapter) is initially a matter for the Bench Training and Development Committee (BTDC) which may later refer matters up to the Advisory Committee.
5. See, e.g. justice.gov.uk/forms/magistappform-int.doc Applications can be completed online or forms printed off. They are processed to match the recruitment cycle.

Advisory Committee and Judicial Appointments Committee compared

In 2006 a Judicial Appointments Commission (JAC) was set up under the Constitutional Reform Act 2005 to select candidates for many other judicial offices, for recommendation to the Lord Chancellor; when selection is also on merit and through fair and open competition from within the widest range of eligible candidates. After many hundreds of years of the Lord Chancellor selecting and then appointing judicial officers, judicial independence (*Chapter 2*) is since 2005 enhanced in those cases where the JAC is involved in that a body wholly independent of Government makes the selection. The Lord Chancellor still makes the formal appointment, but he or she must give reasons if he does not accept a recommendation of the JAC.

It has been suggested that the work of Advisory Committees might eventually be transferred to the JAC. Whereas this would make sense in bringing the appointment of magistrates into line with that of other judicial officers, the number of appointments required annually (upwards of 1,500) and the resources involved (now provided at relatively low cost by Advisory Committees) would have a major impact on the work of the JAC. Much of the local, 'grass roots' involvement might also conceivably be lost.

Eligibility and Selection

As noted in *Chapter 2*, magistrates' jurisdiction now extends across the whole of England and Wales. In line with this, consistent, national considerations apply to the recruitment and selection process. The following personal factors are relevant:

- people under 18 years of age will not be appointed[6]
- people over 65 years of age are not normally appointed: the initial training, mentoring and appraisal process takes some time and appointees are then expected to be able to serve for at least five years before reaching the retirement age for magistrates which is normally 70 years of age[7]
- British nationality is no longer a requirement although an oath[8] of allegiance to the Crown is taken when magistrates are appointed and is a prerequisite to the magistrate being able to sit in court and adjudicate
- the health of applicants is relevant only to the extent that it might prevent them from properly carrying out the duties required
- applications are encouraged from people with disabilities who are able to adjudicate unassisted or with changed working or sitting arrangements within section 6 Disability Discrimination Act 1995 (including people who are sight-impaired, registered blind people, or hearing-impaired)

---

6.   It is understood that the youngest person appointed was 19 years old at the time.
7.   See later in the chapter for exceptions.
8.   Or an equivalent affirmation. But non-nationals still seeking asylum will not be considered.

- local residence is not nowadays the issue it once was: as already seen, there is a national jurisdiction and successful candidates can choose to sit near to their home or place of work. A previous requirement for 'local knowledge' or for established residence in the area of sitting no longer applies.
- close relationship to a serving magistrate is no longer the issue it used to be although such people would not be rostered to sit together in court
- being a freemason (including a woman freemason) must be declared but is not a bar (nor is it any form of qualification) for appointment
- being subject to, or the beneficiary of, a maintenance or child support order will not in itself be an issue if the order is enforceable in another area or if it can be transferred elsewhere for enforcement
- bankruptcy is a statutory bar to appointment and, because of the need for public confidence in the administration of justice, undischarged bankrupts will not usually be appointed[9]
- special considerations apply to Members of Parliament, Members of the European Parliament and Members of the Welsh Assembly as well as to full-time political agents. Similar considerations also apply to people in certain types of public employment (e.g. those whose work brings them into contact with magistrates' courts), to those in certain other occupations (e.g. public house licensees) or who undertake certain types of voluntary work (e.g. for the Citizen's Advice Bureau).
- if an applicant has criminal convictions this may or may not be a bar to appointment: everything will depend on the nature and number of offences and how long ago the were committed by the candidate[10]
- applicants are expected to undertake preferably at least two observations at their local magistrates' court before submitting their application; and
- previous applicants, those who applied in the past but did not demonstrate the 'Six Key Qualities' (below), need not be interviewed for a further three years (although they are not prevented from reapplying at any time).

Where there is no automatic bar to appointment it is for the Advisory Committee to assess whether to call the applicant for interview and then make up its own mind.

The Six Key Qualities

As an overarching consideration, Advisory Committees assess candidates at interview in relation to what are the prescribed 'Six Key Qualities':

---

9. Special considerations apply in respect of directors of companies that have gone into liquidation.
10. The Lord Chancellor's directions provide specific guidance.

- good character
- understanding and communication
- social awareness
- maturity and sound temperament
- sound judgement; and
- their commitment and reliability.

The Interview Process

The Advisory Committee will set up an internal panel to interview all potentially eligible candidates. There is a two-stage interview process.

First interview

This concentrates on:

- going through the application form, including with regard to any personal issues of the kind noted under the last heading
- discussing the applicant's impressions gained from observation visits
- the 'Six Key Qualities' (although certain of these will be explored again in greater depth in any second interview)
- discussion about criminal justice and other related public or social issues such as drug misuse, drink driving or youth crime issues
- what life on the bench will involve
- what used to be called the 'key question' and which is now known as the 'good character and background' question:

Is there anything in your private or working life, or in your past, or to your knowledge in that of your family or close friends, which, if it became generally known, might bring you or the magistracy into disrepute, or call into question your integrity, authority or standing as a magistrate?

Second interview

If the candidate has demonstrated that he or she may have the 'Six Key Qualities' and there are no other matters militating against his or her appointment, then a second interview will be conducted. This concentrates on matters such as:

- going through two case studies[11] with the applicant to assess how he or she might approach judicial decision-making: it is the general approach that is considered and no technical knowledge is demanded or expected
- putting again the 'good character and background' question (above); and

---

11. As approved by the Ministry of Justice.

- explaining the rest of the appointments process from thereon in.

Questioning is probing rather than confrontational. Candidates are given an opportunity to ask questions, reflecting a two-way process. Only 'objective evidence' obtained from the application form or interview can be considered and the Advisory Committee applies a standard scoring system to just four of the Six Key Qualities:

0	not demonstrated: little or no positive evidence
1	demonstrated: generally positive
2	well demonstrated: positive evidence
3	very well demonstrated: very strong evidence

Note: 'Good character' and 'commitment and reliability' are not scored: they are either demonstrated during the application and interview process or they are not.

There is no minimum score for appointment: it is accepted that the requisite qualities can be enhanced through training and appraisal (*Chapter 4*). However, if there are more suitable candidates than are required for local purposes then the relative scores of different candidates may be decisive. Any applicant who is not recommended for appointment can ask the Lord Chancellor to review the matter.

NEXT STEPS BEFORE APPOINTMENT AND SITTING

Where the Advisory Committee proposes to recommend a candidate it will instigate an enhanced-level check with the Criminal Records Bureau (CRB). It will also require the completion of a formal undertaking by the applicant concerning such matters as:

- his or her judicial and personal conduct
- respecting confidences
- participation in training
- keeping up the minimum number of court sittings (below)
- his or her preparedness to resign if he or she becomes disqualified from sitting as a magistrate (e.g. on bankruptcy) or unable to perform the duties involved
- his or her preparedness to answer questions in surveys relating to the composition of the bench
- acting as a magistrate without bias
- notifying any future impending active criminal or civil proceedings against the applicant (or close relatives)
- disclosing when a close relative has subsequently joined certain criminal justice

agencies; or
- that he or she has become or ceased to be a freemason.

Appointment

Successful applicants are appointed to the national Commission for England and Wales. For practical and pastoral purposes they are assigned to one of the various Local Justice Areas (LJAs) (*Chapter 2*) and this will become their 'home' bench.

A certificate of appointment is drawn up and the new magistrate receives both a letter of appointment and initial explanatory paperwork. At the same time a specially trained existing magistrate will be appointed by the local Bench Training and Development Committee (BTDC)[12] (*Chapter 4*) as a mentor for each newly appointed magistrate. The mentor's role is not to train his or her new colleague but to support and guide him or her through their initial training and early sittings in court which lead up to their first appraisal some 12-18 months later (see below and also again *Chapter 4*).

Initial ('Introductory') Training

The next step before being sworn in as a magistrate is to complete the introductory part of 'Initial Training' along with others new appointees. Supported by their mentors, they will undertake an introductory and familiarisation session (around half a day), usually at the local courthouse. It will cover matters such as:

- an introduction to senior bench personnel and other local magistrates and staff with key responsibilities
- the organization of the local bench[13]
- how the courts are administered locally
- the arrangements for magistrates' court sittings
- an introduction to the Magistrates' Association (*Chapter 2*)
- the role of the mentors assigned to each of the new magistrates
- an overview of the full Initial Training programme
- the three formal 'competences' that all 'wingers'[14] must acquire and subsequently demonstrate through appraisal: in summary 'Managing Yourself', 'Teamwork' and 'Making Judicial Decisions'[15]
- a detailed examination of the judicial oath (or affirmation) that new magistrates will soon be required to take, i.e. swear (or make) in due course
- the practical arrangements for their swearing-in ceremony; and

---

12. The shorter abbreviation TDC is often used. BTDC is used for consistency in this work.
13. All local magistrates' courts are known as 'benches': see the *Glossary*
14. This is the name traditionally given to magistrates who sit to either side of the chairperson in court.
15. See Competences 1 to 3 in *Chapter 4*.

- 'domestic' or 'housekeeping' issues such the parking arrangements at the court-house, security, layout of the premises and courtroom, expenses claims (see later in the chapter) and other immediate practical matters.

Swearing-in

The final step before starting full Initial Training is the swearing-in ceremony. At this public ceremony all the newly appointed magistrates, often accompanied by their families and mentors, take two oaths (or make two affirmations):

- the Oath of Allegiance to the Crown; and
- the Judicial Oath by which each person confirms that he or she will:

Well and truly serve our Sovereign Lady Queen Elizabeth the Second, in the office of Justice of the Peace and will do right to all manner of people after the laws and usages of the Realm without fear or favour, affection or ill will.

This is the central to the culture of 'judicial fairness' examined in *Chapter 5*.

Initial ('Core') Training

This second aspect of the Initial Training is more detailed and usually follows hard on the heels of a magistrate being sworn in, so as to maintain the impetus and ensure that he or she starts sitting and gaining experience as soon as is possible. Typically, it takes place over several (not necessarily consecutive) days and is wide-ranging in its content. It is based on nationally provided materials and includes matters such as:

- social awareness
- respecting rights and promoting fairness (see *Chapter 5*)
- avoiding bias, prejudice and discrimination
- diversity issues
- the key skills required of a magistrate, such as attentive listening, team working, assertiveness and structured decision making.[16]

The acquisition and enhancement of these 'soft skills' (examined further in *Chapter 5*) receives high priority. As well as benefitting the delivery of justice, it can benefit the individual magistrate concerned and often also his or her employer (a point Advisory Committees often highlight in their recruitment publicity).

---

16. Structured decision-making began in magistrates' courts the 1980s. It has since been refined to something of both an art and a science. It involves breaking a decision down into its essential stages and making sure that each is completed in sequence, whilst also making sure that there are supporting facts and explanations.

The training then moves on to cover more technical matters and task-based features of the work of magistrate. It will typically extend to:

- further and now more structured observations in court (often with the mentor in attendance and with debriefing in training sessions)
- the jurisdiction of magistrates (*Chapters 2* and *7*)
- the main types of court work in which new magistrates are likely to take part, what is called 'adjudicating'
- structured decision-making [16]
- giving reasons
- the role of the justices' clerk and court legal advisers (*Chapter 6*); and
- magistrates out of court and emergency duties (*Chapter 10*).

It then concentrates on matters such as:

- preparation for the magistrates' first sitting in court
- the third, and final, part of this Initial Training (as below); and
- the nature of future training, including the forthcoming Consolidation Training (explained below).

Observations and Visits

The third and final aspect of Initial Training comprises two main parts:

- structured visits to National Probation Service (NPS) offices and projects which play a role in community sentences; and
- structured visits to penal institutions. [17]

Materials: A Note

To complement the whole of their initial training, new magistrates are provided with the Judicial Studies Board's 'Workbook for Magistrates' which is a set of home study materials to support and supplement their face-to-face training. In addition each is given a copy of the *Adult Court Bench Book* which is a practical, loose leaf reference tool for use in training and also when sitting on the bench in court. [18]

---

17. Penal is a word which is used to connote 'appertaining to punishment'. In this particular context it refers, e.g. to prisons and young offender institutions (YOIs). For purely logistical reasons it is not always possible for a magistrate to complete all such visits in time for their first sitting in court in which case these are completed as soon as possible thereafter.
18. Both of these can be accessed at jsb.co.uk

TAKING TO THE WATER: STARTING TO SIT IN COURT

By the time the Initial Training is complete arrangements will have been made for the new magistrate to undertake his or her first sitting in court (and whilst the training is still fresh in his or her mind). Wherever possible, this will involve sitting in court alongside his or her mentor. Mentors continue to sit with their charges at intervals over the next year or so and on at least six occasions if possible. They may also maintain contact by other means. This allows for a continuing dialogue, explanations and clarifications about what it is that is happening in the wider context of the courtroom.

Whilst the nature and content of the Initial Training will have enabled new magistrates to feel as comfortable as possible in their early sittings and to contribute immediately to the judicial decision-making process they will remain novices for some time. But existing magistrates often value this and find that the contributions of newly trained magistrates and a 'fresh eye' are a useful stimulus and a refresher for themselves. New colleagues will also have received much up-to-date information during their training about which existing magistrates will also need to keep abreast and 'on their toes' vis-à-vis their newer colleagues.

New magistrates sit as 'wingers'[19] and only in *The Adult Magistrates' Court* as described in *Chapter 7*. It is only later that the new magistrate may progress to taking the chair and possibly also to sitting in the other kinds of courts which come under the umbrella of the magistrates' court as noted below.

Consolidation Training

After nine to 12 months of sitting as a 'winger', new magistrates undertake Consolidation Training. This, as its name implies, involves looking back over the initial training and the experience gained during early court sittings. It seeks to reinforce matters and deal with problems or queries. Such training typically lasts for the equivalent of a couple of days and tends to have a particularly practical base. This part of the training also prepares new magistrates for their first appraisal which will follow shortly.

First or 'Threshold' Appraisal

As was noted above, all new magistrates must acquire three formal competences and then demonstrate this fact through their first appraisal and, thereafter, at three-yearly intervals. The first appraisal usually takes place 12 to 18 months after their appointment, following the Consolidation Training noted above. This will also be after their mentor has reported that they appear to be ready for appraisal. The appraisal involves working with a magistrate colleague (and sitting with them in court), who

---

19. See the explanation of this term in an earlier footnote.

has been specially trained as an appraiser. The pair jointly note on a special form aspects of the performance of the magistrate being appraised. The results are then referred to the local Bench Training and Development Committee (BTDC).[20]

The BTDC considers the report and if it decides that the new magistrate has demonstrated 'the three competences' he or she is so informed. Following this successful 'threshold appraisal', the new magistrate may begin to think about appointment to the youth or family jurisdictions described in *Chapters 8* and *9*.

Minor gaps in the competences of a new magistrate may be accepted by the BTDC and addressed through limited and targeted extra training and support. Any major gaps in competence will require this to be more substantial and usually result in the need for a further appraisal after a reasonable period. But a magistrate who continues to demonstrate a significant shortfall in his or her competences can, if he or she does not choose to resign, be referred to the Advisory Committee for it to decide what action to take.

Regular further appraisals of 'wingers' follow at roughly three-yearly intervals and before each such appraisal there is day of Continuation Training comprising refreshers, updates and preparation for the next upcoming appraisal.

SITTINGS REQUIREMENTS

The Lord Chancellor requires every magistrate to sit in court to hear cases for a minimum of 26 half-days per year. A full day's sitting counts as two days. Many magistrates regularly exceed this minimum requirement: to support the work of their local bench, for mentoring purposes, to make sure that they continue to gain experience, that their competences are up to strength and that they are up to date. Since Advisory Committees are keen to ensure the widest social base for the magistracy, they and the court administration will usually try to accommodate magistrates' preferred sitting patterns, e.g. where there is a need to balance other work or family commitments. But there can be problems, when a committee may need to remind the magistrate of the undertakings which he or she gave before being appointed.[21]

Section 50 Employment Rights Act 1996 provides that magistrates are to be given time off work to perform their duties to an extent that is 'reasonable in all the circumstances', based both on what the duties themselves involve and also the

---

20. Often in an anonymised way. Even magistrates who are professional appraisers in their ordinary working life must still undergo specific appraiser training. There are many models of appraisal and familiar work-based models are unlikely to meet the needs of judicial appraisal. However, any existing skills can be harnessed. Other varieties of 'threshold' and three-yearly appraisal will also follow if the magistrate goes on to serve in the youth or family jurisdiction or to take the chair.

21. Special considerations apply if a magistrates starts to take the chair or to sit on youth or family cases and thus faces additional pressures (see later in the chapter). But neither will a magistrate be pressed to sit more than 26 times if he or she is just an adult court 'winger': part of encouraging diversity.

circumstances, e.g. of the employer's business and the effect that the absence of the magistrate will have on it. However, such 'time off' work does not have to be paid leave. Certain loss of earnings allowances can be claimed (below). Magistrates have been known to use annual paid leave to maintain their sittings target.[22]

At the opposite end of the spectrum, although a willingness to sit far more frequently than the bare minimum might be seen as an even greater contribution to civic life, magistrates are not encouraged to sit for more than 100 half-days per year. To do so would detract from the fundamental nature of the role, inhibit participation by a broader range of people and possibly bring those magistrates concerned too close the subject matter with which they are dealing. Whilst a district judge (magistrates' courts) is a lawyer by training and professionally schooled in objectivity and detachment, the risk of a lay person dealing with a continuous 'diet' of prosecutions, offenders and punishments becoming 'involved' is arguably different.

PROGRESSING TO TAKING THE CHAIR

'Wingers' can apply to their local BTDC to attend training for potential adult court chairtakers after their second successful appraisal. Typically this will be five to six years after first appointment as a magistrate, i.e. some time after their first or 'threshold' appraisal and the first of their subsequent three-yearly appraisals.[23]

There is of course a need to ensure a good flow of court chairtakers, so that the Continuation Training that new magistrates will necessarily have undertaken just before reaching this stage will have contained a major input by way of an introduction to taking the chair. Subject to various considerations, most of those who are prepared to train for taking the chair are accepted for this. Any subsequent 'thinning out' will be based on aptitude or continuing interest which arises during:

- the training itself
- supervised sittings as a trainee chair taker over the following months; and
- formal appraisals as a trainee chair taker of which there are a minimum of three and a maximum of six within the year following training for the chair.

Competence for the Chair and Appointment
There is a separate competence for those who take the chair (*Chapter 4*): 'Taking the Chair: Managing Judicial Decision-making' (Competence 4). Those who complete the demanding process described in it are appointed to the local list of approved chairtakers by the BTDC. This appointment is subject to continuing three-yearly

---

22. Thus in effect forgoing any 'loss of earnings'.
23. And provided the application is made within three years of the last three year appraisal.

appraisal against Competence 4.[24] However, if they transfer to another local justice area (LJA) addition to the list of chair takers in the new area is not automatic even though the underlying accreditation of the person concerned can continue.

The Lord Chief Justice has indicated that he anticipates that chairpersons in the adult court will sit in the chair for at least one third of their sittings (still a minimum of 26 half days) although they are encouraged also to sit as 'wingers' on occasions both to continue to see matters from that perspective and also to make way for, or to support, colleagues who are newer to the role.

YOUTH AND FAMILY JURISDICTIONS

As already noted, the jurisdiction of magistrates in the adult court extends, as a result of the Courts Act 2003, across the whole of England Wales. Likewise, magistrates appointed to sit on youth or family cases will also exercise a national jurisdiction.

Appointment to either jurisdiction is no longer by election by the local bench (as it once was) but by way of selection by the Lord Chief Justice who has delegated this function to local BTDCs.[25] In both instances the process is controlled by the Justices of the Peace (Training and Development Committee) Rules 2007 which provide the three statutory criteria for appointment, i.e. the magistrate concerned must have:

- sat in the adult court for at least two years
- been appraised as competent on at least one occasion in the adult court in the last three years; and
- have observed the proceedings in the youth or family court (as applicable) on at least two occasions prior to the application.

It can be seen that eligibility to apply to sit on youth or family cases arises fairly early on in a new magistrate's career and before they are eligible to apply to train and be approved to take the chair in the adult court. The Lord Chief Justice has prescribed the form of application.[26] He has also directed that the 'Six Key Qualities' (above) originally demonstrated to the Advisory Committee do not need to be demonstrated afresh, nor should they be examined again by the BTDC. Instead the BTDC must look at just three personal factors in respect of applicants to ensure that they have:

- a basic understanding about youth or family work (as appropriate)
- an aptitude for undertaking youth or family work (as appropriate); and

---

24. Which can continue until the magistrate concerned retires at 70 years of age (below).
25. There are certain structural variations in the London area although the processes and considerations are essentially the same.
26. See estudo.co.uk/jsbmoodle and follow the link to 'Magistrates'

- a commitment to undertake that work as required along with the requisite training.

In exercising this delegated selection function, BTDCs are, in essence, acting as a form of 'mini Advisory Committee', selecting people to exercise a national judicial jurisdiction and, again, until they retire at 70 years of age or otherwise leave the bench. The main difference is that they select from within an existing 'judicial pool'.

Most of the guidance and values followed by Advisory Committees apply to BTDCs in one form or another when exercising this selection function and the process is, again, a 'two-way' one. Selection or non-selection must again be based solely on objective criteria. The BTDC thus looks at matters such as:

- validated training records
- existing appraisal reports
- comments made on the application form; and
- evidence obtained through any interview with a magistrate conducted by members of the Advisory Committee.[27]

There is dedicated training for both new youth and new family 'wingers' which broadly speaking mirrors, with adaptations, relevant aspects of that for new magistrates. An initial appraisal will again take place in each jurisdiction a year or so in and there will thereafter be additional three-yearly appraisals in each extra jurisdiction. For this reason, if no other, it is not usual for magistrates to undertake *both* youth and family work at the same time on top of their adult court work. It is, however, now sometimes possible for magistrates after five years sitting in this extra jurisdiction to concentrate solely on family matters (but not just on youth justice) if local circumstances permit (certain historical arrangements in London continue to see some magistrates sitting to deal with just youth or family work).

Where magistrates sit on either youth or family cases in addition to their adult court work the Lord Chief Justice suggests a minimum of 15 half-day sittings in each.

If a magistrate who sits on youth work wishes to take the chair in that jurisdiction then the usual route is via adult chair qualification and then 'conversion' to the youth court chair after taking further special training. On the other hand, taking the chair in the family court is more often by way of dedicated training, given the

---

27. Such interviews are not necessarily required for this appointment, but a single interview may now be conducted to address the personal factors above. If interviews are to be conducted then all applicants will be interviewed. Dedicated interview training is given to members of BTDCs. Any authorisation granted by the BTDC will be national and last until the magistrate is 70 years old or otherwise leaves the bench. It will also continue if the magistrate moves to another area of the country.

very different nature of that work. In both jurisdictions the BTDC will oversee the training and formal approval of chair takers.

The removal of a magistrate from these jurisdictions is on limited grounds (e.g. persistently failing to meet minimum sittings in the jurisdiction concerned or to demonstrate competence in that jurisdiction). It will be undertaken not by the BTDC but by the Lord Chief Justice personally on receiving a report from that committee.

EXPENSES

Unlike say local councillors, magistrates do not receive attendance allowances. They have, over the years, collectively resisted suggestions that they should. Most accept being a magistrate as voluntary, unpaid public service. They do, however, receive allowances to cover:

- loss of earnings for those who are employed or self-employed (albeit only up to a set maximum and only when there is an actual loss)
- subsistence (again within certain limits)
- travelling allowances (in the case of motor vehicles based upon a set amount per mile and the type of vehicle in question)
- certain other loss allowances, e.g. where a magistrate has to engage a childminder to cover the period when he or she is sitting.

The Magistrates' Association (*Chapter 2*) provides some up-to-date information for members which can be seen at its website: magistrates-association.org.uk

USE OF THE SUFFIX 'JP'

On appointment, magistrates or 'justices of the peace' (*Chapter 1*) become entitled to use the suffix 'JP', although not all of them choose to do so. It was formerly considered improper to use it for such purposes as business notepaper, but, recognising the voluntary contribution made by magistrates, this is now seen as acceptable provided, always, that there is no attempt in these or any other circumstances to secure any financial or other gain by this means. On retirement at 70 years of age (or sometimes earlier) it remains permissible to continue to use the suffix.

Retirement and the Supplemental List
Magistrates retire from active service when they reach 70 years of age. There are two exceptions, i.e. if they are then:

- chair of the local bench (but not just of the local youth or family panel) they can continue to sit until the end of the calendar year when that term of office automatically expires; or
- currently involved in particular unfinished court proceedings when they can seek authorisation through the Advisory Committee to continue to sit until those proceedings have been concluded.

On retiring from the bench they can apply to be placed on what is known as the 'Supplemental List' and the Lord Chancellor will usually agree to this on the recommendation of the local Advisory Committee which, in turn, will act on the basis of the individual's conduct and performance on the bench.

Magistrates on the Supplemental List do not have the judicial powers of a serving magistrate and have no prescribed functions. Their main role in practice, should they choose to exercise it, will involve witnessing the signing of documents or the countersigning of such matters as passport applications (simply because JPs come within the wider category of people authorised to perform such tasks).

In certain cases, magistrates who resign from the bench for personal reasons before they reach 70 years may also, on application, be placed on the Supplemental List. However, although still technically a JP, they have no automatic right to be reappointed at some later stage.[28]

---

28. Magistrates formerly remained eligible to sit at the Crown Court (see *Chapter 10* under 'Magistrates in the Crown Court') until 72 years of age, although local arrangements would often seek to limit this to those under 70 years of age in practice. The Courts Act 2003 effectively removed this specific extension. So that the only magistrates who can now (theoretically) continue to sit in the Crown Court beyond 70 years of age are those falling within the categories of exception relating to the magistrates' court itself.

Joining the Bench and the Early Years 'At a Glance'

Advisory Committees determine local bench needs and publicise the recruitment round

Advisory Committees hold two-stage interviews and examine the 'Six Key Qualities'

CRB checks and undertakings in respect of those to be recommended for appointment

The Lord Chancellor, in consultation with the Lord Chief Justice, appoints

Appointment of mentor by Bench Training and Development Committee (BTDC)

Start of Initial Training

Swearing-in

Rest of Initial Training, including observations and visits

Start of sittings, including mentored sittings, as an adult court winger

9-12 months

Consolidation Training and preparation for first appraisal

12-18 months

First appraisal

(Eligible to apply to sit on youth work, family work and appeals at the Crown Court (*Chapter 10*))

Continue to sit as an adult winger

Continuation Training, including preparation for three-yearly appraisal and introduction to the chair

First of continuing three-yearly appraisals as an adult court winger

Year 5-6

(Eligible to apply to train for the chair in the adult court)

CHAPTER FOUR

Magistrates Training and Development

Some readers may have come to this book inclined towards what was once a fairly common view that magistrates are 'all of a kind': well-intentioned amateurs armed with common sense and thus able to administer justice. From *Chapter 3* it can be seen that the modern-day appointments process is designed to ensure that they come from diverse backgrounds and that they must also undergo extensive training and appraisal. Similarly, there are nowadays genuine opportunities to progress in their part-time voluntary careers. They only perform the role of magistrate in their spare time, but being a magistrate requires considerable commitment. This chapter looks in greater detail at how their training and development takes place.

THE JUDICIAL STUDIES BOARD

The training and development of judges, magistrates (and members of tribunals) is overseen by the Judicial Studies Board (JSB).[1] Since 2007, the JSB also oversees the legal and judicial training and development of justices' clerks and court legal advisers (*Chapter 6*), with Her Majesty's Courts Service (HMCS), their Civil Service employer, arranging to cover other aspects.

The JSB is an independent body resourced through the Ministry of Justice (MOJ) (see generally *Chapter 2*). It is part of the Directorate of Judicial Offices of England and Wales and is led by judges rather than government officials. It reports ultimately and directly to the Lord Chief Justice who works in close liaison with the Lord Chancellor, including through what is known as 'The Concordat', a mechanism to allow discussions between judges, Ministers of State and others without the fear that this will impinge on judicial independence (see again *Chapter 2*).

One widely drawn JSB committee of magistrates, district judges (magistrates' courts) and others, is dedicated to matters affecting magistrates' courts. The JSB provides national training for the adult court for those legal advisers new to the service, or to youth or family work. The JSB also, from time to time (and subject to resources), provides training to justices' clerks and their legal teams in their role as deliverers of training. Furthermore, in partnership with magistrates, justices' clerks and others, it has produced a number of 'Bench Books'. These are practical reference tools for use in training and when sitting on the bench. There are separate Bench Books for each of adult, youth and family work.[2]

---

1. The JSB is based at based at Steel House, 11 Tothill Street London SW1H 9LJ: jsboard.co.uk
2. These and many of the other materials mentioned in this chapter can be viewed at jsboard.co.uk

MAGISTRATES NATIONAL TRAINING INITIATIVE (MNTI)

In 2003 the JSB produced a second version of what is now known as the Magistrates National Training Initiative (MNTI) handbook (or 'MNTI 2').[3] The term 'national' presaged the nationwide jurisdiction of magistrates since 2005. It also stresses a general move towards consistency at both local and national level in relation to magistrates and their activities. The comprehensive MNTI 2 handbook covers all aspects (adult, youth and family) of the structure, content and arrangement of magistrate training, including the Initial Training and Continuing Training described in *Chapter 3*. It also covers the training and development of those magistrates who apply to take the chair and who are appointed as mentors or appraisers and contains much advice on good practice.

Although the JSB devises and delivers some training itself nationwide and issues suggested national specimen training materials for local use, by far the largest part of the training of magistrates is delivered at local level by or through the justices' clerk. Here, the independence of judicial training and the independence of magistrates and their court legal advisers go hand in hand (see further *Chapter 6*).

Competence Framework

The JSB has, in partnership with magistrates, justices' clerks and others created the Competence Framework for magistrates within which those competences already described in *Chapter 3* fall; and against which magistrates can progress and be appraised. The framework includes elements both of knowledge and of performance criteria. As noted in *Chapter 3*, three of the competences are for 'wingers' (Competences 1 to 3) and one is for chairpersons (Competence 4). These same basic competences apply in all three jurisdictions (adult, youth and family) although the contexts in which they have practical effect differ. Wider summaries of Competences 1 to 3 and 4 are also set out at the end of this chapter so as to give some flavour of their range and depth.

Standards Framework

The JSB has a separate monitoring and evaluation team based in Leeds. This team has produced a Standards Framework for the training and evaluation of magistrate (and court legal adviser) training along with guidance to assist Magistrates Area Training Committees (MATCs) (below) to monitor and evaluate their own training arrangements and activities. The team also provides an internal evaluation service for the activities of its JSB colleagues in London.

---

3. Full and short explanatory leaflets appear at estudo.co.uk/jsbmoodle (follow the link to 'Magistrates').

MAGISTRATES AREA TRAINING COMMITTEES

To preserve the independence of magistrates' training, not only are justices' clerks and their legal teams the main providers of such training but the local training programme for magistrates is, in the main, determined by the magistrates themselves through a Magistrates Area Training Committee (MATC). This is a statutory committee established under the Justices of the Peace (Training and Development Committee) Rules 2007.

The MATC is based, solely for convenience, on Courts Boards areas (*Chapter 2*) and has a number of functions identified by statute and good practice, including:

- undertaking a training needs analysis
- devising training solutions[4] to meet such training needs
- arranging for the creation of local training materials (which draw on the JSB specimen materials already mentioned where relevant)
- creating an annual programme for the delivery of magistrates' training and development
- securing the requisite funding by Her Majesty's Courts Service (HMCS)
- monitoring and evaluating the content and delivery of local training and development
- monitoring and evaluating much of its own activity
- engendering local good practice; and
- producing an annual report each September.

The membership of MATCs essentially comprises:

- the chairs for the time being of Bench Training and Development Committees (BTDCs) across the area
- a justices' clerk from the area[5]
- where available, a family judge, a Crown Court liaison judge and a district judge (magistrates' courts); and
- a representative of the Magistrates' Association (*Chapter 2*).

The last of these is so as to maintain a link with the Magistrates' Association which is itself a significant provider of magistrate training.[6]

---

4. i.e. not just traditional training courses but 'solutions'.
5. The justices' clerk is a full voting member and not just an adviser to the MATC so as to reflect that, as seen in *Chapter 6*, justices' clerks themselves exercise certain judicial powers.
6. Examples of such work can be viewed at magistrates-association.org.uk

Relationship between the MATC and the JSB

The JSB has produced good practice guidance for MATCs. Because MATCs are not budget holders, the JSB, on an annual basis, agrees with HMCS a national statement as to the minimum training provision to be covered for the forthcoming training and financial year, thereby ensuring that any executive controls on budgets do not adversely affect the independence of magistrate training. This agreement extends not just to the front-line delivery of training but to all the necessary supporting structures and services.

Thus, if the MATC plans an annual training programme reasonably based on the agreed national statement, then adequate funding will usually follow. All indications are that HMCS has taken the independence of magistrate training very much to its heart and full and varied programmes take place around England and Wales.

BENCH TRAINING AND DEVELOPMENT COMMITTEES

The broad activities of Bench Training and Development Committees (BTDCs) have already been noted above and in *Chapter 3*. As their name implies, they are based in and around individual local benches of magistrates. BTDCs carry out duties across a range of adult, youth and family matters. However, it should be noted that all parts of the country (and not just Greater London which continues to have its own dedicated family TDC) may, now, on application, set up a separate, dedicated Family Training and Development Committee (FTDC). Inner London (uniquely) has, by retention from the past, a dedicated Youth Training and Development Committee (ILYTDC). The generic term Training and Development Committee (TDC) is now commonly applied to all such committees and is used in that sense in what follows.

TDCs are, like MATCs, statutory creatures under the Justices of the Peace (Training and Development Committee) Rules 2007. Their duties are, within varying remits, essentially the same whatever their individual subject matter. There is, however, in effect also a fourth version of a TDC in Inner London. Because all family TDC work there is undertaken by the Greater London FTDC and because all Inner London youth TDC work is undertaken by the ILYTDC, bench based TDCs in Inner London deal only with adult court training and development.

The broad duties of all TDCs include:

- establishing and maintaining a panel of trained mentors
- establishing and maintaining a panel of trained appraisers
- establishing and administering a scheme for appraising magistrates in relation to the adult, youth or family jurisdiction as appropriate
- arranging for around 20 per cent of local appraisals to be 'cross-bench' appraisals,

i.e. undertaken by approved appraisers from a neighbouring bench so that there is some degree of verification and consistency of approach

- working with the MATC in relation to its own functions and especially by identifying and relaying local training needs
- arranging for magistrates to attend relevant training provided by the MATC (or other training providers)
- identifying possible new chairpersons, arranging their training, supervision and appraisal and subsequently accrediting them as approved court takers and then maintaining a list of people so qualified; and
- sending its own TDC chair as an ex officio member to the local MATC.

TDCs comprise six or nine members, all serving magistrates appointed by or through local bench colleagues. Membership of a TDC is usually for a three-year term with an overall maximum of nine years. As already intimated, the justices' clerk is the adviser to the committee and he or she provides administrative support but, unlike the position in relation to the MATC (above), he or she is not a member.

THE CROWN COURT: A NOTE

Magistrates may in certain situations sit at the Crown Court alongside a circuit judge or recorder. The arrangements for this, together with their role, involvement and preparation for that jurisdiction are dealt with in *Chapter 10.*

MNTI 2 COMPETENCE FRAMEWORK FOR WINGERS

(SUMMARY OF COMPETENCES 1-3 ADULT, YOUTH AND FAMILY)

COMPETENCE 1 - MANAGING YOURSELF

1.1. BEFORE COURT

    1.1.a. Time keeping, questions of legal adviser, reading reports, checking guidelines

    1.1.b. Agreeing roles and responsibilities

    1.1.c. Identifying potential conflicts of interest

    1.1.d. Procedural, legal and case management issues

1.2. IN COURT

    1.2.a. Focusing attention, body language, communication

    1.2.b. Note taking, asking questions as appropriate

    1.2.c. Interacting with court users, including vulnerable, disadvantaged and special needs groups

    1.2.d. Maintaining authority, dignity and impartiality

1.3. LEARNING AND DEVELOPMENT

    1.3.a. Assessing own performance, seeking feedback, identifying own learning needs

    1.3.b. Adapting and developing performance in line with change

COMPETENCE 2 - TEAMWORK

2.1. MAKING AN EFFECTIVE CONTRIBUTION

    2.1.a. Expressing own views

    2.1.b. Questioning views of others

    2.1.c. Equal consideration, listening and understanding

    2.1.d. Non-discriminatory language, challenging stereotyping and discriminatory comments

2.2. CONTRIBUTING TO THE WORKING OF THE TEAM

    2.2.a. Supporting, respecting, communicating and minimising conflict

    2.2.b. Seeking and being receptive to advice of legal adviser

COMPETENCE 3 - JUDICIAL DECISIONS

3.1. USING APPROPRIATE PROCESSES AND STRUCTURE

    3.1.a. Structured decision-making

    3.1.b. Assessing relevance of information

    3.1.c. Analysing information within a structured approach

    3.1.d. Identifying and evaluating outcomes of structured approach

    3.1.e. Formulation of reasons and pronouncements

3.2. MAKING IMPARTIAL DECISIONS

    3.2.a. Identifying, acknowledging and setting aside prejudice and bias

    3.2.b. Challenging bias and prejudice in decision-making

    3.2.c. Recognising relevant and irrelevant factors that may influence decisions

MNTI 2 COMPETENCE FRAMEWORK FOR CHAIRMEN

(SUMMARY OF COMPETENCE 4 ADULT, YOUTH AND FAMILY)

COMPETENCE 4 - COMPETENCE 4 - MANAGING JUDICIAL DECISION MAKING

4.1. WORKING IN PARTNERSHIP WITH THE LEGAL ADVISER TO ENSURE THE EFFECTIVENESS OF THE COURT

    4.1.a. Identifying issues for clarification prior to court session, establishing relevant structures/processes to facilitate routine applications/procedures.

    4.1.b. Agreeing and maintaining their respective roles and responsibilities.

    4.1.c. Reviewing the day's sitting with the legal adviser.

4.2. MANAGING COURT PROCEEDINGS USING APPROPRIATE COMMUNICATION SKILLS

    4.2.a. Ensuring the purpose/framework of the hearing is established/maintained from the outset by giving appropriate directions, setting realistic timetables, seeking explanations for failure to comply with directions and taking appropriate action.

    4.2.b. Giving clear instructions to participants throughout the proceedings and checking that all involved understand everything.

    4.2.c. Addressing those in court fluently, clearly and audibly.

4.2.d. Encouraging participants to contribute constructively and dealing assertively with any inappropriate/inaccurate/unhelpful contributions by restricting representations, speeches and discussion and dealing promptly with any disruptive behaviour.

4.3. SEEKING AND ENHANCING THE CONTRIBUTION OF COLLEAGUES IN ORDER TO ENSURE EFFECTIVE DECISION MAKING

4.3.a. Asking colleagues to take responsibility for key tasks (e.g. checking guidelines and locating appropriate structures).

4.3.b. Facilitating discussion by focusing on structure, identifying/summarising key issues, intervening promptly when disagreement is preventing constructive discussion and progressing/exploring areas of disagreement.

4.3.c. Agreeing the decision, reasons and pronouncement to be given in court.

4.3.d. Reviewing the day's sitting with magistrate colleagues and/or the legal adviser and seeking, receiving and giving feedback.

4.4. ENGAGING IN ONGOING LEARNING AND DEVELOPMENT

4.4.a. Assessing own performance against framework. Regularly seeking feedback and identifying own learning and development needs.

4.4.b. Adapting and developing own performance in light of changes to law, practice, procedure, research and other developments. Keeping own resource materials (e.g. bench book, handbooks, and guidelines) up to date.

CHAPTER FIVE

Respecting and Promoting Fairness and Rights

Everyone expects people in judicial positions to act fairly and not ride roughshod over the rights of people involved in court proceedings, whether as defendants, victims, parties, witnesses or in any other capacity. However, you do not need to look far to see that, in some countries, the Executive may try to bring the Judiciary under its influence, or alternatively judges may have agendas of their own. *Chapter 2* looked at aspects of judicial independence. *Chapters 3* and *4* also showed how such independence is encouraged via appointment and training. *Chapter 6* also emphasises how this is reinforced by the legal advice that a magistrates' court receives.

But how, in what is increasingly a society that demands direct accountability in all aspects of public life, can people in England and Wales remain assured that all of its nearly 30,000 magistrates act fairly and appropriately, both individually and collectively? And how do the aspirations of the Competence Framework described in earlier chapters concerning impartial decisions become a reality?

THE JUDICIAL OATH

The Judicial Oath has been noted in *Chapter 3*: 'I will well and truly serve our Sovereign Lady Queen Elizabeth the Second, in the office of Justice of the Peace and will do right to all manner of people after the laws and usages of the Realm without fear or favour, affection or ill will'. This seems clear and direct enough and has perhaps served well enough and for many years. It recognises the diversity of individuals, the need to make decisions within the law and that it is essential to be fearless and fair in doing so. But how does the oath translate into good practice? And what of the Human Rights Act mentioned daily in the media (often without further or adequate explanation or accurate and informed understanding)?

The Human Rights Act 1998

The European Convention On Human Rights and Fundamental Freedoms (ECHR) was a response to certain horrific events of World War II. Even today many parts of the world continue to experience events of a kind that occurred over half a century before. The need for a human rights culture is as great as ever; and it has relevance even for people living in liberal democratic states not currently directly or personally affected by such events. It is often through small manipulations of public systems, particularly judicial systems, that an overzealous, let alone corrupt, State can inadvertently or intentionally begin to deny the rights of ordinary people.[1]

The Human Rights Act 1998, which in 2000 incorporated the ECHR into UK law, is not a just a high-minded gesture. It is a real and immediate protection for all individuals. It goes to the very root of how a State and its many agencies and public services should treat individuals.

As far as magistrates' courts are concerned, after a flurry of activity in the early days following implementation in 2000, human rights factors have now worked their way into all aspects of court work and are generally honoured without the need for specific consideration. Conscious appreciation of the importance of human rights through training and good practice is now perhaps the main counter to complacency. The Bench Books available to magistrates and referred to in *Chapter 4* each offer human rights guidance whenever a Convention right might be 'engaged' (by which is meant that consideration of the right should follow whether or not the court might ultimately interfere with its application in a given situation). This is part of magistrates taking a structured and reasoned path.

Some Principles of Human Rights

Following the 1998 Act, all new legislation, when being introduced into Parliament, is expressly confirmed as being 'compatible' with Convention's rights. It remains for the courts to later decide whether this is correct when applying the law.[2]

The ECHR contains a number of Articles and Protocols dealing with different rights. It is said to be a 'living instrument', i.e. their meaning and application were not indelibly fixed at the time when the Convention was drafted, but change with the times (unlike the English law of precedent). Thus magistrates, like all other members of the judiciary, need to remain alert and ready to adapt the application of human rights to new situations or circumstances.

Protection of human rights demands a 'purposive approach', i.e. again it looks to the intent (which is quite unlike the historical position in English law where a court largely speaking looks to the 'letter of the law'). What matters with human rights law is the underlying protection of given rights not whether the language was precise enough or a comma or full stop was in the right place. For similar reasons, there is often a 'positive duty' on States to be proactive in the application and preservation of Convention rights.[3]

All public authorities (including not just the courts but public agencies having business in the courts, such as the police, HM Prison Service and the National

---

1. Two classic instances are Nazi Germany and early Communist Russia, where incrementally the judiciary was brought under State control: but it has happened in other parts of the world, usually but not always in countries where judicial doctrines and standards are less well-developed or respected.
2. Principally the High Court and House of Lords: several laws have been found to be incompatible when government has had to consider amending legislation. Judges can adapt secondary legislation.
3. Wither then the UK which has so often been found to have denied or failed to uphold human rights. Holders or former holders of high judicial office have commented on the lamentable nature of this.

Probation Service) must not deny a Convention right; and should promote it.

Courts must try to interpret and apply all laws so as to give effect to Convention rights. The higher courts[4] can declare legislation incompatible with any of the Articles of the Convention.

ARTICLES OF THE CONVENTION

The Articles confer different levels of right according to the nature of their subject matter: absolute, limited or qualified. Limited rights have their limitations expressly stated in the Convention itself, whilst qualified rights may be overridden under principles such as the doctrine of proportionality, which connotes a balancing exercise between public or national and private rights. Due to the Human Rights Act, proportionality has also become a watchword for the actions of public authorities as whole. The Articles with the most day-to-day relevance to magistrates are contained in *Figure 1*. The chart also explains the status of the right involved.

Human Rights in Everyday Operation.

An interesting application of Article 6 (the right to a fair trial) in magistrates' courts arose in respect of section 172 Road Traffic Act 1988. Essentially, that section allows police to require the registered keeper of a motor vehicle, under threat of criminal sanctions, to give information concerning who was driving it at a time when it is alleged that the driver committed one of a list of offences connected with the vehicle. The duty to respond applies even if the keeper was the driver at the time.

However, express aspects of Article 6 are the presumption of innocence (see further below) and protection from self-incrimination (both also age old English principles). On appeal to the House of Lords it was determined that, although Article 6 may have been engaged, it had not, in all the circumstances and final analysis been breached.

Another example concerning Article 6 in magistrates' courts arose in relation to the question 'Just what are 'criminal proceedings?'. Obviously they include those which involve prosecution for clearly defined offences. But Article 6 provides rights to a fair trial in respect of all types of proceedings though, understandably, more specific ones for criminal cases. So can a State avoid some of the criminal case implications of Article 6 simply by designating matters as civil proceedings?[5]

The answer is 'no'. Not that there were any such intentions imputed to the UK government when it introduced anti-social behaviour orders, but it did provide via legislation that they would be civil proceedings. Article 6 quickly came into play and

---

4. In theory any court can, including a magistrates' court. A practice has developed of leaving the matter to the higher courts. It would be a bold magistrates' court which did not defer to this.
5. See also *Chapters 2* concerning civil proceedings in magistrates' courts and *Chapter 10* for examples.

domestic case law soon determined that although the proceedings may have been classed as civil by the legislation, the criminal burden of proof ('beyond reasonable doubt' as opposed to the 'balance of probabilities') applies. In broad terms this is because such proceedings can lead to criminal sanctions: see further *Chapter 10*.

ARTICLE NUMBER	TERMS OF ARTICLE	NATURE OF THE RIGHT
3	Prohibition on subjecting people to torture or to inhuman or degrading treatment	Absolute
4	Prohibition of slavery or forced or compulsory labour	Part Absolute Part Limited
5	The right to liberty and security	Limited
6	The right to a fair trial (incorporating 'reasons')	Part Absolute Part Limited
7	No punishment without law	Absolute
8	The right to respect for family and private life	Qualified
10	The right to freedom of expression	Qualified
11	The right to freedom of assembly	Qualified
14	Prohibition of discrimination in the enjoyment of the other Convention rights	Absolute
First Protocol	Protection of property	Qualified
If a right is *absolute* then there can be no limits or qualifications to its application.		
If a right is *limited* then there may be circumstances when that right will cease to apply, e.g. it is possible to order unpaid work (arguably 'forced or compulsory labour' in other circumstances) as a sentence, albeit only in accordance with clearly defined and reasonable statutory provisions. Similarly, lawful imprisonment or being held in custody is provided for specifically be law and also protected by *habeus corpus*.		
If a right is *qualified* there may be a need, applying proper provisions, to interfere with it in order to balance it with another Convention aims or with the rights of others.		

Figure 1: Summary of Articles, Protocols and the nature of individual human rights

REASONS FOR DECISIONS

Another significant change brought about by the Human Rights Act was that, in determining what was a 'fair trial' for the purposes of Article 6, the public giving of reasons by all courts for their decisions was seen to be an integral feature. Although all courts had previously given reasons to some extent and statute already provided for this in certain specific situations,[6] the process acquired a major new impetus from 2000 onwards, especially in magistrates' courts. As courts of summary jurisdiction (*Chapter 2*) magistrates had hitherto been less involved in the giving of formal reasons save in those situations where they were compelled to do so by law.

This was sometimes argued as being in order on the tenuous basis that 'If you don't say anything, then you can't make a mistake!' People brought up in the human rights era would predictably find this bizarre. Needless to say, as noted in other chapters, the quality of advice and training given to magistrates has moved on.

Giving reasons involves relating the facts and merits of a case to an explanation for the final outcome of a case or at some intervening stage. This must be consistent with both the law which applies and the evidence or information in a case. In a sense, it is a way of testing whether a decision is sound and when reasons are announced it enables to parties to test this also. Human rights rest on open justice of this kind.

BIAS, PREJUDICE AND DISCRIMINATION

In their selection, training, judicial oath and Competence Framework, as well, as in other respects, magistrates are encouraged to focus on recognising, avoiding and challenging prejudice, bias and discrimination in themselves and others. The following informal definitions can be suggested:

- **bias** approaching a situation from a preformed personal opinion rather than judging it on its own facts and merits
- **prejudice** a preconceived negative opinion of someone or something often based on little or no real evidence
- **discrimination** treating people differently when there is no lawful basis for this, in effect less favourably because of certain factors such as their race, skin colour, gender, sexual orientation or disability.

A first line of approach in addressing all such issues is the acquisition of knowledge about people and their lives and cultures. The inherent and increasing diversity of magistrates noted in *Chapter 3* helps in this. Magistrates training in such matters is addressed towards matters such as:

- minority ethnic groups (including what are often termed black or minority ethnic

---

6.   Such as when compensation is not awarded to a victim of crime (*Chapter 7*) or re a decision not to disqualify someone from driving when ordinarily a mandatory requirement. Other examples include: bail (*Chapter 2*) and sentencing generally (*Chapter 7* and see section 174 Criminal Justice Act 2003).

people and matters (BME))

- varying family structures
- religion in all its forms
- disability (physical, mental, blindness, deafness or other reasons)
- sexual orientation
- gender issues
- poverty issues
- literacy and numeracy
- diverse cultures (see further the following paragraph)
- dress and appearance; and
- lifestyle.

All the Bench Books referred to above and in *Chapter 4* contain detailed guidance on such matters. To build on this and to help magistrates to hone their skills against the Competence Framework, the Magistrates' Association (in conjunction with the Judicial Studies Board, Justices' Clerks' Society and others) has produced a number of workbooks. These focus on practical issues and strongly on matters of bias, prejudice and discrimination. They also offer suggestions on how to guard against stereotyping people (placing them in neat categories and then assuming that they have features in common with other people perceived to be in the same category) and give information about different aspects of the make-up of society, communities, groups and individuals. Judges have for many years had available to them an Equal Treatment Bench Book[7] copies of which are widely available in bench libraries at magistrates' courts.

There are many other drivers of anti-discrimination, including a duty which is placed on the Lord Chancellor to publish regular details concerning such matters for the information of all people involved in the administration of justice.[8]

STRUCTURED DECISION-MAKING

One way of ensuring that all judicial decisions are fair and accord with the law and that the reasons given in support are appropriate is to adopt a structured approach to making decisions. For many years, magistrates have been trained in structured decision-making. Following decision-making structures is particularly useful when grappling with the complexities that are inherent in certain judicial decisions. It makes it easier to underwrite findings at each stage within an overall decision and by gathering together supporting reasons at each stage. These can also be used to

---

7. Again, this like the other materials mentioned can be accessed at jsboard.co.uk
8. The duty is contained in section 91 Criminal Justice act 1991. It formerly fell on the Home Secretary.

formulate a public pronouncement[9] at the end of a case. The Bench Books referred to above and in *Chapter 4* also contain suggested decision-making structures (which many magistrates' courts have translated into easily used formats for use on the bench in court). There are also templates which can be adapted to meet the needs of individual pronouncements.

An example of a structured approach to deciding the verdict in a contested criminal case is contained within the questions that a court would ask itself:

1. What are the ingredients of the offence charged?
2. Has the underlying burden of raising all of these in evidence been discharged by the prosecutor?
3. What are the relevant facts that are not in dispute?
4. What relevant facts are in dispute?
5. What admissible evidence has the court received from both prosecution and defence witnesses on those disputed facts?
6. Which parts of that evidence does the court accept as reliable?
7. Have all the ingredients been proved to the requisite *standard of proof* (beyond reasonable doubt: see later in the chapter)?
8. If they have, then the court will find the case proved.
9. If they have not, then it will dismiss the case.
10. What reasons has the court found in support of its decision as demonstrated by and during the structured decision-making process?
11. How can the court formulate those reasons for public pronouncement from the chair in support and explanation of its decision?

Figure 2: Example of how a court approaches a structured decision

It should be noted re *Figure 2* that:

- English criminal proceedings are 'adversarial' as opposed to 'inquisitorial' (as in found in many European countries) or 'problem-solving' (as per restorative justice: see the *Glossary*), i.e. the court's role is not to search proactively for the truth or to find a solution that avoids conflict but to adjudicate for one party or another on the facts and evidence before it.[10]

---

9. 'Pronouncement' is commonly used to describe any announcement in court, especially at the end of a case. The Bench Books (and other materials) contain sample pronouncements for a range of matters.
10. For the adversarial system, see *Fighting For Justice: The Origins and History of Adversary Trial* (2006), Hostettler J, and for Restorative Justice, *Doing Justice Better: The Politics of Restorative Justice* (2007),

- thus defendants are not found 'innocent' but, instead, are 'found not guilty' and the case is 'dismissed' and they are duly 'acquitted' and 'discharged'
- the decision is by a straight majority (magistrates usually sit only in twos or threes and, for obvious reasons, always try to sit in threes for contested cases). Any difference of opinion is not announced, the verdict being presented as unanimous.
- there is no concept of 'benefit of the 'doubt': if there is a doubt in the mind of one or more of the bench then, for them, the case has not been proved. They will have to vote for acquittal but accept the majority view.
- each adjudicating magistrate has an equal vote (new magistrates cannot 'defer to the experience' of longer serving colleagues); and
- the chair, if outvoted by his or her two 'winger' colleagues, will still have to return to court and announce the decision without demur: it is the decision of the bench as a whole, a form of collective responsibility.

FOLLOWING GUIDELINES

The role of magistrates is generally to undertake a series of specific tasks within court proceedings (e.g. consider verdict, determine sentence, etc). Many such tasks have a corresponding suggested structure to work through to assist magistrates in coming to their decisions. There are also often suggested national guidelines, e.g. Mode of Trial Guidelines in relation to either way offences (*Chapter 2*) or Sentencing Guidelines (*Chapter 7*). Such guidelines cover, e.g. the main factors which magistrates' should consider in a given situation and during each step of their decision.

FAIRNESS SUMARISED

It is useful to summarise the wide range of items which in combination are designed to ensure that magistrates' courts to act fairly:

- the judicial oath
- applying and balancing human rights considerations
- training
- a Competence Framework
- independent legal advice
- reference materials
- practical in-court handbooks
- structured decision-making

Cornwell D J, both Waterside Press. Some proceedings before magistrates have restorative elements, e.g. in the youth court (and as supported by the Youth Justice Board) and family proceedings court.

- following national guidelines
- giving reasons publicly
- collective responsibility; and
- creating a culture in which inappropriate matters can and will be challenged.

THE PRESUMPTION OF INNOCENCE

A presumption is a conclusion that follows as a matter of course once some under-lying premise is established. The criminal law involves both presumptions of law (where the law says that something is the case on given facts) and presumptions of fact (that it gets dark early in winter). One presumption of the Common Law is the presumption of innocence: a longstanding rule that an accused person is innocent unless and until found guilty by a court, or until he or she voluntarily pleads guilty to the offence charged.

This is now reinforced by Article 6 of the ECHR. It affects the way in which accused people are dealt with at all stages of the criminal process prior to conviction; and is, e.g. the reason why someone who is interviewed by the police is described as a 'suspect' rather than 'an offender'. It is why prisoners who are awaiting trial are held under a separate and less restrictive regime than those who have been convicted. It is also why even in the most unpalatable of situations, pre-conceptions, trial by media or word-of-mouth, or otherwise pre-judging a case is wholly inappropriate.

BURDEN AND STANDARD OF PROOF

The burden of proof in a criminal case normally rests on the prosecutor. His or her evidence must also reach the requisite standard of proof for a criminal case, i.e. beyond reasonable doubt.[11]

Very exceptionally, the law reverses the onus and the accused person must then raise and establish something by evidence (e.g. that he or she had permission or re certain statutory defences); when the standard applied to that evidence is the lesser civil standard of proof, 'on a balance of probabilities'. The reason for this is that a prosecutor can hardly be expected in all cases to prove, e.g. that someone did not hold a licence or did not have authority or permission to do something. He or she can only present the known facts, leaving it to the accused person to explain matters

---

11. As confirmed in a seminal House of Lords ruling in *Woolmington v. Director of Public Prosecutions* [1935] Appeal Cases 462. Lord Sankey said, 'Throughout the web of the English criminal law one golden thread is always to be seen - that is the duty of the prosecution to prove the prisoner's guilt ... If, at the end of and on the whole of the case, there is a reasonable doubt, created by the evidence given by ... the prosecution or the prisoner ... the prosecution has not made out the case and the prisoner is entitled to an acquittal ... No matter what the charge or where the trial [this principle] is part of the Common Law of England and no attempt to whittle it down can be entertained'. This has been reiterated many times over.

in such a situation. If the latter does not, even then it is still for the court to decide whether or not to convict on the basis of all of the evidence which it has heard. The situation can be usefully compared with that described in *Chapter 2* in relation to 'No Case to Answer'.

In civil proceedings the burden of proof generally lies with the person bringing the case, i.e. whoever is making the application or complaint (see generally *Chapters 2* and *10*); or failing that the individual assertion being made.

When the word 'satisfied' is used

In some instances an Act of Parliament will say that magistrates must be satisfied as to something or other. This may involve the formal burdens of proof described above, but is can also in certain situations mean something less. Magistrates' dealing with bail applications (*Chapter 7*) will need to be satisfied that grounds for refusing bail exists before they deny the accused person his or her right to bail (now reinforced by Article 5 of the ECHR: see further *Chapter 10*). No formal burden or standard of proof is implied here. Naturally, there will need to be evidence or information on which the court can base its decision, but it is a matter for the magistrates how they 'satisfy themselves' concerning the existence of the relevant ground.

CHAPTER SIX

Magistrates and the Law

The Justices of the Peace Act 1361 may still be on the Statute Books but its provision that, within the justices, there should be 'some learned in the law' no longer applies. Indeed the whole rationale behind the modern magistracy is that it should be truly 'lay' in nature (albeit 'professional' in action and approach). The term 'lay', which appears in the Courts Act 2003, is now no longer generally used in practice. As noted in *Chapter 3*, the modern magistracy contains the broadest spectrum of society possible and any prior knowledge of the law is far from being a qualification for appointment.

There may, however, be magistrates who are, as it happens, legally qualified in their private or business lives. They will still undertake the full training, development and appraisal measures as for their colleagues.[1]

'It's Now a Matter for You'

The relationship between magistrates and their legal advisers is perhaps nowhere better demonstrated than via the adviser's traditional response after tendering advice to the bench and culminating in the closing words: 'But it's now a matter for you'.[2] But as will be seen, the adviser can also point out that on given facts a particular finding is inevitable or follows as a matter of law.

It has been noted in earlier chapters when touching on the judicial independence of the magistracy how the provision of independent legal advice plays a vital part in this. *Chapter 2* also covered the role of the justices' clerks and how they, and their legal teams, fit into the wider structure of magistrates' courts. Those who provided clerical assistance (but not legal advice) to magistrates had, from Tudor times onwards, mainly been drawn from within the magistrates' own private staff.

The existence of a professional justices' clerk providing both clerical support and legal advice dates from the early 19th century when the part-time services of a local solicitor in private practice would be obtained by a bench on a fee-attracting basis. This continued well into the 20th century although, by then, the function had turned into a statutory office, held 'at the pleasure of' the local bench and attracting a salary rather than fees. The clerks formed the Justices' Clerks' Society in 1839 and, although the number of justices' clerks *per se* in the country is now less than 50, the

---

1. The author worked with a magistrate who was also a Law Lord, the latter having been appointed as a local magistrate in his younger days. He claimed to be the only holder of high judicial office who sat by virtue of the ordinary Commission of the Peace rather than *ex officio* due to his status as a senior judge.
2. Usually followed by 'Sir' or 'Madam'; and here it is convenient to note that this is the modern way of addressing the court for everyone concerned, i.e. via the chair. The term 'Your Worships' is rarely if ever used nowadays and seems quaintly old-fashioned.

JCS still flourishes and has for some time, admitted to membership all court legal advisers employed to assist justices' clerks.

The beginnings of the modern full-time, employed justices' clerk, occupying an independent statutory office date from the Justices of the Peace Act 1949 which started the process of moving to the form of magistracy in place today. With the arrival of Her Majesty's Courts Service in 2005, the office of justices' clerk as such disappeared and all justices' clerks and their legal teams became civil servants by virtue of the Courts Act 2003. The term justices' clerk is still used however by statute and in practice.

In the lead up to all of this there had been expressed clear, strong and justifiable concerns about how the independence of the magistracy, and of the legal advice it received, could be assured. Furthermore, how could there be a civil servant exercising the judicial powers possessed by justices' clerks and their assistants. The relevance of the fair trials provisions of Article 6 of the European Convention on Human Rights is all too clear (see *Chapter* 5). The matter was addressed through what became section 29 of the Courts Act 2003:

(1) A justices' clerk exercising—

   (a) a function exercisable by one or more justices of the peace,

   (b) a function specified in section 28(4) or (5) (advice on matters of law, including procedure and practice), or

   (c) a function as a member of the Criminal Procedure Rule Committee or the Family Procedure Rule Committee,

is not subject to the direction of the Lord Chancellor or any other person.

(2) An assistant clerk who is exercising any such function is not subject to the direction of any person other than a justices' clerk.

This covers advice in court and also in training sessions, bench meetings or on similar occasions. The above, coupled with the inclusion of justices' clerks within the wider 'judicial family' under the Lord Chief Justice, appears, in practice, to have secured the continuation of the fierce independence of advice and mind which justices' clerks appear to have gained a reputation for. It also covers the work of justices' clerks (and legal advisers in their legal teams) when exercising their own judicial powers (below) and should they become involved in helping to draft national procedural rules. It can, however, be noted that legal advisers in the justices' clerk's legal teams are subject to direction in even legal matters by the justices' clerk, thereby ensuring consistency and competence of advice to justices. Greater consistency of advice is also pursued through the Area Judicial Forum (see *Chapter 2*).

The statutory qualifications for appointment as a justices' clerk are to be found in section 27 of the 2003 Act. The most common route to qualification will now be by way of being a barrister or solicitor who has served for not less than five years as an assistant to a justices' clerk. In turn, the Justices' Clerks (Qualifications of Assistants) Rules 1979 (as amended) set out the basic legal qualification provisions for those who wish to become legal advisers in court acting on behalf of a justices' clerk.

Over recent years, particularly as their numbers reduced from the hundreds of around thirty years earlier and life has become more complex, justices' clerks have been drawn increasingly into management matters and more removed from their in-court role, although they have generally held firmly on to their training role to maintain contact with their benches. However, there is now a move within Her Majesty's Courts Service to try to free them up to be able to work more closely with their magistrates in the courtroom.

THE COMPETENCE FRAMEWORK AND LEGAL ADVICE

It has already been seen in *Chapter 4* that the Competence Framework for both wingers and chair takers, in all of their adult, youth and family jurisdictions, directly addresses how to work with legal advisers and how to seek and receive advice. Justices' clerks and their legal teams have their own competences which in many ways mirror those of magistrates.

The relationship between magistrates and their justices' clerk and the justices' clerk's legal team is at the heart of an effective and fair magistrates' courts system and is a text book example of people working together, complementing each other but at the same time respecting their individual roles and functions. Great efforts are made to establish and nurture this very special and unique form of partnership.

THE KEY PRACTICE DIRECTION

The role of justices' clerks and their teams of legal advisers to magistrates is governed by a *Practice Direction* on the 'The Role of the Legal Adviser'[3] which, in its current form, essentially provides that advisers can advise magistrates on:

- questions of law (including of course human rights law)
- questions of mixed law and fact (e.g. if, in deciding upon their verdict, magistrates find particular facts proved then they must as a matter of law convict since all the

---

3. *Practice Direction on the Role of the Legal Adviser: Guide to the Conduct of Justices' Clerks and Assistant Justices' Clerks* (2007). See also 'The Role of the Legal Adviser' (2008), Justices' Clerks Society (which can be accessed at jc-society.com). Other information is available at hmcourts-service.gov.uk

elements of the offence charged will exist)
- practice and procedure
- the range of penalties available
- relevant decisions of the higher courts (*Chapter 2*)
- sentencing guidelines (*Chapter 7*); and
- decision-making structures (*Chapter 5*)

The tendering of such advice arises both where the magistrates have directly asked for advice from the justices' clerk (or court legal adviser acting in place of the justices' clerk) and also where the latter considers that advice needs to be tendered even though the magistrates may not have thought of this.

In addition, justices' clerks (or a legal adviser acting in place of the justices' clerk) may also, where appropriate:

- inform all present of what is in any note of evidence he or she may have taken
- assist in the formulation of the bench's reasons (*Chapter 5*)
- ask questions of witnesses and parties to clarify evidence and issues
- assist (but clearly not act as advocate for) an unrepresented defendant in formulating any questions he or she may be trying to put to a witness; and
- assist in ensuring the overall fairness of the proceedings.

Advice is usually given in open court and in the hearing of all present but, if given in the privacy of the retiring room will always be summarised on the magistrates return to the courtroom so that, in all cases, the advice can be openly known and challenged if thought necessary.

Following on from human rights considerations, the role of the legal adviser in court in any enforcement proceedings is not to adopt an adversarial or partisan approach but to present the facts fully and clearly, letting those facts speak for themselves, and then to offer advice in the usual way.

It will then be seen that any legal advice proffered to magistrates will not venture into the actual decision to be made, such as:

- what facts to find
- whether or not to grant bail
- verdict (save as noted above); or
- what sentence to impose (save where the law precludes or requires certain sentences when sometimes this may need to be pointed out).

JUDICIAL OFFICERS

For some years now justices' clerks in legal proceedings have increasingly been given the powers of a 'single justice' (one magistrate sitting alone has long been able to undertake certain, albeit limited and essentially procedural, judicial acts).[4] Also in family proceedings courts (see *Chapter 9*) justices' clerks possess extensive judicial powers along broadly related lines.

Justices' clerks have thereafter been able to delegate these powers, through a formal scheme, to appropriate members of their legal teams, thereby giving name to the concept of 'delegated powers' i.e. judicial powers exercised in this manner concurrently with, but independently of, the magistrates. In the criminal courts such powers include:

- issuing a summons
- adjourning proceedings
- extending bail (on existing terms)
- issuing a warrant for failure to answer bail where there is no objection from the defendant (e.g. where the defendant had not asked for an adjournment or had not proffered a reasonable excuse for being unable to attend in answer to bail)
- dismissing a case where no evidence has been offered by the prosecution
- ordering a pre-sentence report (but not giving any 'indication of seriousness' of the offence) (*Chapter 7*)
- committing a defendant for trial in respect of an either-way offence without consideration of the evidence (*Chapter 2*); and
- giving directions relating to the management of the proceedings.

Sometimes justices' clerks and legal advisers sit in court on their own (albeit at their usual desk below or to one side of that of the magistrate: see the 'Example of a Courtroom Layout' on page xiii). On other occasions they may exercise these powers when the magistrates have retired to consider their decision, or even at the end of a court list when there are appropriate cases left to deal with. This helps to expedite the whole court list and to allow magistrates to concentrate on their prime functions. However, this sort of arrangement calls for a careful transition between the giving of advice to others and a judicial role. It also has to operate within the special personal relationship between magistrates and their legal advisers so that magistrates feel supported not undermined.

---

4. And in the case of magistrates' some wholly judicial decisions such as granting bail or sending a case for trial in the Crown Court.

THE 'BANGALORE PRINCIPLES'

In 1988 (even before the UK's own Human Rights Act incorporated the European Convention On Human Rights into UK law) a number of countries, including the UK, held a judicial colloquium in Bangalore to examine how internationally recognised human rights should be applied in local domestic jurisdictions. In respect of judicial matters there emerged what became known as the 'Bangalore Principles of Judicial Conduct' which encompassed matters such as:

- impartiality
- integrity
- propriety
- equality of treatment for all before the law
- competence; and
- diligence.

These principles were already well established in the actions of magistrates and continue to be further enhanced in that respect. They have also been adopted for both the advice giving and judicial roles of justices' clerks and those court legal advisers employed to assist them. They supplement the fairness and rights culture examined in *Chapter 5*.

CHAPTER SEVEN

The Adult Magistrates' Court

'Adult' magistrates' court is the everyday way of referring to the court which deals with allegations against people aged 18 and over (and corporate bodies). If the term 'magistrates' court' is used without qualification then it can normally be assumed that it is this court which is being referred to rather than the youth court arrangements of the magistrates' court (*Chapter 8*) or its family proceedings jurisdiction (*Chapter 9*). Advice and guidance on many of its detailed processes is contained in an *Adult Court Bench Book* published by the Judicial Studies Board (JSB)[1] which:

> is intended to assist magistrates to meet the high standards … expected of them … the Bench Book provides them with a set of tools which will assist them in their work. It [promotes] a consistent approach to decision making and court procedure. The national guidelines, checklists and pronouncements that are included should be of greatest value in helping magistrates undertake the task of decision-making in a fair and structured manner. This will increase the public's confidence in their decisions.

As will be seen in *Chapter 10*, the magistrates' court deals not only with criminal cases but *A Diverse Range of 'Other' Responsibilities*. An adult court sitting may be described in a more descriptive way, e.g. as an enforcement court, crime court,[2] road traffic court, sentencing court or 'non-police court'.[3] HMCS takes the responsibility for overall sitting patterns and the arrangements for 'standard sitting days'. The task of scheduling cases for hearing is known as 'listing'. This is a judicial aspect of case management and is usually carried out by a dedicated listing officer at the behest of its justices' clerk and taking account of any wishes of the bench.

ADULTS, YOUNG OFFENDERS AND JUVENILES

In the context of age the following key points should be noted:

- 'adult' means someone of or above the age of 18 years[4]
- there is, however, an overlap, in that the term 'young offender' is used for those aged

---

1. The *Adult Court Bench Book* can be accessed at jsboard.co.uk
2. Usually meaning that it is dealing with more serious matters such as thefts, assaults, burglaries, etc.
3. Meaning that it is dealing with cases other than those initiated by the police *Chapter 10*. Magistrates' courts long ago ceased to be the 'police courts' of the Victorian era: *Chapter 1*.
4. An 'appropriate adult' (AA) is someone aged 18 or over who is (or sometimes must be) called upon to safeguard the interests of a child or vulnerable person in their dealings with the police, etc. and in particular when in police detention (*Chapter 2*), e.g. a relative or youth worker.

18-20 inclusive even though young offenders are technically adults. This leads to informal use of terms such as 'full adult' or 'adult for all purposes' to distinguish people aged 21 or over from those below that age'; and

- cases involving accused people below 18 years of age are normally heard by the youth court, but juveniles (or 'youths') may appear in the magistrates' court if, e.g. they are charged alongside an adult (although efforts are made to avoid this).[5] The sometimes different terminology of the youth court and other age-related categories, procedures and jurisdiction are explained in *Chapter 8*.

THE THREE CATEGORIES OF OFFENCE

As noted in *Chapter 2*, the jurisdictions of the Crown Court and magistrates' court and related powers, particularly of sentencing, are determined principally by three categories of criminal offence. These are as follows:

- **summary offences** (aka 'purely summary offences') which can normally only be dealt with in the magistrates' court as described in *Chapter 2*

- **either way offences** which can be tried either in the magistrates' court or the Crown Court depending on the outcome of the plea before venue/mode of trial procedures described below; and

- **indictable offences** (aka 'indictable only offences') which can and must only be tried and such an offender sentenced in the Crown Court (after magistrates have processed such cases at the very outset as described in *Chapter 2*).

PLEA BEFORE VENUE (PBV) AND MODE OF TRIAL (MOT)

The provisions described in this section are currently in a state of transition as there are sections (not yet brought into effect) in the Courts Act 2003 which (if and when brought into effect) will introduce new 'allocation and sending' arrangements.

PBV and MOT are descriptions for the procedural mechanisms for choosing between trial in the magistrates' court and trial in the Crown Court (aka 'trial on indictment'). Either way offences include theft; handling stolen property; various deceptions or frauds; those burglaries without aggravating features; criminal damage when the value is high; assault occasioning actual bodily harm (ABH); and the

---

5. Or even in the Crown Court. See also *Chapter 8* for other such situations.

possession or supply of certain prohibited (aka 'controlled') drugs.

In relation to every either way offence, the accused person has an unfettered right to trial by jury in the Crown Court. However, he or she may consent to trial in the magistrates' court where the magistrates are prepared to accept summary trial.

They will listen to an outline of the case by the prosecutor and any representations by the accused person or his or her legal representative. If they consider that the case is more suitable for summary trial, i.e. essentially but not exclusively that, if the accused person is convicted, their own maximum powers of punishment will be sufficient, then it is open to them to assume jurisdiction. As indicated in *Chapter 2*, magistrates' maximum powers extend to imprisonment for up to six months per either way offence[6] up to a maximum of 12 months (pending changes).

Many either way offences are, factually speaking, well within magistrates' powers and may well lead to a lesser sentence: a community sentence or fine rather than imprisonment. MOT guidelines exist to help magistrates in this task: see later.

Plea Before Venue

However, prior to embarking on the mode of trial procedure the court must give the accused person the opportunity to volunteer what his or her ultimate plea to the either-way offence will be. If that plea is stated to be one of guilty then the magistrates will by-pass MOT and move straight to consider sentence themselves or commit to the Crown Court for sentence if they consider their sentencing powers to be inadequate. This process also benefits the accused in later seeking credit at the sentencing stage for an early indication of a guilty plea (see later in the chapter).

Mode of Trial Procedure

If the plea is to be one of not guilty or is not otherwise stated then the mode of trial procedure will follow. This involves the court, as noted above, in hearing an outline of the facts and then listening to representations from both sides as to whether trial before the magistrates or at the Crown Court is more appropriate. The adequacy of the magistrates' sentencing powers will be a major factor but other factors such as the nature of the case will also apply. There are national Mode of Trial Guidelines to assist in this process.[7]

If the court decides that the case should be heard before the Crown Court then it may have to be adjourned for committal papers to be served and the case later formally committed for trial.

---

6. Twelve months per offence when latent powers come into force: see also that *Chapter 2* for aggregate sentences. A new as yet unimplemented regime of custody plus and intermittent custody (aka 'week-day imprisonment' or 'weekend gaol') contained in the Criminal Justice Act 2003 is also 'in limbo'. Custody plus and intermittent custody involve sentences served partly in prison and partly in the community. For a closer analysis of the legal provisions and other ramifications, see *Criminal Justice Act 2003: A Guide to the New Procedures and Sentencing* (2004), Gibson B, Waterside Press.

7. These can be accessed at jsboard.co.uk There are comparable MOT guidelines for Crown prosecutors.

If the court decides that the case can be heard before the magistrates then the accused will be asked to consent to that position (i.e. give up the right to trial before a judge and jury at the Crown Court). If such consent is forthcoming a formal plea is then taken (likely, but not necessarily, one of 'not guilty' given what has gone before in the plea before venue procedure). The court then proceeds in the usual way depending on that plea. If the accused pleads guilty or is found guilty by the magistrates, they have a power to commit to the Crown Court for sentence if they ultimately consider their sentencing powers then to be insufficient (usually in the light of previous convictions which only now will be disclosed).

If such consent is not forthcoming then, again, the case may have to be adjourned for committal papers to be served and the case later formally committed for trial.

Committal to the Crown Court for Trial

Historically magistrates dealing with a committal to the Crown Court (or Assizes and Quarter Sessions as it was on the old days) were known as examining justices. Even, e.g. in a murder case they critically examined the evidence for the prosecution, as given by live witnesses, to see whether there was a sufficient case to 'send up'. Under a series of reforms beginning in 1967 it became possible to have a 'paper committal' under which the same process was conducted using statements and related exhibits, but essentially amounting to a largely formal mechanism for transmitting cases 'upwards'.

The accused person continued to have certain rights to challenge both the nature of the case against him or her and the strength of the evidence, if need be by having some or all of the prosecution witnesses called to give evidence. This has now become yet more streamlined. In essence, the case is nowadays conducted solely on the papers and the only real issue is whether the statements disclose at least some evidence of each and every ingredient of the offence charged. If so, any later decisions concerning the progress and management of the case, or its strength are made by the Crown Court.

Magistrates still deal with issues of bail (below) or legal aid at this stage; but in most cases the committal itself has become something of a formality; and if the accused person or his or her legal representative does not wish to raise any issues it is largely a matter of the prosecution, defence and court making sure that the bundle of papers complies with modern-day committal procedures.

HOW CASES COME BEFORE MAGISTRATES

As described in *Chapter 2* in relation to criminal cases, a hearing before a magistrates' court involves a number of stages. Within the processes of detection, investigation and prosecution and subsequently the carrying out of any sentence, the court must arrive at a verdict and where the offender is guilty sentence him or her.

Suspects are interviewed by the police, who make a decision whether or not to arrest and charge them with an offence. In some instances they may wish to detain the individual concerned whilst investigations continues, when, after they have exhausted their own internal statutory limits, they will, if they would like to hold the suspect for further questioning or whilst the investigation continues elsewhere, need to apply to magistrates for a warrant of further detention (below).

Once charged, the accused will be allowed police bail to appear before a magistrates' court on some future date; or will be brought before the court for the magistrates to decide whether there is a need for him or her to be held in custody pending the next stage in the proceedings. The following mechanisms should be noted:

- **information and summons**: here the person making the allegation 'lays an information', i.e. submits a document[8] setting out details of the accused, the allegation in outline and saying what particular criminal law the conduct, failure, omission or events contravene. A summons is issued by a magistrate or justices' clerk and served on the accused person requiring the accused person's attendance at court;
- **arrest and charge**: here the police issue the accused person with a charge sheet, transmit a copy to the court, and either release that person on bail (below) or bring him or her before the court in police custody; and
- **charge and requisition**: a relatively new procedure (yet to be fully implemented nationwide) for public prosecutors was introduced by the 2003 Act, whereby the charge serves as the CJS-related paperwork and the requisition signals to the accused person when and where he or she should attend court.

Where someone is already before a magistrates' court (e.g. due to some other matter) a charge can be put to him or her directly (often referred to as an information 'on sight') subject to fairness in terms of allowing adequate time for it to be considered (see generally *Chapter 5*). This might occur, e.g. where a charge is substituted or added in the courtroom following discussions between the lawyers in the case (although, in most instances, any such matters should normally, nowadays, be 'trapped' earlier under the arrangements described under the next heading).

PRELIMINARY HEARINGS AND CASE MANAGEMENT

The next stage in all but straightforward or lesser cases is for a preliminary hearing to be held. This will assess future progress and is a form of 'case management'.

---

8. Technically, an information need not be in writing provided a court knows what is being alleged. It will of course be 'reduced to writing' if made orally. The situation is not typical, but it can occur in the courtroom when substitute charges have been under discussion or negotiation (including as part of a plea bargain).

Disclosure

Both the prosecutor and accused person are under various duties of disclosure, meaning that they must give prescribed information to each other concerning their case, the defence only, compulsorily, since 2003. Before that, 'advance disclosure' was, legally speaking, generally a matter for the prosecutor only and the principle was that the accused could reserve his or her defence, even to the extent of 'springing a defence' at the last moment or revealing it only as the case proceeded.[9] He or she might lose any sentencing discount (see later) but equally the case against him or her might 'cave in' altogether.

Victims of crime in particular found such developments to be an affront to justice, just as they to an extent still do in relation to certain aspects of the adversarial system of justice. In contrast, prosecutors tended to disclose their case automatically in either way cases (and this was obligatory on request) and in relation to many lesser contested cases. Disclosure is now integral to case management.

Unused prosecution materials

There are further rules about disclosing unused materials (those known to the prosecutor relating to the case but which are not to be used or relied upon by him or her to prove the case).[10]

Keeping the case under review

Throughout criminal proceedings, the Crown prosecutor has a continuing duty to keep the case under review; which may lead to a decision to discontinue it if it no longer satisfies the prosecution tests set out in the Code for Crown Prosecutors.[11]

CIVIL AND FAMILY CASES: A NOTE

Here it is the party bringing the claim who makes an application (aka in some cases a 'complaint') to the court office. A summons or notice is then served on the other party for him or her to attend court on a given date to answer whatever claim is being made. See further *Chapter 9* (re family proceedings) and *Chapter 10* (re civil cases) for the kind of matters involved. It was in family cases that more extensive processes of preparation for court, disclosure and case management began. Only in modern times have criminal courts begun to 'catch up'.

---

9. Except, notably, for a defence of 'alibi' which since 1967 had to be disclosed at the time a case was sent to the Crown Court for trial. Nowadays this former exception looks rather quaint.
10. At least so far as either way cases are concerned: but in practice most contested cases. In 2009, three defendants who had served 16 years apiece as part of life sentences were freed by the Court of Appeal after it was revealed that evidence which might have cleared them had been withheld. Some 14 police officers were later arrested on allegations of perverting the course of justice (pending).
11. The Code for Crown Prosecutors can be viewed at cps.gov.uk

THE LIBERTY OF THE SUBJECT

Two key procedures affect the liberty of people at the 'front end' of the criminal process and demand particular care and attention in view of the fact that they will not have been convicted of the offence with which the investigation or charge is concerned and are entitled to the 'Presumption of Innocence': *Chapter 5*.

Detention and Further Detention

Police detention (or that of other authorised law enforcement agencies) of suspects as per the Police and Criminal Evidence Act 1984 (PACE) is also known as detention without charge. When someone is arrested (other than on a court warrant) and taken to a police station, the police custody officer must release him or her unless there is enough evidence to support holding that individual for questioning about a criminal offence. Release may be on (police) bail for that person to return to a police station. It is possible for a police officer to grant 'street bail' (i.e. without taking the suspect back to a police station) which has a similar effect.

The detention process is governed by the Police and Criminal Evidence Act 1984 (PACE) and the PACE Codes made under that Act which were introduced in response to a number of high profile miscarriages of justice in earlier years.

The custody officer must keep the situation under review and once it becomes clear that detention is no longer justifiable the suspect must be released. But further detention can be authorised by a court under a series of applications and processes up to a maximum of 96 hours. This power is exercised by issuing what is called a warrant of further detention (WFD). Police powers have been greatly increased with regard to terrorism. Such suspects can be held for up to 28 days.[12]

Bail and Custody

The Bail Act 1976 gives a right to bail to people once charged with offences, i.e. not to be held in custody unless a statutory exception to that right exists. If a court finds that an exception (also known as a 'ground') does exist, the accused person can be refused bail and remanded in custody, usually for not more than eight clear days at a time *before* conviction.[13] Longer remands in custody are possible, up to 28 days (including after a case reaches the Crown Court after a decision of that court).

Following conviction and pending sentence, the custody limit is normally 21 days; but this is renewable. Most courts operate without the need for renewal.

---

12. This is a specialist area. Notoriously, a Government move to increase this to 42 days was defeated in the House of Lords in 2008. European Court of Human Rights criticism of executive powers of detention without trial led to the control order re terrorism under the Prevention of Terrorism Act 2005. This allows the Home Secretary to make someone subject to stringent requirements going well beyond those normally associated with bail. The control order is subject to judicial oversight, not by magistrates or the ordinary courts, but via the Special Immigration Appeals Commission (SIAC).
13. Eight clear days covers an inclusive span of ten days, i.e. one day either side of the eight.

People who are refused bail by magistrates can appeal to a judge of the Crown Court or a High Court judge; and prosecutors can appeal against the granting of bail (sometimes shortened to 'a grant') in certain instances.

Bail information and bail support schemes exist for people facing court hearings; many operated by the NPS and/or HMPS and/or youth offending teams (YOTS). They seek to provide information relevant to a bail decision to the CPS and defence. Matters not previously considered are looked into, e.g. a fixed address, or the possibility of a temporary one, or of a surety or security (below). The results are put to the court at the next hearing; and may be linked to referral schemes.

Some Key Aspects of Bail

Failure to surrender to bail is a criminal offence in its own right. An absconder also risks being arrested and the failure or absconding will also become a basis for refusing bail in the future (below).

Conditional bail, i.e. bail with conditions attached to it, can be granted, e.g. for the accused person to live at a particular address; report to the police; to keep away from the victim, witnesses or named people (aka a 'non-association condition'); or to stay away from a specified location. Reasons must be given by the court for imposing conditions. A defendant can be arrested without a court warrant for breach of a bail condition. Unlike failure to surrender to bail (above) a breach of a bail condition is not an offence.

Refusal of bail: grounds and reasons

Bail can normally only be refused if a court is satisfied that a statutory exception to the general right to bail exists. Any ground for refusing bail, and reasons in support, must be announced in court. A written copy of the grounds and reasons is given to the accused on request (but usually automatically). Under the Bail Act 1976, the principal bail statute, bail can be refused before conviction in respect of any offence that carries a possible sentence of imprisonment[14] if there are 'substantial grounds to believe' that if set free the accused would:

- fail to surrender to custody (above)
- commit an offence; or
- interfere with witnesses.

The scope for refusing bail is greater *after* conviction; less if the offence does not carry possible imprisonment.

Accused people can always be held in custody for their own protection whatever the offence concerned; or if there has been a previous breach of bail by absconding

---

14. Known as an 'imprisonable' offence: see the *Glossary*.

and the court believes that the accused would abscond again. An offender need not be granted bail if the offence is indictable only or an either way offence (both above) if already on bail for one offence when another was (allegedly) committed. Offending on bail, i.e. committing a criminal offence is not itself an offence. It may be a reason for refusing bail, cancelling it or treating the underlying offence more seriously at the sentencing stage.

Reasons for *granting* bail must be given in the case of murder and certain other prescribed offences; whilst bail cannot be granted at all re murder, attempted murder, rape, attempted rape or manslaughter if the accused already has such a conviction.

Since 2003, the police can grant most types of conditional bail (above) and street bail, literally 'on the street' at the discretion of the arresting officer rather than at the police station by a custody sergeant.

Repeat bail applications using the same arguments are restricted by law.

A security can be deposited with the court by an accused person or third party, i.e. some valuable item as a guarantee that the accused will attend court for his or her next scheduled appearance; failing which the security can be forfeited by a court.[15] A requirement that the accused 'find a surety' is a frequent bail condition, i.e. a responsible individual who will, in effect, vouch for the accused's re-appearance. The surety enters into a recognizance: see the *Glossary*.

An adult who is refused bail can be held for short periods in police cells, but normally and for anything longer than a day he or she will normally be held at a local prison. There is often a separate remand wing or prison landing where unconvicted prisoners are kept apart from (and under a different and relatively relaxed prison regime to) sentenced prisoners. People aged 17 to 20 inclusive[16] who are refused bail are held in a remand centre (RC) young offender institution (YOI) or prison. Below the age of 17, a refusal of bail operates as a remand to local authority accommodation unless, exceptionally, strict criteria for more secure custody are met.

Custody time limits

Where an accused person is held in custody there is a limit on the length of time that he or she may be held pending the start of the case. This varies according to the circumstances. If a time limit expires, he or she must be released. This does not affect the question whether the case can proceed; but it prevents the accused being held in custody before conviction during the future progress of the case.

---

15. English bail arrangements do not mirror those in the USA where 'bail bonds', possibly purchased from the private sector are commonplace. Forfeiture of a security is aka 'estreatment'.
16. Note the anomaly here. People do not become adults until they are 18 (see the start of the chapter).

KEY STAGES OF A CRIMINAL TRIAL

The procedures in magistrates' courts and the Crown Court fall within the remit of a Criminal Procedure Rule Committee (CPRC) headed by the Lord Chief Justice. The CPRC is all the time working to enhance, simplify, standardise and integrate the quite extensive rules of criminal procedure across the criminal courts. These are a bedrock of the work of court legal advisers.

The central focus of criminal proceedings is the trial of an alleged offender, i.e. by a judge (aka trial judge) and jury at the Crown Court or by magistrates (aka 'summary trial': *Chapter 2*). The term trial court (or 'court of first instance') is commonly used to describe the court of trial (i.e. as contrasted with an 'appellate court').

The trial follows the same pattern in whichever court it takes place, increasingly so due to the work of the CCRC. Taking the magistrates' court and in broad outline:

- the charges are read out by the court legal adviser
- any necessary or outstanding consents to summary trial are obtained (see 'Mode of Trial' above)
- the accused person is asked to enter a plea to each charge (or to each count in the indictment in the Crown Court)
- the presumption of innocence applies and unless he or she pleads guilty there must be a full and fair trial
- the prosecutor must prove the allegation to the required standard of proof (*Chapter 5*) and failing this the accused must be discharged; and
- the accused is not obliged to give evidence in his or her own defence, but a court may nowadays draw appropriate inferences if he or she declines to explain matters (as it may also do following silence at earlier stages in the criminal process).[17]

'Cracked trials' and Equivocal Pleas

Cases listed for a contested hearing can turn into guilty pleas at the courtroom door: hence the expression 'cracked trial' to describe one that 'caves in' at that late stage. This may be due to an eleventh hour decision by the accused because, e.g. all the prosecution witnesses have in fact turned up.

On the other hand the case may also 'crack' and have to be withdrawn because a witness has disappeared, possibly following intimidation or threats (when a police investigation may follow).

---

17. Which still begs the question what inferences might properly be drawn: a matter for the magistrates or jury on the whole of the evidence in the case, its quality, reliability, strength and weight. Note also that, as explained in *Chapter 5*, ultimately it is the prosecutor who will always need to discharge the burden of proof to the criminal standard, beyond reasonable doubt.

Sometimes, the prosecutor may have reason to change his or her view after reviewing the case file in the light of defence disclosure and will decide to discontinue the case. An effect may be to waste CJS resources. It is such disruptive and avoidable events that 'Preliminary Hearings and Case Management' (above) seek to avoid.

Other matters that case management seeks to eliminate are equivocal pleas, i.e. pleas of guilty which are not truly so because the accused also says something inconsistent with guilt, such as 'I just want to get it over with', 'I took the goods but I was going to give them back'. Equivocal pleas cannot be accepted. If after the accused person has had an opportunity to consider his or her position the situation remains the same, a trial will need to be held so that the magistrates (possibly now a different bench in the interests of fairness) can decide whether or not, in the second example given, the accused person was acting dishonestly or had any intention to permanently deprive some other person of his or her personal property. This is because under the Theft Act 1968 these are essential ingredients of the offence of theft. In all cases an offence is only made out if each and every ingredient is proved to exist.

Order of Evidence and Speeches

Assuming that a case does proceed as a 'not guilty plea', the trial process can be summarised as follows:

- as a matter of good practice, many benches will, at the outset, make sure that everybody agrees the elements of the particular offence(s) being heard
- the prosecutor will outline the case (known as an opening speech)
- he or she will then call his or her evidence which may be in the form of testimony (the sworn evidence of witnesses on oath ot affirmation in the courtroom), witness statements (subject to certain procedures), documents and exhibits[18]
- the defence will then have the opportunity to cross-examine 'live' witnesses
- at the end of the prosecution case the accused may, if he or she considers it appropriate, submit that there is 'no case to answer', i.e. even if no explanation were to be given by the defendant: that some essential ingredient of the charge has not been covered at all by the evidence (a matter of mixed fact and law usually, so that the court legal adviser may need to be called upon) or, e.g. that the witness or witnesses are so unreliable that no court could properly convict on the basis of their evidence (a question of fact and judgement)
- the court itself may reject the prosecution case at this stage on the same basis, i.e. of its own motion and indeed should be alert to this in all cases
- the magistrates (or the judge rather than the jury in the Crown Court) will decide

---

18. There are other possibilities, such as admissions and confessions by the accused.

whether there is a sufficient prosecution case and either dismiss the charge (or the judge will withdraw it from the jury in the Crown Court).

This is the key half-way stage in a trial. Until now the court will not have been concerned with the ultimate issue of 'guilty' or 'not guilty', simply whether enough evidence exists for the case to proceed further. Assuming that the court decides that there is enough evidence, the accused must then decide whether:

- to remain silent (and risk any inferences that the court may draw from this)
- give evidence himself or herself if desired
- subsequently call witnesses of his or her own (whereupon the prosecution will have a corresponding right to cross-examine any 'live witnesses'); or
- simply address the court.

The last word in a criminal case is reserved for the defence, usually by way of a 'closing speech'. But the prosecutor can answer any matters of law raised by the defence or his or her legal representative at this late stage, or challenge any misleading impressions which arise from what the defence now says.

There is no equivalent in the magistrates' court to a judge's summing-up to the jury and their being directed on matters of law. As explained in *Chapter 5*, both fact and law are a matter for the magistrates'. Where they need advice to help them to arrive at a conclusion, they will call on their court legal adviser.

CONVICTION AND BEYOND

The next stage is for the magistrates (or jury) is to weigh the evidence in order to decide whether the criminal standard of proof, 'beyond reasonable doubt', described in *Chapter 5* has been met. If not, then the accused must be acquitted. He or she will be discharged from court (and from custody if being held) and is normally entitled to his or her costs from public funds (so far as they are not covered by legal aid).

Sentencing

If the court decides to convict the accused,[19] it will move directly to the sentencing stage. In straightforward, relatively minor summary cases it will be able to deal with the case by way of a fine and will sentence the offender straight away. With more serious or complex matters it will often, as a step in assessing sentence, need to consider a pre-sentence report (PSR): see 'Role of the Probation Service' later.

---

19. From which point onwards it is becomes appropriate to refer to him or her as 'the offender'.

THE SENTENCING FRAMEWORK

This is the description given to overall arrangements for sentencing. The first statutory sentencing framework appeared in the Criminal Justice Act 1991. It was replaced by that in the Criminal Justice Act 2003. In summary, it contains four different levels of sentence each with its own 'seriousness' threshold as per *Figure 1* overleaf:

- discharge
- fine
- community sentence (aka the 'generic community sentence'): and
- imprisonment.

Compensation and ancillary orders (e.g. disqualification or costs) may be added in all cases and, in appropriate cases, compensation may be a sentence in its own right. With fines, there is also a victims surcharge (below).

Figure 1 has been adapted and updated from *The Sentence of the Court*.[20] It shows the framework in diagram form together with the relevant sentencing thresholds.

Discharges

Discharges can be used where punishment is 'inexpedient'. An absolute discharge marks offending but involves the offender in no further liability (other than that it ranks as a sentence for the purposes of a criminal record). Under a conditional discharge, i.e. conditional on the offender not committing another offence within a period of up to three years (determined by the court),[21] this sentences lapses if there is no such further offence. Otherwise, the offender can be sentenced for both the new offence and that in respect of which the conditional discharge was made.

Fines and financial orders

Fines are monetary penalties imposed by a court (but the term can also be viewed as including fixed penalties: below). Financial orders also include matters such as compensation (below) or costs. Fines are unlimited in the Crown Court (but must be reasonable and proportionate). In the magistrates' court, maximum fine values occur on one of five levels, a level five fine (the highest) has a ceiling of £5,000 per offence (April 2009). The level for an individual offence is set by the Act of Parliament creating that offence (usually).

---

20. A seminal work not republished for some years. It was issued by the Home Office in five editions (1964-1990) (something readers might find strange given modern day sensitivities concerning judicial independence: *Chapter 2*). It was later published in four editions (1996-2003) under the auspices of the Justices' Clerks' Society. Backlist titles are available for research purposes from Waterside Press.
21. This is the sole condition in relation to a conditional discharge.

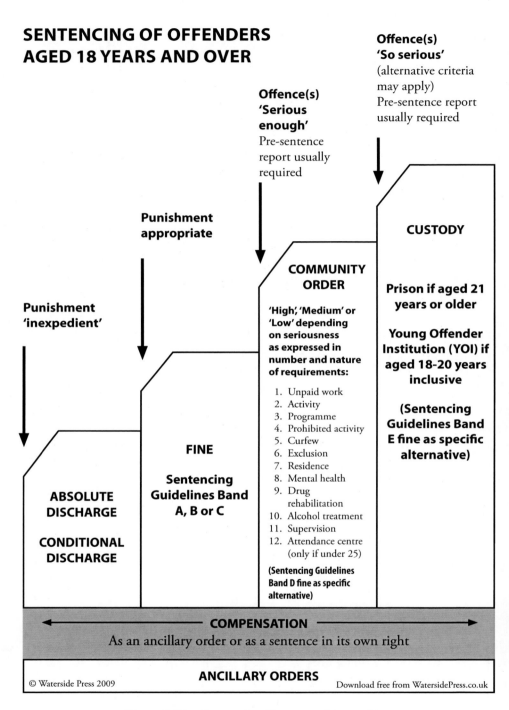

Figure 1: The Sentencing Framework in outline

Notes on *Figure 1*:

- **The relevant threshold tests** are, for a *community sentence*, that the offence (or the offence and any offences associated with it) is (are) *serious enough* to warrant such a sentence; and for *custody*, that such offence(s) is (are) *so serious* that neither a fine nor a community sentence can be justified for it (them).
- **Alternative criteria may apply** which cannot be covered in a short outline, and there are also rules affecting the amount of punishment rather than its type.
- **Fine bands**[22] were instituted by the 'Magistrates' Court Sentencing Guidelines' (2008) as was the concept of relevant weekly income (RWI): see later under 'Sentencing Guidelines' for further explanation of RWI and an example.
- **With regard to community sentences**, electronic monitoring may (or in some instances must) be added. The meanings of 'High', 'Medium' and 'Low' community sentence are dealt with in the guidelines: see sentencing-guidelines.gov.uk

The court will also require payment forthwith, but if this is not possible it will set terms, e.g. for the fine, etc. to be paid within a month or by weekly or monthly instalments. Courts will usually look for fines to be cleared within a 12 month period. Collection of financial orders takes place via the magistrates' court (including of fines imposed by the Crown Court). The court administration has certain enforcement powers but, in other circumstances and given that enforcement is nowadays a priority, defaulters are likely to be summoned to a 'fine enforcement' court to explain non-payment.

Enforcement methods include: an attachment of earnings order (AEO) requiring the employer to make deductions and send these to the court; distress warrant (sending in the bailiffs) (and in other situations a vehicle can be seized and sold to cover what is due); money payment supervision order (MPSO) under the National Probation Service (NPS) (usually); attachment of State benefits; or committal to prison for willful refusal to pay (subject to legal restrictions and procedures). Maximum committal periods reflect the balance due on a statutory scale.

People who are unlikely to remain in a place in the UK long enough for standard enforcement methods can be imprisoned immediately. However, in the case of non-nationals, there are increasingly enhanced reciprocal enforcement arrangements as between some States whereby fines can be enforced across national borders.

Variation of payment terms

Magistrates and certain court officials can vary the terms of payment and the former

---

22. Fine bands should be contrasted with fine levels mentioned earlier. Fine levels are set by statute and determine the maximum financial penalty available to the court. Fine bands are a decision-making tool.

can in some circumstances order remission of fines, etc. (i.e. their cancellation or reduction to reflect a later deterioration in personal financial circumstances: but not normally re compensation without consulting the victim). The court can compel disclosure of means by making a financial circumstances order.

Fixed Penalties and 'Administrative Fines'

Many public authorities have powers to issue fixed penalty notices (FPNs) (extending to what are known as fixed penalty notices for disorder (FPNDs)). Others have wide powers to levy administrative fines, which can in some instances be far higher in value than magistrates will ever order.[23] Fixed penalties are regularly enforced via the magistrates' court as if they were fines; and in many instances there is a right to have a fixed penalty superseded by criminal proceedings where the recipient wishes to challenge the FPN (and assuming that the prosecutor wishes to pursue matters).

Community Sentences

Since 2003, community sentence means a generic community sentence: a broad-based form of order containing requirements selected by the court from a 'menu' of twelve (with three being the usual practical maximum and then only for more serious offending). As noted within *Figure 1*, these cover supervision; unpaid work; activities; programmes; prohibited activities; a curfew; exclusion requirements; those re residence, mental impairment, drugs[24] or alcohol treatment; or to attend an attendance centre (the latter only for people under the age of 25).

Enforcement of a community sentence follows if there is a breach of the order, i.e. a failure to abide by its terms; when a court takes into account the extent to which the existing order has run, the level of compliance by the offender and his or her response to the sentence before deciding what action to take. Note also the 'sentencing threshold' for community sentences in *Figure 1* and 'Role of the Probation Service' below. Reoffending during a community sentence does not, of itself, breach the order but may lead to its revocation and to resentencing.

Since the Criminal Justice and Immigration Act 2008, a community sentence can only be used where the offence is 'imprisonable': see the *Glossary*.

Community sentences often involve attendance at projects, programmes, courses or similar ventures focussed on crime prevention or the protection of the public. As with similar arrangements in prison they may have a drugs or alcohol component according to the needs of the offender or be directed towards 'life skills' or 'cognitive thinking' (i.e. affecting such things as reasoning, perception, intuition and appropriate responses if an offender finds himself or herself in a 'tricky' situation).

---

23. And with much less public visibility..
24. Including in substitution for a former Drug Treatment and Testing Order introduced in 1998. The origins of other community sentences lie in the probation order (1907 onwards) and the community service order (1974): see historical works.

Imprisonment

Magistrates maximum powers of imprisonment have already been noted in *Chapter 2.* and the criteria and 'sentencing threshold' for imprisonment in *Figure 1* above. Quite apart from statutory criteria, imprisonment is generally regarded as 'a sentence of last resort'. As noted in *Chapter 3*, magistrates visit penal institutions as an integral part of their training and this will normally include their local prison.

Suspended sentence of imprisonment

Magistrates can order imprisonment to be suspended so that is will not be 'activated' by the offender actually being sent to prison unless the he or she commits another offence which is punishable by imprisonment during the currency of the suspended sentence. This suspension can be for up to two years. A fine must also be considered in addition and suspended sentences can, since 2005, have requirements added to them of a kind normally found in relation to community sentences (above).

Ancillary Orders

Orders ancillary to sentence are regularly made in addition to or to run alongside a sentence. These take various forms and their exact nature will depend on the circumstances of the case (and sometimes the level of court). They include:

- the costs of bringing the prosecution (or a contribution to these)
- compensation (see further below)
- disqualification, e.g. from driving (see further in *Chapter 11*), or from keeping an animal or acting as a company director, etc.
- confiscation of property (including a vehicle)[25] or items representing it
- forfeiture and or destruction of items cash, weapons, drugs, forged documents, tools used to commit or attempt crime, etc; and
- restitution of stolen, etc. property, i.e. its return to a person who is entitled to it.

Some further orders can be made as an adjunct to criminal proceedings or 'in their own right', i.e. as free-standing disposals. Examples are contained in *Chapter 10*. When considering such matters it is important to bear in mind the underlying status of the powers in question which may affect procedures, standards and processes.

Criminal anti-social behaviour order

The criminal anti-social behaviour order (CRASBO) should perhaps be specifically mentioned at this point. It is similar to the anti-social behaviour order (ASBO) noted in *Chapter 10* under the heading 'Preventive Justice', but is made in criminal proceedings as an adjunct to or possibly instead of any of the ordinary sentences

---

25. The police also now have power to seize and destroy a vehicle in relation to certain offences.

noted in this chapter. In other words, it is made 'on the back of' a criminal conviction. It will contain prohibitions individually tailored to the prevention of anti-social behaviour or criminal acts, e.g. concerning association with certain people who may be an influence on unacceptable behaviour; entering defined areas in the community or certain buildings, or shopping areas; or leaving home at given times.

COMPENSATION

This is a form of financial recompense to a victim of crime for injury, loss or damage caused by an offence. It must take precedence over a fine and should be an automatic consideration in all cases. It may be an ancillary order (above) or a stand alone sentence, also known as 'compensation in its own right'.

Reasons for *not awarding compensation* must be given by a court which does not make such an award if in the circumstances it could have done so.

The Criminal Injuries Compensation Authority (CICA) (which operates independently of the courts to deal with certain situations where compensation is not otherwise forthcoming for a victim) operates discretionary scale payments for victims of violence, e.g. where no or inadequate court-based compensation occurs. This is known as the Criminal Injuries Compensation Scheme (CCCS): see cica.gov.uk

Victims of Crime

A victim is anyone who suffers directly as a result of a criminal offence, i.e. the person injured or whose property is stolen, damaged, destroyed or lost.[26] Often a victim liaison officer (VLO), a police officer (usually), acts as a go-between re the victim and the investigating officers or Crown prosecutor. A victim personal statement (VPS) is one made by the victim for the attention of magistrates at the sentencing stage (or the judge if the case goes to the Crown Court). It describes the effect that the offence had on the victim and his or her family, including the anger, anxiety and stress that it caused as well as any financial harm.

This does not directly affect sentence, but ensures that the victim is not excluded from the criminal justice process. The *Victims Charter* (1990) was the original, Government-led initiative ultimately leading to a Victims' Advisory Panel and Commissioner (yet to be fully implemented). A victims surcharge is routinely added to each fine imposed; to fund improved services and compensation schemes.[27]

---

26. Hence, also, the (non-technical) term 'secondary victim': someone who suffers at one remove.
27. £15 per case in April 2009.

Victim Support

Central to the victims' movement[28] is Victim Support (VS). This is a key example of the work of the voluntary sector: an independent charity helping people affected by crime by providing free, confidential support (and whether or not the crime is reported to the police). Citizens can also use Victim Supportline. From 2008, various local member charities across England and Wales began to merge to form a single, nationwide body. For further information, see victimsupport.org.uk

SENTENCING PRINCIPLES AND SOME GENERAL POINTS

Quite apart from the specific provisions already noted in relation to individual sentences, the Criminal Justice Act 2003 introduced the first statutory purposes of sentencing for adults. These underlie all sentencing decisions. They are:

- the punishment of offenders
- the reduction of crime (including through deterrence)
- the reform and rehabilitation of offenders
- protecting the public; and
- reparation by offenders to people affected by their offences.[29]

Individual sentences also often involve more specific criteria for their use than can be summarised in a book of this kind. As already noted, there are various thresholds for sentencing as displayed in *Figure 1* but also further twists and turns which the reader should explore in other texts as his or her understanding progresses. In its essentials,[30] sentencing involves an assessment of the serious of the offence (or, and especially, e.g. in relation to offences of violence or sexual offences issues of public protection). It involves looking at the facts of a case and applying aggravating factors and mitigating factors to arrive at a just and fair outcome.

Punishment is sometimes described as 'restriction of liberty', legitimately so provided that it does not involve torture, cruel and unusual punishments or other unlawful, unjustifiable or disproportionate intrusions on fundamental rights: *Chapter 5*. Traditionally, it has also been balanced by welfare-based considerations, as per expressions such as 'punishment and rehabilitation'. But this has varied throughout history according to the political or judicial temperature or pressure for reform. As can be seen from the statutory purposes of sentencing above, rehabilitation (which is partly a welfare-based concept) is integral to sentencing considerations.

---

28. The 'victims movement' is a feature of the modern-day Criminal Justice System (CJS). It encompasses a range of support groups and has links to initiatives in restorative justice and victim-offender mediation.
29. For further details of this key provision see section 142 Criminal Justice Act 2003.
30. And of necessity quite superficially for present purposes. Specialist works should be consulted.

The primary governing mechanisms for sentencing are:

- legislation such as the Criminal Justice Act 2003 already mentioned
- other sentencing law: the rulings of the Court of Appeal or other higher courts as reported, e.g. in the Criminal Appeal Reports (Sentencing) or learned texts; and
- nowadays the work of the Sentencing Guidelines Council (SGC) (below).

Previous Convictions and Other Sentencing Considerations

Following conviction a list of any previous convictions is handed to the court by the prosecutor and a note concerning the defendant's previous convictions and a separate list of any cautions. There may be a list of other offences to be taken into consideration (TICs), i.e. which the offender also admits but with which he or she has not been charged. With all the more serious matters there will usually be a pre-sentence report (PSR) (below). Normally, an offence will be regarded as more serious where the offender has a record (especially similar offences) and there are a number of specific situations in which an offence must be treated by law as being more serious, e.g. where it was committed whilst on bail, or various forms of hate crime.

Sentencing Discounts

The principle and legal duty of giving credit (also known as a sentencing discount or credit for a guilty plea), to reflect a timely guilty plea and that the offender has saved time, expense, resources and not put a victim or witnesses through the ordeal of giving evidence in a trial is nowadays embedded in legislation and sentencing guidelines (below). The court must take into account the stage in the process (including during police interview) when an intention to plead guilty was *indicated* and the surrounding circumstances (see also 'Plea Before Venue and Mode of Trial' above).

Mitigation of Sentence

This is the description usually applied to representations to a court by an accused person or his or her lawyer in an attempt to persuade it that a lesser sentence than it might otherwise give is appropriate. It may relate to the offence or the offender and the situations in which it is appropriate to reduce a sentence vary according to which as well as the overall facts and merits of the case. Closely associated, courts may exercise mercy or leniency where this is consistent with the broad interests of justice.

Deferment of Sentence

Deferment of sentence involves postponing sentence to allow the court to have regard to the offender's conduct, situation, attempts to 'go straight' and possibly whether he or she has made reparation to the victim (as well as to any changes to his or her circumstances). The arrangements were revised in 2003 to allow certain activities by the offender to occur during the period of deferment and for the court to consider 'how well the offender complied'.

Sentence can be deferred (for up to six months) but only if the offender consents and undertakes to comply with any requirements. Deferment must be in the interests of justice not simply a way of 'ducking' coming to a decision.

The court may appoint a supervisor (a probation officer usually) to monitor compliance. It can deal with the offender before the end of the period of deferment if satisfied that he or she has has failed to comply with one or more requirements or if he or she commits another offence.

Sentencing in the Crown Court: A Note

The maximum sentencing powers of the Crown Court range up to life imprisonment, which is the mandatory sentence for murder (and in certain other situations). It is a discretionary sentence, e.g. for manslaughter or rape. Many more serious offences attract a maximum sentence of 14 years imprisonment, an indeterminate sentence for public protection (ISPP) or extended sentence for public protection (ESPP). The Crown Court has unlimited powers to fine offenders subject to reasonableness, fairness and proportionality.

SENTENCING GUIDELINES

In *Chapter 5* the structured approach to decision-making whereby magistrates seek to ensure matters such as fairness and consistency was noted. Whenever possible they do so following nationwide guidelines. Nowhere is this more important than in relation to the 1.3 million or so sentences imposed annually by magistrates' courts. Sentencing guidelines contain considered advice and, e.g. suggested starting points for sentences in given situations, including aggravating and mitigating factors.

Sentencing Advisory Panel (SAP)

The SAP was originally set up under the Crime and Disorder Act 1998 and now supports the Sentencing Guidelines Council (SGC) (below). It is appointed by the Lord Chancellor in consultation with the Lord Chief Justice; who also appoints its chair. It is responsible for research, reports and related information. Its findings go to the SGC. The SAP may make proposals to the SGC which the SGC must consider. In turn, the SGC must notify the SAP of any proposed or revised Sentencing Guidelines and the SAP must consult various people and respond.

Sentencing Guidelines Council (SGC)

The SGC was established by the Criminal Justice act 2003. It promulgates advice and guidance to judges and magistrates on a range of sentencing matters. It is headed by the Lord Chief Justice and comprises further judicial members (the majority) and non-judicial members.

The SGC has produced guidelines on a range of sentencing matters which are freely available to view at its website: see sentencing-guidelines.gov.uk

Once the SGC decides that a sentencing guideline is a definitive (rather than a proposed or draft) sentencing guideline, then all courts must have regard to it or explain why they have departed from it in a given case. The Lord Chancellor consults with the SGC at arms-length, and can appoint an observer to attend and speak at its meetings, and put forward proposals in relation to the SGC's work.

The Magistrates Court Sentencing Guidelines

In 2008, the SGC produced the 'Magistrates' Court Sentencing Guidelines'. These are openly available at its website above. They cover offences commonly encountered by magistrates In essence the guidelines are a simple, but effective, step-by-step guide to working through what might otherwise appear to be an overwhelming collection of statutory rules and *offence* or *offender* based factors. The process involves looking at and considering matters in the following sequence:

- looking at the page within the guidelines which applies to the offence under consideration: sample pages for 'criminal damage' and 'speeding' are reproduced by kind permission of the SGC on the pages which follow
- taking the most appropriate of the various starting points aided by common practical examples of the offence (as set out on the relevant page) and as best meets the facts of the offence before the court
- noting that all guideline sentences are based on a first-time offender (previous convictions are considered later in the process) who has pleaded not guilty (any credit for pleading guilty will also come into consideration later: see below)
- using this to obtain a guideline sentence or a sentencing range within which the court can work when looking at the facts of the particular case
- considering aggravating or mitigating factors relating to *the offence in question* (as well as those which apply *more generally to all offences*, such as culpability, the harm caused by the offence, previous convictions, racial aggravation, or whether there was a vulnerable victim (all as set out in the general rubric to the SGC guidelines))
- taking any *offender* mitigation into account
- giving credit for any guilty plea on a sliding scale (up to a usual maximum of a third) depending, e.g. on when a willingness to admit the offence was first indicated
- arriving at the final sentence
- considering whether to make any ancillary orders; and
- preparing and making a public pronouncement of the outcome along with the reasons for it, based upon national suggested sentencing pronouncements.

Criminal damage (other than by fire)
Racially or religiously aggravated criminal damage

Criminal Damage Act 1971, s.1(1)

Crime and Disorder Act 1998, s.30

Criminal damage: triable only summarily if value involved does not exceed £5,000:
Maximum: Level 4 fine and/or 3 months

Triable either way if value involved exceeds £5,000:
Maximum when tried summarily: Level 5 fine and/or 6 months
Maximum when tried on indictment: 10 years

Racially or religiously aggravated criminal damage: triable either way
Maximum when tried summarily: Level 5 fine and/or 6 months
Maximum when tried on indictment: 14 years

Where offence committed in domestic context, refer to page 177 for guidance

Offence seriousness (culpability and harm)
A. Identify the appropriate starting point
Starting points based on first time offender pleading not guilty

Examples of nature of activity	Starting point	Range
Minor damage e.g. breaking small window; small amount of graffiti	Band B fine	Conditional discharge to band C fine
Moderate damage e.g. breaking large plate-glass or shop window; widespread graffiti	Low level community order	Band C fine to medium level community order
Significant damage up to £5,000 e.g. damage caused as part of a spree	High level community order	Medium level community order to 12 weeks custody
Damage between £5,000 and £10,000	12 weeks custody	6 to 26 weeks custody
Damage over £10,000	Crown Court	Crown Court

Offence seriousness (culpability and harm)
B. Consider the effect of aggravating and mitigating factors
(other than those within examples above)
Common aggravating and mitigating factors are identified in the pullout card –
the following may be particularly relevant but **these lists are not exhaustive**

Factors indicating higher culpability	Factors indicating lower culpability
1. Revenge attack 2. Targeting vulnerable victim **Factors indicating greater degree of harm** 1. Damage to emergency equipment 2. Damage to public amenity 3. Significant public or private fear caused e.g. in domestic context	1. Damage caused recklessly 2. Provocation

Form a preliminary view of the appropriate sentence
If offender charged and convicted of the racially or religiously
aggravated offence, increase the sentence to reflect this element
Refer to pages 178-179 for guidance

Consider offender mitigation
Common factors are identified in the pullout card

Consider a reduction for a guilty plea

Consider ancillary orders, including compensation
Refer to pages 168-174 for guidance on available ancillary orders

Decide sentence
Give reasons

Speeding

Triable only summarily:
Maximum: Level 3 fine (level 4 if motorway)

Must endorse and may disqualify. If no disqualification, impose 3-6 points

Offence seriousness (culpability and harm)
A. Identify the appropriate starting point
Starting points based on first time offender pleading not guilty

Speed limit (mph)	Recorded speed (mph)		
20	21 – 30	31 – 40	41 – 50
30	31 – 40	41 – 50	51 – 60
40	41 – 55	56 – 65	66 – 75
50	51 – 65	66 – 75	76 – 85
60	61 – 80	81 – 90	91 – 100
70	71 – 90	91 – 100	101 – 110
Starting point	Band A fine	Band B fine	Band B fine
Range	Band A fine	Band B fine	Band B fine
Points/disqualification	3 points	4 – 6 points OR Disqualify 7 – 28 days	Disqualify 7 – 56 days OR 6 points

Offence seriousness (culpability and harm)
B. Consider the effect of aggravating and mitigating factors
(other than those within examples above)
Common aggravating and mitigating factors are identified in the pullout card –
the following may be particularly relevant but **these lists are not exhaustive**

Factors indicating higher culpability	Factor indicating lower culpability
1. Poor road or weather conditions 2. LGV, HGV, PSV etc. 3. Towing caravan/trailer 4. Carrying passengers or heavy load 5. Driving for hire or reward 6. Evidence of unacceptable standard of driving over and above speed **Factors indicating greater degree of harm** 1. Location e.g. near school 2. High level of traffic or pedestrians in the vicinity	1. Genuine emergency established

Form a preliminary view of the appropriate sentence,
then consider offender mitigation
Common factors are identified in the pullout card

Consider a reduction for guilty plea

Consider ancillary orders
Refer to pages 168-174 for guidance on available ancillary orders

Decide sentence
Give reasons

FINE BANDS

BAND	STARTING PRECENTAGE OF 'RWI'	PERCENTAGE RANGE OF 'RWI'
A	50%	25% to 75%
B	100%	75% to 125%
C	150%	125% to 175%
D Alternative to Community Order*	250%	200% to 300%
E Alternative to Custody*	400%	300% to 500%

*In appropriate circumstances it may be possible to consider other forms of alternative e.g. community order in place of custody

As far as fines are concerned (the most common sentencing disposal by magistrates), then as has already been noted earlier, the maximum amount which magistrates can impose is fixed by law on five levels. These range from £200 to £5,000.

The 'Magistrates' Court Sentencing Guidelines' advise magistrates how to set about determining the actual amount of the fine within those limits. This the SGC bases on a mix of fining 'bands' linked to a starting percentage and percentage range which produces what in effect is a multiplier in relation to the offender's 'relevant weekly income' (RWI). The table for this is set out above. Note that the greater the seriousness of the offence, the higher the band and starting percentage. Discretion is then reflected by the range in the right hand column within which courts are advised to work. RWI is a broad-brush concept. The 2008 guidelines describe it as (paraphrased):

- the offender's actual income (or expected income) after deduction of income tax and National Insurance contributions for those who are employed or self-employed
- £100 p.w. if his or her income is less than £100 p.w.
- £100 p.w. if the offender is on State benefits
- £350 p.w. if there is no direct, reliable information as to financial circumstances and the court is unable to determine a figure on any information available to it.

There are special considerations for people who have no income of their own but rely on the income of other people. Tax credits, housing benefit and child benefit are not brought into the equation. The figures already have built into them an allowance for the usual range of domestic outgoings as well as an element for discretionary expenditure. Special provisions exist for people with unusually low outgoings or out of the ordinary levels of expenditure (but, in the case of the latter, only where such outgoings substantially reduce the ability to pay the fine and would lead to undue hardship if not taken into account).

> As an example, for someone with an RWI of £200 p.w. and a guideline fine of Band A, the starting point would be a fine of (RWI x 50%) £100. But the range (25% to 75%) could mean that the fine could be as low as £50 or as high as £150 according to the precise circumstances of the particular offence.[31]

In the final analysis, the court will not necessarily slavishly follow this mathematical approach but will always look at the totality of its sentence, its proportionality to the offending and more general sentencing advice contained in the guidelines.

Sentencing Commission

This is a further proposed independent body. A Sentencing Commission Working Group (SCWG) is currently in being and collecting information and evidence. The SCWG is seeking views on how a structured sentencing framework could be adapted for England and Wales, drawing also on experiences in the USA. The aim is to develop a set of proposals to improve the operation of the CJS in relation to sentencing and the SCWG is looking at such possibilities as having sentencing grids or matrices to assist the application of sentencing factors to outcomes.[32]

ROLE OF THE PROBATION SERVICE

The role of the National Probation Service (NPS) as discharged by probation officers working on the front line and in the courts includes:

- meeting with accused people after they are first charged with a view to bail information and bail support
- writing pre-sentence reports (PSRs) (below)
- making or taking part in risk assessments as to whether someone is likely to offend or reoffend
- in some instances interviewing victims and or arranging for someone to take part in victim reparation schemes

---

31. Not surprisingly, magistrates have adopted ready reckoners. Calculators are often available in courtrooms.
32. See judiciary.gov.uk

- delivering community sentences either directly of through third parties, using NPS or other resources, facilities and staff (e.g. at a probation centre)
- managing offenders in the community, whether during their community sentences or whilst the offender is on parole following release from prison or subject to some other form of release licence
- carrying out supervision of offenders where this is a requirement of a community sentence or licence
- cooperating with HM Prison Service (HMPS) concerning end-to-end sentences of the kind described in *Chapter 2*
- the enforcement of NPS-related sentences or licences where the offender does not comply with their terms, i.e. by bringing breach proceedings in the magistrates' court or Crown Court, or participating in the process of recall to prison
- supervising people who are subject to money payment supervision orders (MPSOs) (see under 'Fines' above).

Pre-sentence Reports (PSRs)

A PSR can be requested by a sentencing court from the NPS (or a youth offending team (YOT) or social worker re a juvenile: *Chapter 8*). This is especially and normally the case where a community sentence or custody is in mind, or if there is some other valid reason (e.g. suspected mental impairment: when a psychiatrist may also be asked to prepare an assessment).

PSRs are routinely obtained in all the more serious cases although they can be 'dispensed with' if the court considers that one is 'unnecessary'. Their content is the subject of National Standards: see the *Glossary*. PSRs are confidential, but since the Pre-Sentence Report (Prescription of Prosecutors) Order 1998, Crown prosecutors are entitled to see a copy, whilst there can be disclosure to other public prosecutors at the discretion of the court. A copy is provided to the offender or its contents brought to his or her attention.

Typically, a PSR contains basic information about the offence and offender and a note of the sources used and steps taken to validate data. It will include relevant information about the offender's background, day-to-day activities, abilities, associates, attitudes, responsibilities and any known problems, e.g. re drugs, alcohol, mental impairment, employment (or lack of it) and debts. It may contain a risk assessment as to potential future harm to the public or likelihood of re-offending. It may also contain a sentence proposal (but not a recommendation as such).[33]

---

33. Probation officers us an Offender Assessment System (OASys) which incorporates risk-assessment mechanisms and builds on evidence-based research (and eOAsys with regard to assessment for electronic monitoring). An aim is to enable courts to impose 'sentences which work'.

There are two basic types of report: a fast delivery report (FDR) (usually provided on the same day as it is requested or within a couple of working days and often presented orally) or a standard delivery report (SDR) (which is used in relation to more serious offending behaviour and is more often than not in writing and produced within 15 working days, or ten working days if the offender is in custody). Naturally, sentencing is adjourned for the appropriate length of time.

LEGAL REPRESENTATION

Professional advice from a lawyer may often be essential if an accused person (or a convicted person) is to adequately understand and put forward his or her case, including making an informed decision whether he or she should plead guilty or not guilty and the potential consequences of delaying making that decision (see, e.g. under the heading 'Sentencing Discounts' above).

In the magistrates' court, solicitors and barristers have what are called 'rights of audience'. All defendants have the right to use reasonable support materials and resources including a 'friend' (the so-called McKenzie Friend after the case which first introduced the concept) being someone who assists an unrepresented accused to deal with his or her own case. But this 'friend' does not acquire the right to address the court and the facility can withdrawn if abused.

More rarely, a member of Queen's Counsel (QC) might be seen in the magistrates' court, a senior barrister or 'silk'. QCs tend to feature in the more serious cases in the Crown Court where barristers predominate.

Legal Aid

In concept, legal aid allows every accused person to obtain legal representation at public expense in certain circumstances; under the auspices of the statutorily empowered Legal Services Commission (LSC). The LSC replaced the Legal Aid Board in 2001.

The reforms, based on the Access to Justice Act 1999 and the Criminal Defence Service (Advice and Assistance Act) 2001, had various effects: 'legal aid'[34] as such was abolished and replaced by 'State-funded legal representation'; legal aid orders by 'representation orders'; and free representation in the magistrates' courts.

The Criminal Defence Service (CDS) provides legal assistance and advice to people in police detention or accused of crimes through a mix of contracts with private and salaried defenders so as to ensure access to justice. It operates under the auspices of the LSC and uses solicitors with a franchise from the LSC or who work for the CDS directly.

---

34. But the term 'legal aid' has persisted.

Where a case ends in the Crown Court, the judge can order the accused person to pay some or all his or her 'legal aid' costs, known as a 'recovery order'.[35]

Duty Solicitors

For many years there have been local duty solicitor schemes under which a particular solicitor will take part on a rota to meet and give preliminary advice (and often limited representation) to people appearing at the magistrates' court. This is especially the case where accused people are in police cells, possibly having only recently been arrested or they may have been held overnight, when the duty solicitor may also be on stand-by to be called out to the police station at all hours.[36]

---

35. Other reforms have involved effectiveness and efficiency savings in line (some would argue ahead) of comparable ones across the CJS; leading to controversy, claims that access to justice is arguably being curtailed and some solicitors leaving the scheme on economic grounds.
36. It is worth noting that this is in effect a 'first-aid' scheme and there may be limits to the advice that can be given in this way or the extent of the actions which the solicitor can take.

CHAPTER EIGHT

The Youth Court

At the time going to press it had been reported that certain provisions of the Criminal Justice and Immigration Act 2008 which significantly affect juvenile sentencing[1] might be brought into effect late in 2009. This would be accompanied by new youth-specific sentencing guidelines from the Sentencing Guidelines Council (SGC) (*Chapter 7*).

This chapter reflects existing law and practice. But readers should see the summary of the pending provisions at the end and check for any commencement dates or newer or transitional provisions.

A nationwide training programme for youth magistrates and court legal advisers is set to precede any such changes.

Aspects of Youth Offending

'Hug a hoodie' or 'street rat' encapsulate modern media and public perceptions of young offenders. It used to be said that most young offenders 'burned themselves out' by their mid-twenties. Even if true, this hardly justifies a reactive approach to youth justice: society still has to bear the brunt of such offending and young offenders will continue to bear the adverse consequences of any offending behaviour into at least early adulthood, if not for longer. Nonetheless, there is nowadays a generally more forward-looking approach to juveniles and this is reflected in the totality of the arrangements. Many of these are designed to keep juveniles out of the youth court altogether or to divert them towards the most constructive outcomes in terms of their lives and future.

Generally speaking, the arrangements for youth justice come under the Youth Justice Board which is primarily a responsibility of the Ministry of Justice (MOJ), even if many of its day to day functions fall to the Department for Children Schools and Families (DCSF). The YJB has no say whatsoever in how courts are run or what magistrates' decide, other than in terms of general liaison and consultation functions. But is also has to be recognised that in conjunction with other youth-oriented public authorities it determines what resources are available to tackle such matters. It is also highly influential in the work of all (non-court) youth justice services.

The Impact of an Early Life Experiences

Official statistics point to the fact that events and factors in someone's early years can have a considerable impact on future offending behaviour; e.g. it has been suggested that:

---

1. The term 'juvenile' is used in this work. Some people call them 'youths' and this may have gained ground

- only one in five adult prisoners can complete a job application form
- 48 per cent of adult prisoners are at or below the reading level of an average eleven year old
- 65 per cent of adult prisoners are at or below the numeracy level of an average eleven year old
- 82 per cent of adult prisoners are at or below the writing level of an average eleven year old; and
- nearly half of adult male prisoners were excluded from school.[2]

Society is, therefore, rightly concerned with addressing youth crime and often in a proactive way, even if it cannot always agree a common, unemotional standpoint. Future considerations are likely to focus on matters such as the:

- increasing incidence of offending by young women in areas such as violence, disorder, damage and theft from shops
- relative over-representation of black juvenile offenders (of African-Caribbean and other black ethnic origins)
- relatively high use of custody for juveniles in England and Wales (for remand purposes as well as sentence): at any one time around 3,000 juveniles will be in some form of custody; and
- wider issues arising from the European Convention On Human Rights (ECHR) (see *Chapter 5*) and United Nations Convention On the Rights of the Child.

Apart from all the standard pressures of growing up and going through puberty, certain major factors have been identified as putting young people at greater risk of offending such as:

- a troubled home life
- school issues, including poor attainment, truancy and school exclusion[3]
- drug or alcohol abuse
- mental health issues
- peer group pressure
- poor or inappropriate parenting
- having family members or peers who have offended
- deprivation; and
- poor housing: in 2007 it was suggested that one in five young people seen by youth

2. Two useful general accounts in this field are *Criminal Classes: Offenders at School* (1995), Devlin A and *Children Who Break the Law: Everybody Does It* (1999), Curtis S (a JP) (both from Waterside Press).
3. Just as social exclusion generally is seen as a significant cause of crime.

offending teams (YOTs) (below) displayed a housing disadvantage.

As with most things, the reality varies from individual to individual and there is a mix of factors within the overall spectrum where early and appropriate intervention and attention can sometimes bring both short term and long term benefits.

As one example of the recognition given to the often transient nature of youth offending, the rehabilitation periods applicable under the Rehabilitation of Offenders Act 1974 (a provision whereby it is possible, after a period of non-reoffending, legally not to disclose a conviction in many circumstances) are halved where they apply to juveniles. This then assists juveniles into responsible adulthood if they are able to leave their earlier offending behind them.

A PREVENTIVE[4] APPROACH TO YOUTH OFFENDING

In recent years many dedicated measures have been taken to support the development of juveniles with a view to removing some possible causes of youth crime, e.g:

- 'Sure Start': support services to young families in disadvantaged areas
- 'Connexions': a school-based programme to provide support and advice to young people and to improve behaviour and reduce truancy
- 'Neighbourhood Renewal': improving community services in areas that struggle economically
- 'schools mentors' whereby, in participating schools, volunteers try to create a positive and totally independent relationship with pupils who may not be fully engaging with their educational or other life opportunities; and
- a specific duty placed on YOTs (below) to work on general youth crime prevention and crime reduction measures not just those referred to them by the courts.

A DIVERSIONARY APPROACH

A police non-statutory practice of cautioning appropriate young offenders as a way of diverting them from the mainstream CJS was established long ago. Cautioning as such of youths was exchanged under the Crime and Disorder Act 1998 for a system of 'reprimands' and 'warnings' often supported by input from YOTs.

Reprimands
The police can give a reprimand only if all the following criteria are satisfied:

---

4. As with he use of this word in *Chapter 10*, some people say 'preventative'

- there is evidence of guilt
- there is a realistic prospect of conviction
- the juvenile admits the offence
- he or she has not been previously reprimanded or warned
- he or she has not previously been convicted by a court of an offence
- it is not in the public interest for the offender to be prosecuted; and
- the offence is not so serious as to warrant a (more serious) warning (below).

Warnings

A warning (often referred to as a 'final warning' as it can only normally be given once to the same person) can be used if:

- there is evidence of guilt
- a realistic prospect of conviction
- the juvenile admits the offence
- he or she has not been previously warned (a previous warning given more than two years before the present offence can be disregarded if the present offence is not so serious as to warrant criminal proceedings)
- he or she has not been previously been convicted before a court of an offence
- tt is not in the public interest for the offender to be prosecuted; and
- the offence is so serious as to warrant a warning.

In the case of both reprimands and warnings, the practical effect is to divert the juvenile away from criminal proceedings. The local YOT will have to assess anyone given a warning and a programme of rehabilitation will be built into this unless that is inappropriate. Future criminal proceedings for *that* offence are precluded regardless of future conduct, although:

- previous reprimands and warnings (and failure to participate in any support programme arranged) can be cited in proceedings for any later offending; and
- if later convicted of a further offence committed within two years of a warning the court will be precluded from ordering a conditional discharge save in 'exceptional circumstances'.

A dilemma occasioned by such diversionary measures remains for those juveniles who consider themselves to be not guilty of the offence: they must either 'admit' the offence to the police if a reprimand or warning is on offer or maintain their lack of guilt and risk prosecution.[5]

---

5. There is in respect of adult offenders a statutory form of 'conditional cautioning' whereby, as the name

In respect of certain specified types of offending (e.g. public order, retail theft under £200, criminal damage under £500 and being drunk and disorderly) by those aged 16 or 17 years it is possible for the police to issue a fixed penalty notice. Over 19,000 such notices were issued in 2007.

In some instances, whether during diversion, referral or a sentence, use is made of acceptable behaviour contracts (ABCs) between members of a YOT and juveniles who are at risk of offending (or further offending) whereby advice, guidance, support and services are made available in return for a promise of acceptable behaviour.

Diversions from Custody and More Intrusive Outcomes

Other forms of diversion seek to avoid the potentially damaging effects of other early CJS experiences (partly in view of the kind of factors mentioned at the start of this chapter). Naturally, some young people can be a danger to themselves or others and need to be removed from society for this reason, but it has also been long recognised that offending in early life can represent a phase which passes with maturity and a growth in personal values and standards

Historically, and particularly in the 1980s the 'alternative to custody movement' was strong in relation to this age group and the number of juveniles experiencing custodial sentences fell dramatically. It led to the development of various pioneering community-based sentencing schemes.[6]

This momentum may not be what it was and public attitudes may have hardened since the 1990s,[7] but a legacy remains in much of the work of YOTS in particular.

MODERN-DAY YOUTH JUSTICE METHODS

The Crime and Disorder Act of 1998 which set up the national Youth Justice Board (YJB) also stated that its functions include (paraphrased):

* oversight the Youth Justice System (YJS) of England and Wales
* preventing offending and reoffending by children and young people below 18 years of age

suggests, certain forms of condition (including undertaking rehabilitative or preventive activities) are attached to the caution and prosecution can subsequently follow if the conditions are not complied with. It has been suggested that this may be extended to offenders aged 16 or 17 some time in 2009.

6. Which to an extent became a template for work with older age groups: the pre-1992 juvenile court was the first in which statutory reasons had to be given for using custody. For an account, see *Growing Out of Crime: The New Era* (3rd. edn. 2002), Rutherford A. Waterside Press.

7. The high profile Bulger case of 1992 in which a toddler was murdered by two ten year old boys is often seen as marking the watershed (and was a contributing factor to the wider ensuing politically charged 'prison works' mantra of those times). Most commentators point to its misleading and wholly disproportionate effect on public attitudes to juvenile crime. Some 50 children per year kill someone else and this is not just a UK phenomenon: see *Children Who Kill* (1996), Cavadino P (ed.), Waterside Press. This is not condone matters, but it is important in all CJS and YJS matters to take an informed and balanced view.

- ensuring that any custody provisions for those under 18 years old are safe, secure and work to address the cause of their offending behaviour
- promoting good practice
- obtaining and publishing information; and
- advising the Secretary of State on youth services and the YJS.

The 1998 Act at the same time introduced other related measures requiring:

- local authorities to set up dedicated YOTs (below)
- local authorities to produce annual youth justice plans; and
- other public bodies such as the police, local probation boards and health authorities to cooperate with YOTs and provide staff to work as part of them.

Not only do YOTs, like their counterparts within the National Probation Service, provide pre-sentence reports (PSRs) (or 'assessments') to criminal courts and work with convicted offenders to address offending but as already indicated they also have a direct role in wider youth crime prevention initiatives.

THE YOUTH COURT AND ITS CHANGING CULTURE

The formation of dedicated courts to deal with younger offenders dates back to the Children Act of 1908. The modern youth court is based on the reforms of the Children and Young Persons Act 1969 and takes its name from the Criminal Justice Act 1991. Its powers were refined by other statutes, including the Crime and Disorder Act 1998, whilst as already noted significant changes contained in the Criminal Justice and Immigration Act 2008 are pending (see the end of the chapter).

In the early days, 'juvenile courts' dealt with both criminal proceedings against young offenders as well as civil proceedings relating to their welfare on the basis that there would often be clear cross-over considerations between the need for care or supervision and offending. The Children Act 1989 saw the civil aspects move to the family proceedings court (see *Chapter 9*) although welfare is still very much to the fore in criminal proceedings in the youth court due to the welfare principle contained in the Children and Young Persons Act 1933 (see later in the chapter). This applies across the court system and obliges judges and magistrates to have regard to a juvenile's welfare, no matter in what capacity he or she finds himself or herself in a court of law.

Save in very limited circumstances, all prosecutions of juveniles (i.e. those aged ten to 17 years inclusive) are conducted in the youth court rather than the adult court and the criteria which determine when a youth case can go to the Crown Court are highly restrictive (see further below).

Youth courts are comprised of a minimum of two and not more than three youth court magistrates, with at least one man and one woman sitting to hear a case (save for certain emergency situations). Alternatively a district judge (magistrates' courts) (*Chapter 1*) may, as in the adult court, sit alone.

Chapter 3 explained how youth court magistrates are selected by local Bench Training and Development Committees (BTDCs) against set criteria from applicants within the adult bench who wish to play a part in the nationwide youth court jurisdiction. *Chapter 4* also dealt with how such youth court magistrates are trained and developed.

Although the youth court is a criminal court, its ethos and culture, largely driven by the two special statutory aims noted below, have changed considerably in modern times to include features such as:

- 'engagement' by the bench with the defendant and any parents or other family members in attendance. This involves explaining matters in much greater detail and also what the court is trying to achieve and why. It particularly involves direct communication with the parents and the juvenile even if the latter is represented by a lawyer, so that he or she feels part of the process and not just the subject of it. This applies especially after any conviction, so as to try to make juveniles confront their offending behaviour and any underlying factors that might be contributing to it. Parents are also be invited to address the court or to make representations at any appropriate stage. Those taking the chair in the youth court receive special training in respect of engagement in addition to that re their general chairtaking skills.[8]
- the physical layout of the courtroom (and especially in any 'new builds') receives special attention so that it is less formal and more conducive to an inclusive style of hearing. For instance, magistrates will try to sit at the same level as everybody else, parents will sit next to the defendant and everybody will remain seated. There may be a large conference-style table around which the various participants sit (but with the magistrates at a suitable distance, yet often on the same level as everyone else).
- defendants are addressed by their first name
- special attention is paid to the general environment created by the bench and court officials
- the 'opening up' of the youth court is, e.g. allowing victims to attend even if not required as witnesses; and
- youth courts tend to be receptive to feedback from the YJB and local YOT on matters such as reconviction rates and the effectiveness of different types of sentencing.

---

8. As seen in *Chapters 3* and *4* they will normally have acquired these before becoming a youth court chair.

Youth court magistrates have their own equivalent to the *Adult Court Bench Book* mentioned in *Chapter 4*, the *Youth Bench Book*.[9] Some other special features which are applicable in the youth court follow later in the chapter.

STATUTORY AIMS AND PURPOSES

There are two main statutory directives in relation to the Youth Justice System:

- 'Every court in dealing with a child or young person who is brought before it, either as an offender or otherwise, shall have regard to the welfare of the child or young person and shall in a proper case take steps for removing him from undesirable surroundings and for securing that proper provision is made for his education and training' (section 44 Children and Young persons Act 1933); and
- 'The principal aim of the youth justice system … is to prevent offending by children and young people' (Section 37 Crime and Disorder Act 1998).

The first of these, although clearly still valid in itself, now appears to be somewhat dated in its terminology and is in practice usually applied solely to offenders and more in terms of a general 'welfare' goal than as to its precise terms. The case management arrangements in the youth court (below) pick up on both aims.

The approach to sentencing based on 'seriousness' set out in the Criminal Justice Act 2003 applies to juveniles as it does to adults but also has to sit alongside the above aims. But it should be noted that the usual statutory purposes of sentencing (punishment, reduction of crime, reform and rehabilitation, protection of the public and reparation: see *Chapter 7*) do not currently apply to offenders under 18 years of age when convicted (and see later in this chapter for forthcoming changes).

When it comes to balancing all these factors, youth courts typically take into account further considerations such as:

- the accepted wisdom that sentencing is most effective when it follows as closely as possible on, and clearly relates to, the offending behaviour involved
- young people may need extra help to learn from their mistakes
- young people's lives can change rapidly and they can often have moved on from the factors applicable when the offence was committed
- despite the relatively protective stance of the Rehabilitation of Offenders Act 1974 as noted earlier in the chapter, a sentence may have a disproportionate effect on the juvenile's later ability to gain work etc; and

---

9. As with similar publications this is accessible at jsboard.co.uk

- juveniles can be particularly vulnerable if they mix with other young people involved in offending, e.g. through a custodial sentence.[10]

UNDERLYING CONSIDERATIONS AND DEFINITIONS

The age of criminal responsibility in England and Wales is ten years, with the result that criminal proceedings cannot be taken in respect of any behaviour which occurs when someone is below that age, even if it might otherwise constitute an offence in the case of someone aged ten years or older. Put another way there is a presumption of law (*Chapter 7*) that a child below the age of ten cannot commit an offence. Any such behaviour by someone aged under ten years would have to be addressed through other social provisions and the civil welfare system, e.g. in proceedings in the family proceedings court (*Chapter 9*) rather than via the criminal courts.

Children and Young Persons

Until people reach the age of 18 years when they will appear in the adult court (*Chapter 7*)[11] they fall within one of two age groups for the purposes of criminal proceedings:

- **children:** aged ten to 13 years inclusive; and
- **young persons**: aged 14 to 17 years inclusive.

The distinction used to be particularly relevant because there was a presumption, to be rebutted by the prosecution, that 'children' did not have the ability to distinguish between right and wrong and, therefore, lacked the underlying capacity to commit an offence. However, the Crime and Disorder Act of 1998 repealed this provision. On a related note, the previous long-standing Common Law presumption that a boy under 14 years of age (and therefore a 'child') was physically incapable of sexual intercourse and thus of rape had already been repealed by the Sexual Offence Act 1993.

The distinction between 'children' and 'young persons' is still relevant to matters such the powers of the court (e.g. the maximum fine that can be imposed) but legislative measures appear to be moving towards less rigid age demarcations. Care must always be taken to check all applicable age limit provisions when dealing with juveniles as they can vary for different purposes.

---

10. The routine University of Crime argument concerning penal institutions in general, but perhaps more pertinent the younger and more impressionable people are.
11. And subject to any forthcoming changes: see later in the chapter.

The General Ethos of the Youth Court

There are certain other measures that reflect the different ethos and environment of the youth court such as:

- having separate, dedicated youth court buildings, youth courtrooms and/or 'youth court days' where possible (consistent with resources and the scheduling of other court sittings)
- powers to require parents to attend court
- exclusion from the youth courtroom of people not directly concerned with the proceedings (although, as already intimated, this is now being viewed less strictly as part of the agenda to 'open up' of the youth court)
- automatic restrictions on what the press may report of proceedings in the youth court (including re the names of anybody, defendant, witness etc, who is under 18 years of age: although, again, courts are now encouraged to be more ready to make an order permitting the reporting of the names of juveniles if this is in the interests of justice)[12]
- proposed sentences are to be mentioned to the juvenile, his or her parents and legal adviser before being imposed so that representations can be made about these, especially in the light of the two statutory aims referred to earlier
- the right for the court, albeit only in appropriate circumstances, to address the youth in the absence of the parents or vice versa; and
- the ability, in many cases, of the court to impose a 'parenting order' on a parent or guardian of a convicted juvenile.

CASE MANAGEMENT AND FAST-TRACKING

The dual aims of welfare and preventing offending noted above are enhanced by the proper, fair and expeditious management of cases. Most of the considerations in the standard Criminal Procedure Rules 2005 (*Chapter 2*) have equal application to the youth court. An anticipated Youth Court Case Management Framework is under consideration but has yet to be published. It will doubtless mirror in many respects the adult Criminal Case Management Framework and, in the meantime, the latter is often used for general guidance.

---

12. But note that, should a youth be mentioned in the adult court as a victim or witness or appear under certain circumstances in the adult court as a defendant (below) then reporting restrictions will not be automatic and the adult court will have to make a positive order if it feels that similar reporting restrictions are justified. Accredited members of the press have certain rights to address the court in respect of reporting restrictions where they could be lifted or might be about to be imposed.

Fast tracking Persistent Young Offenders

There is a non-statutory, but somewhat involved and technically drawn concept of a persistent young offender (PYO). In its current application it relates roughly to offenders aged ten to 17 years inclusive who have three or more separate prior sentences on their criminal record. Cases involving PYOs are subjected to a form of fast tracking through the youth court (and Crown Court, if relevant) with all of the YJS services giving priority to such cases. The aim is for the period from arrest to final outcome to be less than 71 days.[13] The intention is to deal proactively and speedily with the small, but significant, number of highly active and comparatively serious young offenders who commit a disproportionate number of offences.

The following target periods will usually be set so as to keep well within the overall timescale:

- seven days from arrest to first court appearance
- 28 days from entry of a not guilty plea to trial; and
- 14 days to sentence from guilty plea or conviction following a trial.

Care is taken to ensure that, if the case is to be contested, the court of trial will not became aware that the defendant is a PYO because that would clearly disclose the fact of previous convictions and inhibit a fair trial (*Chapter 5*).

Other youth court cases still receive many of the standard case management considerations as it is always important in the case of any juveniles (be they PYOs or not) that any sentence should follow as quickly as possible after the event.

BAIL AND REMAND

The provisions of the Bail Act 1976 (*Chapter 7*) broadly apply to juveniles in the same way as they do as to adults. But there are significant variations such as:

- a special Intensive Supervision and Surveillance Programme (ISSP) bail support package condition is available for juveniles to help to keep them on bail and in the community if at all possible rather than in custody during any remand period
- any remand other than on bail is to local authority accommodation rather than a penal institution (save for 17 year old defendants who go to remand centres)
- in certain limited circumstances it is possible to order a remand to a secure version of local authority accommodation; and
- other non-bail remands may be subject to other criteria relating to age and/or sex.

---

13. A halving of the previous 142 days when the concept was first applied in 1997.

MODE OF TRIAL AND OFFENCE CATEGORIES

The three-tier classification of offences, summary, either way and indictable only described in *Chapter 7*, still technically applies to juveniles but there are significant variations and ramifications when it comes to determining 'mode of trial'.

The starting point is that *all* offences are dealt with summarily (i.e. by magistrates sitting as a youth court) except that the case *must* be sent to the Crown Court for trial in certain circumstances, i.e:

- concerning offences of 'homicide' (as specifically defined; including murder, manslaughter, attempted murder or manslaughter and maybe arguably also causing death by dangerous driving or causing death by careless driving while under the influence of drink or drugs); and
- where the juvenile is aged 16 or 17 years and the charge involves a firearm and carries the compulsory minimum three-year sentence for adults on conviction.

In the following circumstances the court has a duty to *consider* committing case to the Crown Court for trial:

- where the offence and its circumstances constitute a 'grave crime' (as defined) and a potential sentence of two years or more might be a realistic prospect: examples would include serious sexual offences or offences carrying 14 years imprisonment or more in the case of an adult, such as arson or wounding with intent; or
- where the defendant is initially assessed as a 'dangerous offender', i.e. someone charged with certain serious violent or sexual offences *and* there is a significant risk to the public of serious harm being caused by the offender by further offences.

There is a later duty to commit juvenile offenders to the Crown Court for sentence if it subsequently appears that they are a 'dangerous offender.'[14]

Juveniles in the Adult Court and the Crown Court

Juveniles can be tried (and to a limited extent sentenced) in the adult court or Crown Court in certain other circumstances, although to the extent that it may be possible, efforts are made to avoid this :

- a juvenile jointly charged with an adult *must* be tried in the adult court. However, if convicted, he or she must be remitted to a local youth court for sentence save

---

14. All of these provisions are complex and youth court magistrates, their legal advisers and prosecuting and defending lawyers invariably need to refer to flowcharts such as those contained in the *Youth Bench Book*.

that only the following orders can be made in the adult court: absolute discharge, conditional discharge, parental recognisance for the juvenile's good behaviour or a referral order. Other than in the clearest of cases, most adult courts will, in practice, usually remit even if such disposals might suffice;

- should the adult be committed for trial then the adult court, magistrates have a discretion also to commit a jointly charged juvenile for trial, but only if necessary in the 'interests of justice' (which encompasses a range of considerations and will be wider than just the interests of the juvenile concerned); and

- a juvenile may be tried in the adult court if connected, but not jointly charged, with an adult, e.g. where one is the main offender and the other is an accomplice.

SENTENCING IN THE YOUTH COURT

It will have become apparent that sentencing in the youth court can be somewhat more intricate than sentencing as it applies to adults as described in *Chapter 7*. There are various additional or different types of sentence which are available only in respect of juveniles. Although the 'seriousness' considerations and thresholds of the Criminal Justice Act 2003 usually apply as for adults, as has already been noted welfare and crime preventive considerations are also prime factors.

As with other magistrates, youth court magistrates follow a structured approach to sentencing and other decisions. There are currently no comprehensive guidelines from the Sentencing Guidelines Council (SGC) relating to juveniles as there are for adults (but see the notes at the end of this chapter for developments). There are some commonly used 'unofficial' guidelines dating from 2001.[15]

It is not possible in a single chapter of a book designed as an introduction to magistrates' courts in general to give any simple overview of the youth sentences available and their various criteria, let alone anything which can be guaranteed to be wholly up-to-date in an imminently fluid context. Useful points of reference are the *Youth Bench Book* already mentioned a list of youth court sentences given at its website (yjb.gov.uk) by the Youth Justice Board under the heading 'Sentences, Orders and Agreements' which usually takes account of changes as they occur.

If the law is, indeed, to change significantly towards the end of 2009, it is better in the context of this work, to look ahead. The note in the shaded box on the page opposite gives a broad picture of likely forthcoming arrangements.[16]

---

15. These are referred to in the *Youth Bench Book* which again can be accessed at jsboard.co.uk
16. *The Youth Court and Youth Justice System: An Introduction* (2009), Watkins M and others is scheduled for publication to coincide with the changes. For up-to-date information see WatersidePress.co.uk

Three main developments scheduled to occur late in 2009 include.

- a single new generic 'youth rehabilitation order' (YRO) would replace many of the current non-custodial sentencing options for juveniles
- a new over-arching statutory youth court sentencing framework
- new statutory purposes of sentencing for juveniles; and
- new youth-specific sentencing guidelines from the SGC.

It is worth noting the range and flexibility of the YRO and how it tries to balance considerations relating to the statutory purposes of sentencing for juveniles and deal with issues around welfare, preventing offending and the seriousness of the offence (all of which are features of the new sentencing framework).

It will be possible within the YRO (reflecting the approach taken vis-à-vis the adult generic community order: *Chapter 7*) to select, in accordance with criteria and guidance, from a menu of 18 potential requirements relating to:

- activity
- supervision
- unpaid work (16 and 17 years olds only)
- a programme, e.g. to attend and follow
- attendance at a community-based 'attendance centre'
- prohibited activity
- a curfew
- exclusion from a particular location
- residence stipulations (16 and 17 years olds only)
- local authority residence
- treatment for mental impairment
- drug treatment
- drug-testing
- stipulations in relation to 'intoxicating substances'
- electronic monitoring
- education
- intensive supervision and surveillance (ISS) (to provide a clear alternative where a custodial sentence might otherwise be imposed); and
- fostering.

Custodial sentences for juveniles will expressly become a sentence of 'last resort' and there are tightened criteria relating to when custody may be ordered.

CHAPTER NINE

The Family Proceedings Court

It is perhaps reasonably well-known by members of the general public that, when parents separate and cannot agree matters, such as with whom their children under 18 years of age should reside, or when and where an absent parent should have contact with those children, the parents may apply to the local magistrates' court for an order. When they do so it is to the family proceedings court (FPC). As noted in *Chapter 2*, the FPC is part of a system of family courts that extends to the local county court and Family Division of the High Court.

DEALING WITH MODERN FAMILY PROBLEMS

It may be less well-known that, when the tragic death of a child at the hand of a parent or carer results in a major and very public review of child protection services, there may, in due course, be significant implications for the work of magistrates' courts. The 'Laming Report' of March 2009 following the death of 'Baby P' was wide-ranging and comprehensive and noted, in particular, that:

- as at 31 March 2008 some 60,000 children were looked after by local authorities
- of them, some 37,000 were the subject of care orders
- as at the same date, a further 29,000 children were the subject of child protection plans; and
- during 2007-2008 some 55 children were killed by their parents or someone known to them.[1]

These statistics, distressing enough in themselves, may, regrettably, be just the tip of an even more worrying iceberg. In the aftermath of such tragedies as 'Baby P' or Victoria Climbié (in 2003, on which Lord Laming also reported)[2] there will inevitably, and rightly, be calls for changes in social work practice, including as to the amount of time social workers can devote directly to supporting vulnerable children and concerning the numbers deployed on child care work. All of this can result in the possibility of more care proceedings finding their way to the local magistrates sitting as a family proceedings court and changes in the way evidence is gathered and is presented to the court.

The 2009 Laming Report went on to emphasise two other key things:

---

1. This 2009 report can be accessed at everychildmatters.gov.uk
2. 'The Victoria Climbié Inquiry Report of an Inquiry by Lord Laming (2003), Cm 5730.

- 'When the state is seeking to make a care order, there should be no budgetary impediment to this'; and
- 'The Secretary of State for Justice[3] should take action to shorten the time taken in court proceedings relating to the care of children'.

Alongside this, a 'Family Justice in View' paper laid before Parliament in 2008 led to regulations being made in 2009 whereby all levels of family court were 'opened up' to accredited members of the media. There is an exception in relation to adoption proceedings and the court can restrict attendance if the welfare of the child requires it, or for the safety and protection of parties or witnesses. Announcing the move in April 2009, the Lord Chancellor, Jack Straw noted that:

> Public confidence in the justice system is a necessary and vital part of a democratic society. I want to ensure that reforms to the family courts system increase their accountability to the public ... People need to trust the justice system. One important way is by creating a more open, transparent and accountable system while protecting children and families during a difficult and traumatic time in their lives.

This mirrors analogous sentiments in respect of youth courts (*Chapter 8*) and suggests that magistrates' child protection and family work is likely to attain a new profile as it enters the second decade of the twenty-first century.

WHAT ARE 'FAMILY PROCEEDINGS'

In respect of magistrates' courts this term is defined widely[4] to include a range of proceedings relating to spouses, partners, families and children. This includes, in particular, proceedings in relation to:

- adoption
- certain hearings relating to maintenance payments
- non-molestation orders
- occupation orders relating to family homes
- private law applications under the Children Act 1989 (below); and
- public law applications under the Children Act 1989 (below).

The full list runs to some 15 different types of case that are automatically 'family proceedings' and magistrates themselves have an option to treat certain other matters as 'family proceedings' also. It is not possible in a single chapter to cover all types of

---

3. i.e. the Lord Chancellor wearing his day-to-day hat as the Justice Secretary: *Chapter 1*.
4. See section 65 Magistrates' Courts Act 1980.

work coming before family proceedings courts, let alone go into detail with regard to any one kind of case. Some cases will seek to determine matters between adults within a family context but the greatest number will probably focus on children and their upbringing, welfare or protection.

This chapter concentrates on the Children Act 1989, its underlying principles and the two broad classifications of case which arise within that Act. Useful tools for readers wishing to further explore the full range of the FPC work include the:

- *Family Court Bench Book* (a special version of the kind of Bench Books used in the adult and youth courts); and
- Family Court Reference Cards.[5]

FEATURES OF FAMILY PROCEEDINGS COURTS

FPCs generally consist of not more than three family court magistrates, with at least one man and one woman sitting to hear cases (save for certain emergency situations). Alternatively a district judge (magistrates' courts) (*Chapter 1*) may sit with two magistrates, or he or she may sit alone. Justices' clerks have certain case management powers which they can also delegate to appropriate members of their teams of court legal advisers.

In some situations it is possible, subject to safeguards, for certain urgent matters to be heard *ex parte* (i.e. without notice to the other party or parties).

It was explained in *Chapter 3* how FPC magistrates are selected by local Bench Training and Development Committees (BTDCs) against set criteria and from applicants within the adult bench; whilst *Chapter 4* deals with how FPC magistrates are trained and the arrangements for their development.

The FPC exercises a nationwide family court jurisdiction. As with the youth court, there are certain tenets around the arrangements which here include:

- trying to separate court sittings to deal with family proceedings from sittings for other types of work
- the physical layout of the courtroom (and especially in any 'new builds') will receive special attention so that it is a less formal arena than the ordinary adult magistrates' court and more conducive to a less adversarial style of hearing (e.g. magistrates try to sit at the same level as everybody else and everyone remains seated)
- special attention is paid to the general environment created by the bench and court officials; and

---

5. Both of which can be found at jsboard.co.uk

- statutory provisions cover who may be present and what may be reported (subject to progress with the 'opening up' initiative already mentioned).

THE CHILDREN ACT 1989

The 1989 Act was a landmark in the way the interests of children are viewed, supported and protected. For FPC purposes a 'child' means someone under the age of eighteen years (i.e. there are no sub-categories like those which operate in the youth court: see *Chapter 8*).

Under the Act, children are seen more as individuals in their own right rather than, taking a stark analogy, something to be considered along with the house, its contents and finances when a relationship breaks down. Thus, e.g:

- there is since 1989 no longer an order for 'custody' but an enquiry to determine what a child's needs are in respect of a home and upbringing. Efforts are made to ensure those needs are met, e.g. by a 'residence order'
- parents no longer have 'access' to their children but the court tries to determine those people with whom it would be in the interests of the child (rather than their parents) for the child to have 'contact'; and
- usually, with the formal leave of the court, children are able to make applications to the court themselves, as may wider members of their family in the child's interests.

The 1989 Act contains a number of fundamental principles which directly affect all considerations under the Act. These are noted in what follows.

The Welfare Principle
The Children Act 1989 starts with a simple, yet direct and forceful statement that pervades all relevant courts and court proceedings and establishes a main tenet of such cases: that it is the child who is at the heart of all relevant considerations and deliberations and not the feelings or wishes of the parents or others. Not only will the court pay heed to this principle in all circumstances and in all ways but it will also expect everyone else involved in the proceedings, whether as parties, witnesses, report writers, advocates etc, to adopt similar approach. The task of upholding the principle is supported by the use of two statutory welfare checklists.

Welfare checklists
To 'add meat to the bones' of the 1989 welfare principle,[6] these checklists set out

---

6. Compare and contrast the welfare principle in the Children and Young Persons Act 1933 which is concerned with how children are treated in all courts so as to make that experience bearable: *Chapter 8*.

factors to be taken into account whenever a court is considering a child's welfare. On occasions it may well be necessary to consider the welfare of more than one child in a family and there will then have to be separate applications of the welfare principle and checklists although factors may turn out to be interconnected or even conflicting.

For instance it may be deemed necessary to remove one child from an abusive parent but possible to leave another with that parent (albeit perhaps under supervision). The need to remove the one child would then possibly be at the cost of depriving the second of the company of a sibling and vice versa. In such cases, special arrangements for continuing contact would need to be put in place.

The first, general checklist provides that a court must pay particular regard to:

- the ascertainable wishes and feelings of the child concerned (considered in the light of the child's age and understanding)
- the child's physical, emotional and educational needs
- the likely effect on the child of any change in the child's circumstances
- the child's age, sex, background and any relevant characteristics
- any harm that the child has suffered or is at risk of suffering
- how capable each of the child's parents, and any other person in relation to whom the court considers the question to be relevant, is of meeting the child's needs; and
- the range of powers available to the court under the Children Act 1989 in the proceedings in question.

The contents of the 'Welfare Checklist' are expressly not exhaustive and just because a court, or anybody else involved, has considered everything on it does not mean that all aspects of an individual child's welfare will necessarily have been addressed.

Adoption proceedings
In respect of adoption a special version of this general checklist refers to:

- the child's ascertainable wishes and feelings regarding the decision (considered in the light of his or her age and understanding)
- the child's particular needs
- the likely effect on the child throughout his or her life of having ceased to be a member of the original family and become an adopted person

- the child's age, sex, background and any of the child's characteristics
- any harm that the child has suffered or is at risk of suffering; and
- the relationship that the child has with relatives and with any other person in relation to whom the court considers the relationship to be relevant, including:
  - the likelihood of any such relationship continuing and the value to the child of it doing so
  - the ability and willingness of any of the child's relatives, or of any such person, to provide the child with a secure environment in which the child can develop and otherwise meet the child's needs; and
  - the wishes and feelings of any of the child's relatives, or of any such person, regarding the child.

The no order principle

The Children Act 1989 recognised that, generally speaking, it is better for parents and families themselves to make decisions about their children and their upbringing and that courts or public bodies should, wherever possible, not be involved in the making of those decisions or in the carrying out of them. It also recognised that the mere fact of involvement of courts and welfare services in the life of a family and of a child can, of itself, often serve to create extra pressures.

The Act thus introduced the 'no order' principle which provides:

Where a court is considering whether or not to make one or more orders under this Act with respect to a child, it shall not make the order or any of the orders unless it considers that doing so would be better for the child than making no order at all.

Not only does this acknowledge where the general decision-making should lie, it also discourages parties from coming to the court for an order just to 'get a bit of paper'. Bits of paper can be divisive. They can soon be out of touch with a child's ever-changing needs. The mere fact of a court order can, itself, be intrusive.

The no 'order principle' applies just as much when a local authority applies for child protection measures (what is called a 'public law case' (below)) as when parents apply for one if, e.g. they separate. This does not mean that the child will not receive protection, but that methods are always explored to see if a satisfactory outcome can be achieved, say, by agreement between all concerned in the life of the child

The 'delay' principle

The 1989 Act also recognised that the needs of children can change rapidly and that doggedly striving for some sort of 'perfect' outcome may well serve only to worsen the short-term needs of the child and, even if arrived at, may then have become irrelevant to the child's changed needs.

The purpose of the Act is not to superimpose some idyllic or subjective view of childhood but to recognise that families live very different lives and thereafter to make sure that, save where circumstances give rise to child protection issues, families are helped to reach their own decisions about their children.

Thus, sometimes a simple, immediate solution may be better than imposing the whole weight of court and welfare services onto the family.

The role of magistrates re 'welfare', 'no order' and 'delay'

Magistrates will often, at the very start of family proceedings, make sure that all parties involved, especially if they are not represented, are aware of these three principles and that the court will expect everybody to work within them. This then helps matters such as:

- concentrating everybody's mind directly and exclusively on the child's needs
- creating an inquisitorial rather than adversarial atmosphere and process[7]
- encouraging parties to try to reach their own solutions without a full hearing which might then enable the court to allow the proceedings to be withdrawn and without a formal order
- discouraging parties from seeking that 'bit of paper'; and
- explaining how the proceedings, if they are to continue, will be managed.

Parental Responsibility

Under the 1989 Act, parents do not have 'parental rights' as such but have a 'parental responsibility' to safeguard and promote the interests and welfare of their children. Any rights that the law may give to parents are there primarily to enable them to discharge this responsibility.

Where a child's father and mother were married to each other at the time of his or her birth then each will automatically have parental responsibility. This can be exercised separately as well as jointly. Where the child's mother was not married to the child's father at the time of a child's birth then she will automatically have parental responsibility but the father will not unless:

- his name is or becomes entered on the registration of birth; or
- he and the mother enter into a formal agreement for him to get parental responsibility.

---

7. Contrast the adversarial approach of criminal proceedings: *Chapter 2.*

Application may be made to the court for the grant of parental responsibility by the following:

- a natural father who does not have parental responsibility as above
- the spouse of a parent who has parental responsibility (i.e. a step-parent); and for
- the civil partner of a parent who has parental responsibility.

In such situations the welfare principle (above) will come into play automatically and the 1989 Act adds certain further considerations.

Where a child is taken into care, the local authority automatically acquires parental responsibility. However, that of the parents (or others) continues in force but is now exercised jointly with that of the local authority. Thus, on a care order being made by a court, the State does not, by that fact alone, take over decision-making in respect of the child. It will usually work with the parents towards an outcome that is in the child's best interests (as to which see further below).[8]

Where a 'residence order' (below) provides for a child to live with a father who does not otherwise have parental responsibility then the court must give him such responsibility as if he had made an application for it.

If, on the other hand, the residence order is in favour of some other person who does not have parental responsibility (e.g. a grandparent, aunt or uncle) then that person automatically acquires parental responsibility for the duration of the order.

Parental responsibility will usually last until the child reaches 18 years of age but can, in certain circumstances, be brought to an end earlier.

Section 3(5) of the Children Act 1989 provides, in essence, that a person who does not have parental responsibility for a child but otherwise has care of that child may, in accordance with the Act, 'do what is reasonable in all the circumstances of the case for the purpose of safeguarding or promoting the child's welfare'. This is not an alternative to parental responsibility, nor does it permit excluding those with parental responsibility or going against their decisions, but it may, in real emergencies, provide a long stop route to ensuring the welfare of a child.

PUBLIC LAW APPLICATIONS UNDER THE 1989 ACT

As the name might suggest, these are applications brought by a public body and will include the possibility of considering orders such as:

---

8. On adoption, parental responsibility passes to the adoptive parents.

- an emergency protection order (EPO)
- an interim care order (i.e. a temporary care order: see below)
- a care order
- an interim supervision order (i.e. a temporary supervision order: see below)
- a supervision order; and/or
- a placement order.

Case management of Public Law Applications

A *Practice Direction*, 'Guide to Case Management in Public Law Proceedings' sets out the main principles by which public law cases in respect of children should be managed by every member of the family judiciary.[9] The aim is to ensure that such cases are heard both expeditiously and appropriately.

Emergency Protection Order (EPO)

This is sought by the local authority, often where agreed informal child protection arrangements with the family have significantly broken down or in some other true emergency situation. The seeking of an EPO will often, although not necessarily, be the precursor to an application for a full care order.

The application can, with the leave of the justices' clerk, be made *ex parte* (i.e. without prior notice to potential parties such as the parents) although such leave will always be considered doubly carefully given the very nature of such an order. If notice is to be given then it will usually be no more than one day.

The test for such an order is whether there is 'reasonable cause to believe that the child will suffer significant harm if not removed or kept in a safe place'.

It is possible at the same time to apply for an 'exclusion requirement' to be added so as to exclude a suggested abuser from the child's dwelling and thereby permit the child to stay at home in the care of someone else who can and will care for the child during the period of the EPO.

At this stage the welfare principle will apply but not the welfare checklist as, of its nature, this is just a temporary and brief response to an emergency situation. Human Rights considerations (see *Chapter 5*) will, as in all family proceedings deliberations, be very much to the fore.

The effect of the EPO will be to give the local authority the power to remove the child to a safe place if necessary and to exercise limited parental rights.

An EPO lasts for a maximum of eight days but can be extended on application for a further seven days. However, if full care proceedings are envisaged then the court will usually push for them to be expedited so that the full merits of the application can be explored as soon as possible.

---

9. 'The Public Law Outline: Guide to Case Management in Public Law Proceedings' (2008) is openly available at judiciary.gov.uk

Care Order, Interim Care Order and Placement Order

Application for a care order will be made by a local authority and the effect of such an order is to place the child in the care of the local authority until he or she is 18 years old. As noted above, the local authority will acquire parental responsibility but will share it with anybody else who already has it.

The purpose of the care order is not to remove the child (unless necessary), nor to make any removal long-term or permanent (again unless necessary). The goal will be to keep the child with its family or, if removed, to return the child as soon as possible. If removed, then continuing contact with the family will usually be the starting point and must be encouraged and facilitated unless against the child's best interests.

However, in some circumstances the needs of the child may be best served by looking for a long-term or permanent solution away from the original home and in such cases adoption may be seen as the best arrangement. In such circumstances it is later possible for the local authority to apply for a placement order which effectively starts the process of reducing the parents' parental rights as the child is placed for adoption.

In all cases where a care order is sought the local authority must present a care plan to the court so that future intentions for the child are known and open to comment; or to challenge by all concerned.

The test for a care order is based on that for an EPO but is now, rightly, more demanding in its two-part application:

- at the time the applicant first took protective measures was the child suffering or likely to suffer significant harm; and
- was it attributable to a lack of parental care or the child being beyond parental control.

It should be noted here that, as seen in *Chapter 8*, offending behaviour by children under the age of criminal responsibility (ten years) may need to be addressed via the 'child welfare' route. Serious 'offending' behaviour by someone under ten years of age might be seen as putting the child at risk of serious harm and the above proceedings and tests may come into play.

As its name suggests, an interim care order can be made (for up to eight weeks and subject to certain provisions concerning extension) where, in essence, the local authority satisfies the court that when it first took protective measures there were reasonable grounds for believing that the criteria for a full care order existed. In other words, the full criteria may yet fall to be established but there are reasonable grounds for bringing the proceedings and, therefore, for considering an interim order, temporarily, while the matter is being fully worked out.

Supervision Order and Interim Supervision Order

Here an application will again be made by a local authority. The effect of a supervision order is to place the child under the supervision of the local authority, in effect of a social worker, youth worker or a probation officer who will assist and befriend the child. A main aim will be to try to avoid the need for a care order (above).

The order will last for one year (or through a separate application for extension for one year at a time up to an overall maximum of three years). It cannot have effect once the child is 18 years old.

An interim supervision order can be made for up to eight weeks but can be extended on application for limited periods.

The respective criteria for supervision orders and interim supervisions orders are as for their care order equivalents and such orders may also be made if the original application was in fact for a care order.

EMERGENCY MEASURES BY THE POLICE

Section 46 Children Act 1989 gives the police the power, without a court order, to secure the removal and accommodation of a child where a police officer has reasonable cause to believe that the child would otherwise be likely to suffer significant harm. This will have effect for no longer than 72 hours. The officer has to inform the local authority as soon as reasonably possible afterwards of what has taken place and also has other duties relating to the child and parents.

Although this might be seen as a practical way to avoid the demands of applying to the FPC for an emergency protection order (above), the power tends to be used by the police in only extreme emergencies and where some significant and unexpected factor has arisen. If need be, the police themselves can subsequently apply for an EPO if the local authority does not.

CHILDREN'S GUARDIANS, SOLICITORS AND CAFCASS

As soon as possible, even at any EPO stage (above) if possible, the court will usually appoint an independent children's guardian. He or she will safeguard the child's interests throughout the whole proceedings and, to a certain extent, afterwards if an order is made. The court will also, often with the help of the guardian, ensure that a solicitor is appointed for the child, usually at public expense, and the guardian and solicitor will work together to promote the child's welfare.

The guardian will have access to the files of the local authority on the child and be able to undertake an independent professional assessment of their contents. He or she may also address case management issues and will provide an independent report to the court which may possibly counter what the applicant local authority has put before the court, including in some instances suggesting different outcomes for consideration.

The guardian is appointed from a panel of trained and qualified people which exists for that purpose independent of the local authority. This is the responsibility of the independent Children and Family Court Advisory and Support Service (CAFCASS).

PRIVATE LAW APPLICATIONS

Again, as the name suggests, these are applications that can be brought by parents or (with the leave of the court) other private individuals such as grandparents and even, in some circumstances, by children themselves. The most common are for 'section 8' orders under the Children Act 1989:

- residence orders (where the child should live)
- contact orders (who the child should have contact with)
- prohibited steps orders (parental responsibility steps to be taken only with the leave, i.e. permission of the court); and/or
- specific issues orders (re how certain parental responsibility steps should occur).

There is a national Private Law Case Management Framework which seeks, as with public law cases, to concentrate the minds of all concerned on the issues relevant to the child's welfare and to expedite the proceedings. Fundamental to this is that at the first hearing of a private law application the possibility of reconciliation will be raised, if relevant. In any event, the possibility of an agreed outcome or conciliation (including withdrawal of the proceedings if appropriate) will be explored.

Many courts have a duty CAFCASS officer (above) at such first hearings and many matters can be resolved at this stage both to the benefit of the child but also to that of all others concerned. If the case is to proceed then directions will be given for the management of the hearing and the evidence and a welfare report may be requested from a CAFCASS officer.

The other most common other type of private law applications are for adoption orders. Such orders may now be applied for by a wide range of people aged 21 years or over, including:

- married couples
- people in a civil partnership
- people who are cohabiting
- single people; and
- divorced people.

CHAPTER TEN

A Diverse Mix of 'Other' Responsibilities

It would be impossible in a book of this kind to chart all aspects of magistrates' jurisdiction. Quite apart from criminal cases, youth and family proceedings as described in earlier chapters, they deal with many matters which are not so readily compartmentalised This chapter looks at some of these extra responsibilities.

CIVIL CASES

As noted in *Chapter 1*, a fundamental distinction exists as between criminal cases and civil matters.[1] The civil courts deal with private claims involving such things as negligence, nuisance and tort (which covers a range of 'civil wrongs'). The civil standard of proof is 'on a balance of probabilities' not 'beyond reasonable doubt' (*Chapter 5*). There are a number of situations in which the adult magistrates' court deals with cases of a civil nature, but some of which also exhibit features normally found in the criminal sphere as described below. It is also instructive to consider the term 'preventive justice'. In all cases the items noted are intended as indicative, for the purposes of familiarity and presented in simple outline only.[2]

Civil Behaviour Order

Civil behaviour order (CBO) is a generic term for a range of orders based initially on civil powers but that are backed by criminal sanctions if breached. The Crown Court or a magistrates' court can, after complying with the Criminal Procedure Rules 2005 (as amended in 2008) make CBOs under various powers (sometimes even following an acquittal), e.g. under the Domestic Violence, Crimes and Victims Act 2004; Football Spectators Act 1989; Protection From Harassment Act 1997; Crime and Disorder Act 1998; Sexual Offences Act 2003; Serious Crime Act 2007; or in some situations where an accused person or offender is mentally impaired.

Preventive Justice[3]

By preventive justice is meant an attempt by those concerned with crime prevention, crime reduction and law enforcement or the control of anti-social behaviour (ASB) to pre-empt the worsening of a situation until it becomes a criminal matter,

---

1. 'Civil' is a word also used, e.g. to distinguish everyday matters from military matters, as with the civil police as opposed to the military police; just as the word civilian may be used in various context to indicate non-military, non-police services or other non-professional personnel; especially those working behind the scenes, e.g. in purely administrative roles, or from the private sector.
2. Each attracts its own body of law concerning which specialist works need to be consulted.
3. Some people prefer to use the word 'preventative".

possibly leaving victims in its wake and ultimately 'criminalising' the perpetrator. It is not hard to think of situations which 'simmer' rather than 'explode' immediately into offending, where there are real questions about whether anyone should intervene at all, but where experience shows that left to themselves problems may either peter out or deteriorate, sometimes with devastating consequences. This area is one where magistrates may need not simply a sure judicial touch but in some instances the Judgement of Solomon. Nonetheless, magistrates have a long tradition of using preventative measures and this area of their work has, if anything, expanded quite significantly in modern times. The following will serve as examples:

Binding over to keep the peace

This historic power of magistrates dates from the Justices of the Peace Act 1361. A court may bind over anyone who appears before it, whether as a defendant or witness, but most commonly in practice the defendant in a criminal case as an order ancillary to sentence. They may also do so following the making of a complaint (by the police or, e.g. a neighbour who is concerned about given behaviour).

The consent of the defendant is required, but if he or she fails to agree to the bind over, he or she may be committed to custody (subject to various legal considerations). The bind over must be for a fixed period. It can name individuals for whose protection it is made. People being bound over enter into a recognizance (a promise to pay a sum of money in the event that the order is breached: see the *Glossary*).

A breach of the peace must involve violence or the threat of violence, whether from the defendant or a third party as a consequence of the actions of the person being bound over; and the court must be satisfied that in all the circumstances the conduct of the person it intends to bind over was unreasonable. In assessing conduct prospectively, it must be shown that there is a real risk, not just a possibility, of that conduct continuing into the future so that a breach of the peace might happen.

The power is civil in nature but with sanctions equating with punishment, such that at one stage it faced challenges under human rights law and is now more focused, subject to clearer procedures and attracts quasi-criminal standards in terms of evidence, fairness and explanations. The power is actively used but has been partly superseded in practice by the anti-social behaviour order (below) in terms of 'preventative justice' as opposed to any initial punishment.

Restraining order in respect of harassment

The Protection From Harassment Act 1997 created the offence of harassment to make it easier to deal with, e.g. stalkers and other people involved in related forms of pestering and annoyance; both as a criminal offence of harassment and a parallel civil wrong (which can be pursued in the county court); each based around a then new remedy known as the restraining order, i.e. an order to prevent continuation of a given course of conduct (there must be more than just a 'one-off' occurrence before harassment is made out). Criminal offences of harassment are progressively more serious the longer the conduct continues or repetitive it becomes. The restraining order was the first civil behaviour order (CBO) backed by criminal sanctions if breached; and a blueprint for other such laws.

Anti-social behaviour order

A modern dimension to crime prevention and crime reduction is the targeting of anti-social behaviour (ASB). The development of the anti-social behaviour order (ASBO) began with the Crime and Disorder Act 1998 in order to deal with minor misdeeds by young people (not necessarily criminal in kind and originally described by Government as 'nuisance-type' or 'low-level' behaviour). Since then the use and range of ASBOs has expanded. Tackling ASB was a central tenet of the Government's Respect Agenda from 2000 onwards; and such strategies have become central to CJS work despite some criticisms. ASBOs can also be made in the county court.

An application to a court for an ASBO is a civil matter following liaison between the police and local authority and often using mechanisms established under Crime Reduction Partnerships (CRPs). If an ASBO is not complied with this becomes a criminal offence punishable with up to five years' imprisonment in the case of an adult (custody for up to two years for older juveniles).

The Police Reform Act 2002 allowed on the spot fines for a range of (here criminal) behaviour loosely categorised as anti-social. Hence also the development of fixed penalty notices for disorder (*Chapter 7*). An ASB-related 'premises closure order', introduced in 2003, was strengthened by the Criminal Justice and Immigration Act 2008 (see below).

The criminal anti-social behaviour order (CRASBO) which is comparable in substance and effect to a civil ASBO can be made when a court is sentencing in criminal proceedings (see generally *Chapter 7*).

Serious crime prevention order

The serious crime prevention order (SCPO) is targeted at higher end crimes such as those involved in organized crime, drug-trafficking and money laundering. Hence it has been dubbed the 'gangster ASBO'. It was introduced by the Serious Crime Act 2007. Again, it is initially a civil order. It can be used, e.g. to impose conditions restricting where an individual can live and limiting their work, associations with other people and/or their travel arrangements. SCPOs can last for up to five years and breaching them can result in imprisonment for up to five years.

Premises closure order

The ASB-related 'premises closure order' was first introduced by the Anti-social Behaviour Act 2003 when the police were given powers to issue a closure notice in respect of premises believe to be being used for the production, supply or use of

Class A drugs and causing serious nuisance or disorder. Within 48 hours the police must then apply to the court for a closure order. To make the order the court must be satisfied that: the premises have been used in connection with the production, supply or use of Class A drugs; they are associated with disorder or serious nuisance; and that an order is necessary to prevent disorder/serious nuisance.

The Order can apply for up to three months (and may be extended to a maximum of six months) during which time it is an offence to enter or remain in the premises.

Football banning order

Since the Football (Disorder) Act 2000 (and subsequent legislation) a court must make an (criminal) football banning order (FBO) if the offender is convicted of a football-related offence with regard to a 'regulated football match'.[4] This will be as an ancillary order and thus additional, as a preventative measure, to any punishment for the offence concerned. Thus in an early case, e.g. a fan who yelled 'Paki' at a Port Vale v. Oldham Athletic game was fined and also banned from grounds nationwide for three years. The events were clearly 'football-related' and the High Court ruled that the term was intrinsically racially offensive even if the offender lacked malice.

Alternatively, the police can apply for an FBO independently of any prosecution, including where no prosecution is brought. Before making an order on the complaint of the police, the court must be satisfied that the respondent has (at any time) caused or contributed to violence in the UK or elsewhere and that there are reasonable grounds for believing that an FBO would help prevent violence or disorder at or in connection with a regulated football match.

Orders made on application can be for a maximum of three years and a minimum of two. Those following conviction (above) depend on whether defendant is given a custodial sentence (when the maximum order is ten years and the minimum six) or some other sentence (when the maximum is five years and the minimum is three).

Ministers of State have power to ban named supporters from travelling to matches abroad (a power which has been used on various occasions including in relation to the World Cup).

Foreign travel restriction order

As can be seen from the explanation under 'Football banning order', it is possible for football 'supporters' to be prevented from travelling abroad in certain circumstances at the behest of the Minister of State. A dedicated foreign travel order (FTO)[5] is available to the courts directly as one of a number of preventative mechanisms in relation to sex offenders.[6] It is meant to prevent offenders with convictions for sexual

---

4. Meaning one at home or abroad involving a team from the Premier League, Championship, League One, League Two or the Blue Square Conference.
5. Sometimes called a foreign travel restriction order (FTRO) as per the sub-heading
6. Including a sexual offences risk of serious harm (ROSH) order, the effect of which is to prevent the

offences against children below 16 years of age travelling outside of the UK if there is evidence that they intend to commit sexual offences against children abroad.

Application may be made on complaint by the police in respect of someone who is within, or intends to come to, their police force area. The court may make an FTO if satisfied that:

- the defendant is a qualifying offender (someone convicted, cautioned etc. in respect of certain scheduled sexual offences); and
- the defendant's behaviour since then makes it necessary to make an FTO for the purpose of protecting a child or children generally from serious sexual harm from the defendant outside of the United Kingdom.

The order can prohibit the offender from travelling to a specified country outside of the UK, any foreign country, or any such country except one specified in the order. It can lasts for up to six months. Breach of the order is an either way offence attracting a fine, community sentence or imprisonment (but not a discharge).

'NON-POLICE' CASES

This is a term that is commonly used to describe any case prosecuted or otherwise brought to a magistrates' court (since some of these cases may be civil in nature) which does not stem from a police report, investigation or detection work. Such cases are often, as a matter of court listing and case management (*Chapter 2*), channelled into a separate courtroom, similarly often called a 'non-police court'. Examples of such cases include those brought by:

- TV Licensing, the nationwide agency charged with the collection and enforcement of payment for TV licences
- local authorities, e.g. where the offence is one against one of its bye-laws or involves enforcement of a compliance notice, e.g. with regard to planning law
- the Royal Society for the Prevention of Cruelty to Animals (RSPCA) with regard to ill-treatment or wrongful keeping of animals[7]
- the Serious Fraud Office (SFO), usually en route to the Crown Court as this, under the SFO's own criteria, will involve a case with a value of over £1 million and possibly aggravating features: see 'Plea Before Venue and Mode of Trial' in *Chapter 7*

---

person concerned being involved in certain activities relating to children: see specialist texts.

7. Laws relating to the breeding, rearing, keeping, movement and slaughter of animals (including from time-to-time emergency provisions) are extensive and specialist. Animals are partly a Home office responsibility via its Animals Scientific Procedures Division: scienceandresearch.homeoffice.gov.uk

- HM Revenue & Customs in relation to the evasion of taxation or duty or other offences provided for with regard to increasingly extensive systems of economic and other financial regulation
- the Department of Work and Pensions concerning benefit fraud; and
- those brought by purely private prosecutors as mentioned in *Chapter 2.*

EMERGENCIES

Emergency is a word with many CJS-connotations, various offences being themselves in the nature of an emergency and requiring the intervention of the police, etc. particularly those involving public safety, violence, many sexual offences and threats to public order. Other uses of the term refer to the emergency situation that an accused person or victim may find himself or herself in, possibly leading to a defence based around 'necessity' or self-defence. When such a defence fails, the emergency nature of the situation may still mean that the offender can use this as offence-based mitigation (*Chapter 7*). Magistrates may become involved in out-of-hours emergency applications as described under the next heading, 'Out of Court Matters'.

Whilst in the normal course of events court business is marshalled between normal business hours, an emergency court may nonetheless need to be held outside usual business hours (aka a 'special court' or 'occasional court') or a magistrate may need to be approached in his or her own home as described in the next section.

Certain family applications may need to be made urgently, including by the police under section 46 Children Act 1989 as described in *Chapter 9.*

OUT OF COURT MATTERS

Magistrates deal with some matters which may take place outside the courtroom and in some instances in a place other than a courthouse, such as a magistrates' own home. The Judicial Studies Board (JSB) advises magistrates as to the level of care needed before, e.g. signing a document or concerning the need to contact a member of the court legal team whenever there is any doubt about whether a document should be signed. They are advised always to do so where the application is for a warrant. As demonstrated below, warrants may be requested for a wide range of purposes related to entry to premises, seizure of property and evidence. If unable to contact staff, magistrates are advised not sign such documents and to ask the applicant to attend at their local courthouse during normal working hours.

Many statutes contain provisions for applications of this kind and some of these may of necessity have to be considered in the evening or at a weekend due to their general urgency (see also the comments under 'Emergency' above). Common applications of this kind include:

- **search warrants**: although the majority of applications are made by police officers, these may also be requested, e.g. by officers of a local authority, HM Revenue & Customs or the Royal Society for the Prevention Cruelty to Animals (RSPCA). Common warrants include those to search for stolen property, controlled drugs and firearms.
- **entry warrants**: to enter premises and search for evidence under procedures contained in the Police and Criminal Evidence Act 1984 (PACE) (subject to strict limitations, some requiring an application to a higher court). Such applications normally also require higher authorisation within a police force before being made.[8] As with all warrants, a magistrate acting alone and having to use his or her discretion unaided, verifies the identity and veracity of the applicant, by questioning him or her if need be and making sure that human rights are safeguarded, (a warrant may, e.g. involve interference with private and family life: *Chapter 5*) or being legitimately overridden, e.g. in the interests of national security, public health, terrorism or crime prevention.
- **energy disconnection warrants**: representatives of a gas or electricity supply company may apply for warrants to enter premises to inspect and/or read a meter, install pre-payment meters or disconnect a supply (including in an emergency).[9]
- **mental health orders**: a representative from social services or a mental health team may apply for warrants to remove someone to a place of safety, usually meaning to a hospital and to enter premises, by force if necessary to remove that person. Comparable provisions also apply to people incapable of looking after themselves and refusing assistance.[10]
- **noise**: applications can be made by the local authority where 'noise nuisance' is alleged, including e.g. in respect of burglar alarms activated where the premises are empty or the occupier cannot be located.

Bearing in mind in particular the *ex parte* nature of such applications (they are inevitably made in the absence of the other party or in many instances what is in mind would be defeated by giving prior warning) reasons should normally be given and recorded for granting or refusing a warrant and a personal note kept. Many courts supply magistrates with guidance notes and a pro forma. Other relatively more straightforward out of court functions include witnessing a signature, or counter-

---

8. The police, etc. do have certain powers to seize evidence themselves, e.g. when they are already lawfully on premises, which they may be in an emergency or, e.g. under terrorism powers.
9. Re which the Justices Clerks' Society and Magistrates Association have issued guidance.
10. No-one studying the work of the CJS as a whole should underestimate the impact of mental impairment on offending, imprisonment, self-harm the need for emergency powers and the longstanding difficulties that the CJS has had in coming to terms with this: see specialist works. It has been estimated that as many as four out of every ten people in prison suffer from some kind of mental health problem.

signing or validating documents or certificates, including those designed to prevent fraud and money laundering (*Chapter 2*). Similarly, statutory declarations under the Statutory Declarations Act 1835. Here it is not the truth of the contents of the document that the magistrate is attesting to, but the person concerned will need to understand, if need be by a warning given by the magistrate, that if anything false or untrue is stated by them then they could be guilty of a criminal offence.

The signature of items such as passport applications and those for firearms certificate do or may require direct knowledge of certain matters, or confirmation of given facts, by the magistrate. Here the magistrate is not acting as such, but simply as one person from of a list of the kind of people who may countersign such applications.

MAGISTRATES IN THE CROWN COURT

The Crown Court deals with cases at some 90 locations in England and Wales (aka Crown Court Centres).[11] As noted in *Chapter 2*, the administration of the Crown Court is a function of HM Court Service (HMCS) alongside its responsibility for magistrates' courts. A member of HMCS staff acts as a court clerk in the Crown Court but, unlike the position in the magistrates' court, not as legal adviser.

As described in *Chapter 2*, appeals against conviction and against sentence from the adult court (and also the youth court: *Chapter 8*) go to the Crown Court.

Magistrates themselves have an additional jurisdiction to sit with the judge in the Crown Court to hear such appeals. There are local selection criteria for inclusion on the list of magistrates approved for this purpose, based on national guidance. The criteria are analogous to those for applying to sit in the youth or family jurisdictions as described in *Chapter 3*. The process of authorisation involves the bench chairman, justices' clerk and the Bench Training and Development Committee (BTDC). Only youth magistrates are able to sit on appeals from the youth court.

At the appeal hearing the Crown Court judge will have precedence in respect of matters of law although the magistrates sitting with the judge (usually two magistrates but possibly up to four in adult cases) will have an equal say on matters relating to the facts, general merits and sentence. The final decision is by a straight majority but, in the case of a tie, the judge has a casting vote.

Clearly, magistrates will not sit on a case which they personally heard first time round in the magistrates' court (i.e. out of fairness: see generally *Chapter 5*) but they can sit on cases heard by their local colleagues. The Crown Court will, however, hear appeals from a number of magistrates' courts and not just those from the court from which a particular magistrate sitting on an appeal might come. The Crown Court may thus also draw on magistrates from a wide range of local benches.

---

11. It replaced Assizes and Quarter Sessions in 1972 following the Beeching Report and Courts Act 1971.

The appeal bench decides the matter afresh ('de novo' as it is often put) and there is no suggestion that the magistrates hearing the appeal are there in any way to 'defend' the earlier decision of their magistrate colleagues. A brief form of additional training is normally be given although magistrates will essentially be dealing with familiar work albeit in a different setting. It is the usual practice for magistrates not to undertake a disproportionate number of sittings in the Crown Court (a maximum of one in five has been suggested by the Magistrates' Association).

MAGISTRATES' APPELLATE JURISDICTION

As can be seen from the diagram in *Chapter 2*, magistrates' courts occupy the first rung on the ladder of courts of law. Their former designation 'petty' (or small) sessions courts conveys much in this regard. But surprisingly they also act a 'court of appeal' in respect of a wide range of decisions by certain other public (but non-judicial) bodies or officials. The following are examples:

- the refusal by a local authority to grant a guard dog licence (or in respect of conditions placed on such a licence if granted) under the Guard Dogs Act 1975
- the refusal by a highway authority to grant permission for a door or gate to open onto a street under the Highways Act 1980
- the refusal by a local authority to grant a sex establishment licence (or in respect of conditions placed on such a licence if granted) under the Local Government (Miscellaneous Provisions) Act 1982
- the requirement of a local authority to remove or alter building work that does not comply with building regulations under the Building Act 1984
- the requirement of a local authority or local highway authority that the part of a building intended to be erected at the corner of two streets be rounded off
- many decisions of local authorities in respect of public houses, clubs, restaurants and so on under the Licensing Act 2003;[12] and
- conditions placed on bail granted by the police – on application (a form of appeal albeit not so called) the magistrates' court may vary or remove the conditions.

The general rule is that the case is heard *de novo* (afresh) on the circumstances appertaining at the time of the hearing. In a similar vein, someone aged 16 or 17 wishing to marry whose parent (or other relevant person) is refusing consent can apply for magistrates' consent (when they will sit as a family proceedings court: *Chapter 9*).

---

12. Prior to the 2003 Act, much of this work was initially considered by magistrates' courts themselves, with appeals going to the Crown Court.

CHAPTER ELEVEN

Road Traffic

People who witnessed the birth of the 'horseless carriage' can hardly have envisaged that its arrival would give rise to one our largest bodies of Parliamentary legislation and case law. The law relating to motor vehicles is extensive and detailed: consider, for instance, regulations dealing with 'newtons per square millimetre' or the absence of water in a plastic bottle under a car bonnet to facilitate washing the windscreen. In many respects, the minutiae are nowadays to meet common European standards.

ROAD TRAFFIC OFFENCES

Offences relating to motor vehicles are *criminal* offences like any other. The same burden and standard of proof apply as described in *Chapter 5* and, indeed, various wider rules of criminal law, evidence and procedure have been determined by the higher courts in what began as outwardly simple everyday cases relating to motor vehicles. A main difference, however, is that the vast majority of road traffic offences usually do not require any particular *mens rea* (i.e. criminal intent) in the ordinary sense, or at all. Some of them may involve a mental element in the sense of knowledge or failure but many do not even require that. Speeding is speeding even if the speedometer is faulty (which is a further offence in itself!).

Many road traffic offences attract fixed penalties (described in *Chapter 7* and to which this chapter returns later) as an alternative to prosecution. It is quite possible to commit an offence in respect of a motor vehicle whilst having the best of intentions, without leaving home and with the car safely locked in the garage. As an example, if someone receives a V11 road tax reminder from the Driver and Vehicle Licensing Agency (DVLA),[1] he or she must renew the tax or make a Statutory Off-Road Notification (SORN). If he or she does nothing an offence is committed purely by omission (and he or she can be fined up to £1,000), even if the car will not start.

Endless debates may occur behind the scenes between magistrates as they try to reconcile and compare the culpability involved in motoring offences with that with regard to 'crimes proper'; whilst many members of the general public tend not to like being treated as 'criminals' or having to deal with the criminal courts for what they may regard as relatively minor aberrations or 'slip ups'.

It is, of course, hard to make sense of a scheme of punishments which must serve in relation to both dishonesty, assault or disruptive behaviour and parking on

---

1. Or 'Swansea' as it is commonly called after its location in that Welsh city.

double yellow lines, having no insurance or a defective rear light. Sound across-the-board comparisons are elusive; and people involved in framing sentencing guidelines (*Chapter 7*) tend to resort to treating road traffic offences as a species apart.

But some road traffic offences are very serious indeed, such as causing death by dangerous driving, when it is perhaps easier for all concerned to recognise relative culpability. Others are deceptive. It is perhaps only necessary to stand on a street corner for a few moments to witness a driver unlawfully using a hand-held mobile telephone whilst driving (which is an offence in itself as well as being potentially dangerous). Some drivers think road traffic law is 'for other people'. It is serious or repeated offending that the disqualification and endorsement system described later in the chapter targets; as a way of disabusing drivers of their misplaced ideas. It was the reported arrogance of early motorists which brought about the earliest road traffic laws.

Categories of Offence
Road traffic offences come in three broad categories targeting:

- the manner of driving a vehicle: e.g. driving without due care and attention, speeding, failure to comply with traffic lights etc.
- the state or condition of the vehicle: e.g. defective tyres, defective brakes, lights not working and so on (often described as 'construction and use offences'); and
- regulatory matters: e.g. no insurance, no vehicle excise licence (car tax), failure to notify change of ownership and so on.

The Highway Code
The Highway Code was introduced in 1931 when the number of vehicles on British roads was less than a tenth of the number today (and yet the number of people killed on the roads was around twice the current number). The Code has certainly played its part in the overall drive to improve road safety and is still published today under statutory provisions. Virtually every experienced driver will be aware of the existence of the code but may not be up-to-date with its changing contents and modern-day advice. Many people may have forgotten or not even realised that it contains advice for other types of road users (e.g. pedal cyclists and horse riders and even for pedestrians).

Failure to comply with the code is not an offence in itself but non-compliance may be relied upon, for instance, to support an inference of driving without due care and attention. This is because the code underpins standards of driving.

Vehicle Defect Rectification Schemes (VDRSs)
Many police forces operate a non-statutory VDRS in respect of relatively minor offences relating to the condition of a motor vehicle (e.g. defective windscreen wipers). The driver is given the opportunity to have the defect rectified at an approved

MOT Testing Centre with the VDRS notice being duly endorsed by the centre and returned within (typically) 14 days by the diver to the police. Compliance saves the driver from any fixed penalty or prosecution and also provides a quick and effective way of putting right the original defect and securing road safety.

Driver Improvement and Speed Awareness Schemes

Many police forces, again on a non-statutory and purely discretionary basis, now run driver improvement schemes or offer driver improvement courses for people who might otherwise be prosecuted for a minor offence of, say driving without due care and attention. There are also speed awareness schemes are for those who might otherwise be prosecuted for a low-level speeding offence.

Motorists have the option to decline attendance, when they then risk prosecution for the underlying offence. However, payment of the appropriate scheme fee and attendance at (and proper engagement in) an event provided under such a scheme will result in there being no prosecution and, of course, no conviction or licence endorsement (see later). Further information is available from the Association of National Driver Improvement Scheme Providers.[2]

Perhaps unfortunately, the schemes are not available as an ancillary or alternative order of the court when sentencing those more serious (or indeed other) offenders who are prosecuted. However, the ability to order a retest (see below) may still be a way of addressing any underlying lack of driving skills.

FIXED PENALTIES

To provide a quick and easy mechanism to deal with the mass of everyday road traffic offences (both 'moving offences' and others) legislation has long been in place to enable the police and other authorised public bodies to issue fixed penalty notices (FPNs) to alleged road traffic offenders.

The FPN will, as its name suggests, be for a fixed financial amount (usually set at figure lower than what a court fine is likely to be so as to make acceptance of the FPN an attractive option)[3] and, if the offence carries endorsement, then penalty points will also apply if the FPN is accepted and paid. If such those points are 'variable' (see later) then the lowest figure in the range will apply (again to encourage acceptance). The section headed 'Endorsement and Penalty Points' below gives a general overview of the penalty points system.

If the recipient of an FPN decides to accept it and complies with its terms then the penalty will, generally (but not always) be payable to the local magistrates' court which will also, where relevant, require production of any driving licence for

---

2. See driver-improvement.co.uk
3. But not always so which has been a bone of contention.

endorsement. Failure to accept the offer of a fixed penalty notice will usually result in formal prosecution for the original offence.

Examples of common fixed penalty offences

Some of the more common offences for which a fixed penalty can be used include:

- various parking restrictions
- speeding
- no insurance
- not wearing seat belts
- failure to comply with traffic signs or directions
- the condition of a vehicle; and
- not displaying a tax disc.

For a body of law that is intended to simplify and speed up matters, the provisions relating to fixed penalties can, themselves, be detailed and complex and are not covered here in any greater detail. Such provisions are increasingly being introduced to deal with what are seen as low-level non-motoring offences, particularly those involving disorder: hence a fixed penalty notice for disorder (FPND) (*Chapter 2*).

COMMENCING PROCEEDINGS

Prosecution for road traffic offences, as is the case with regard to many other offences where the defendant has not been arrested, has traditionally been by way of the 'information and summons' procedure described in *Chapter 2*. That chapter also notes a new form of procedure, requisition and charge, which is in the process of being introduced for public prosecutors. Most prosecutions for road traffic matters (save the more serious ones) must be begun within six months of the alleged offence.

Service of the summons by the prosecutor will usually be by way of normal post to the last known address of the defendant. In many instances, in the absence of any reply from the defendant and on service of the summons being proved, application is made to hear the case in the accused person's absence.

If the case is proved in this manner, a defendant who claims not to have received the summons may subsequently have the right to make a 'statutory declaration' of non-awareness of the proceedings and thereby have the conviction nullified (and thus his or her sentence) and the proceedings reopened (again see *Chapter 2*).

Other procedural matters

In road traffic cases the prosecutor will often use what is know as the 'written plea', 'guilty by letter' or 'section 12' procedure.[4] This gives defendants and the court a brief written summary of the facts alleged (known as a statement of facts) and defendants the opportunity of writing in to the court to plead guilty without attending, and by accepting those facts (which cannot then be amended by the prosecutor without notice) and producing their driving licences if offences carry endorsement (below). The defendant can also submit a written note of mitigation (*Chapter 2*) if desired and is required to provide a written statement of his or her financial circumstances.

Another procedure often used in respect of road traffic prosecutions (as also in other criminal proceedings) is the 'section 9 statement' procedure.[5] Here the prosecutor serves, either with the summons or as soon as it looks as though a defendant will not be responding to it or is positively pleading not guilty, formal written statements from witnesses. If not specifically objected to by the defendant, these can be read out as if the witnesses concerned were present giving live evidence. This expedites the proceedings and saves the unnecessary attendance of witnesses (who are often police officers who might otherwise be out on duty) at court.

ENDORSEMENT AND PENALTY POINTS

On conviction, many road traffic offences require that the counterpart[6] of the offender's driving licence (or any subsequent one if one is not already held) be endorsed with certain details of the conviction. In such cases, penalty points will also have to be imposed, either as a fixed number or from within a range of numbers ('variable points') whereupon the actual number will be based on the seriousness of the offence when compared with others of its kind.

If there is more than one offence *committed on the same occasion,* the number of points will be that applicable to the offence which carries the highest number, but each set of occasions will carry its own number. Endorsements remain on a licence as follows:

- eleven years from *conviction* for driving involving drink/drugs and causing death offences
- four years from *conviction* for dangerous driving offences and offences for which disqualification (including a retest) is ordered; or

---

4. After section 12 of the Magistrates' Courts Act 1980. It was originally introduced as long ago as 1957.
5. After section 9 of the Criminal Justice Act 1967.
6. Modern licences are in two parts: a photocard and a paper counterpart. Old-style licences are paper licences until renewed, e.g. due to a change of address. Penalty points are endorsed in writing on the counterpart and are also notified to the DVLA (aka 'Swansea': see the *Glossary*). This applies to main UK licences not foreign licences (but all penalty points are recorded at the DVLA and taken into account re any further offending in the UK).

- four years from the *offence* in all other cases.

After this time, application can be made to the DVLA if their removal is desired, otherwise they will be removed automatically only when a licence is renewed or updated for other reasons such as a change of name or address.

Penalty points do not arise in respect of limited companies but where, say a sole trader or member of a partnership is convicted of aiding and abetting an offence committed by an employee, the licence of such an individual who is convicted will also be endorsed, along with that of the main offender.

See also generally *Figure 2* at the end of this chapter.

'Special Reasons' for Not Endorsing

The court has a discretion if the defendant, usually on oath, satisfies the court that 'special reasons' exist. These must satisfy *all* of the following criteria, i.e. they must:

- constitute a mitigating or extenuating circumstance
- not, in law, amount to a defence (in such cases the original plea would be considered 'equivocal': *Chapter 7*)
- relate directly to the commission of the offence itself and not to the offender; and
- be something which the court ought properly to take into consideration when sentencing.

For example a young driver relying on a parent's reasonable assurance that the parent had insurance to cover the former's use of the parent's vehicle might be accepted as a special reason depending on all the circumstances (and assuming that there was no 'connivance'), whereas lack of financial means, no matter how real, to afford insurance would not be. Neither would the fact that a job as a driver was 'on the line'.

The prosecutor has a right to cross-examine a defendant who puts forward special reasons and also to address the court on the legal and factual merits of the matter. The court legal adviser will also have a role in offering advice concerning what is usually a matter of mixed fact and law (see generally *Chapter 6*).

The court will need to give its own reasons for its final decision on the matter and, if special reasons are found, these must be entered in the court register.

DISQUALIFICATION

Offenders can be disqualified from driving or holding a driving licence in the following broad sets of circumstances:

- obligatory for the offence itself (e.g. driving with excess alcohol in the blood)
- at the court's discretion for the offence itself (e.g. a one-off high speeding offence)
- following repeated convictions for endorsable offences ('totting up': below)
- by way of an interim disqualification (i.e. post-conviction and pending sentence)
- until a test is passed (aka a 'retest' order)
- for any offence where the court, with reason, 'thinks fit';[7] and
- where a vehicle was used for the purposes of crime (a Crown Court power only).

OFFENCE	MINIMUM PERIOD OF DISQUALIFICATION
Dangerous driving	12 months 2 years if had two or more disqualifications of 56 days or more in the 3 years preceding the commission of present offence
Driving with excess alcohol	12 months 2 years if had two or more disqualifications of 56 days or more in the 3 years preceding the commission of present offence 3 years if convicted of similar or related offence within 10 years of commission of present offence
Failure to provide specimen for analysis (driving or attempting to drive) Unfit through drink/drugs (driving or attempting to drive)	12 months 2 years if had two or more disqualifications of 56 days or more in the 3 years preceding the commission of present offence 3 years if convicted of similar or related offence within 10 years of commission of present offence

Figure 1: Common examples of obligatory disqualification.

It should be noted that disqualification cannot be imposed in the absence of the offender unless, after conviction, the case has been adjourned to require the offender's presence and the offender is specifically warned in writing that disqualification

---

7. As introduced by section 146 powers of Criminal Courts (Sentencing) Act 2000.

is under consideration and that failure to attend might result in its being imposed in his or her absence. Note, however, that a defendant who is not before the court but is represented by a solicitor is not deemed to be absent although, as a safeguard, the court would usually make sure that advice has specifically been given by the solicitor that disqualification could take place in the offender client's absence.

Obligatory Disqualification for an Offence

Certain specified offences require the court, unless it finds 'special reasons', to disqualify for a *minimum* period, whereupon penalty points will not be imposed for the current offence. See *Figure 1* on the previous page.

Special Reasons

In obligatory disqualification cases, the defendant may plead 'special reasons' against the same four criteria as for endorsements (above). For example, someone driving with excess alcohol in a true medical emergency where no other option was available *might*, depending on all the circumstances, be able to escape compulsory disqualification or secure a shorter period of disqualification (since these are matters relating to the offence rather than the offender).

Even a doctor convicted of driving with excess alcohol would not succeed with such a plea solely because of a medical emergency (unless perhaps there were some quite unusual explanation as to why he or she and nobody else could drive or attend what would need to be a sufficiently proportionate and serious situation). Neither he nor a travelling salesperson would escape disqualification just because it would affect an ability to work, a matter clearly relating to the offender and not the offence.

Alcohol awareness course

Where the disqualification is for alcohol-related offences and for not less than 12 months (i.e. special reasons were not pleaded or found by the court) then the court has the discretion (usually exercised in the defendant's favour) to offer a reduction in that disqualification of not less than three months and up to a maximum of one quarter if the defendant satisfactorily subsequently completes an approved alcohol awareness course (compare the other discretionary, informal courses already noted earlier in the chapter).

The court sets a latest date by which the course has to be completed: at least two months before the end of the potentially reduced period of disqualification.[8] The following conditions apply in respect of offering these alcohol awareness courses:

- the offender must be aged 17 years or over (not an issue in the adult court where offenders to be sentenced will be aged 18 years and above)

---

8. Most courts, not surprisingly, have 'ready reckoners' to help calculate the necessary periods and dates.

- a place on a course must be available and in time (originally this was an issue when the courses were first being set up incrementally across the country)
- the court must have explained in ordinary language to the offender the nature of the course, its effect and the fee to be paid by the offender in advance to the course provider; and
- the offender must have agreed that the order should be made (not really an issue in practice as agreement, and even later attendance, are not compulsory if the offender does not wish to obtain the reduction).

Discretionary Disqualification for the Offence Itself

On sentencing for any endorsable offence the court, unless it finds special reasons (above) for not endorsing has a general discretion to impose disqualification for any period, whereupon penalty points will not be imposed for the current offence.

This power of disqualification should not be exercised arbitrarily and, as suggested earlier, will most typically be considered where the offence is a particularly serious example of its kind or there is multiple offending which comes before the court on a single sentencing occasion. If the court is considering exercising this power, defendants should be warned of the position and invited to make representations.

The power might be used where the defendant needs to be 'taught a quick lesson' and periods of less than 56 days disqualification are the most common, because such periods also avoid the subsequent possibility of the increased periods of disqualification noted in the table above or in the case of 'totting up' below. If a totting up disqualification is an issue then courts are advised to consider disqualification in that respect and not via the discretionary route so that Parliament's intended minimum period described below will come into play.

This discretionary power expressly also applies to the non-endorsable offence of taking a vehicle without consent (TWOC or 'twocking').

Totting Up

When a defendant is convicted of an endorsable offence (but not one carrying compulsory disqualification for the offence itself unless such disqualification is not imposed for 'special reasons') the court must then add together:

- the penalty points applicable to the present offence (if there is more than one offence, only the highest number from the group will apply)
- if there is more than one set of current offences (i.e. different dates or occasions when the offences were in fact committed), the penalty points applicable to each such set; and
- any penalty points already imposed for other offence within the time frame that is noted next below.

If the number of points then amounts to 12 or more, 'totting up' arises, save that any points for an offence committed more than three years from the commission of another must are disregarded in the equation.

The minimum period of disqualification will be:

- six months if no previous disqualification is to be taken into account
- one year if one previous disqualification is to be taken into account; and
- two years if two or more previous disqualifications are to be taken into account.

The previous disqualifications to be taken into account must satisfy *both* of the following criteria, i.e. it must:

- be for a fixed period of 56 days or more; and
- have been imposed within the three years preceding the *commission* of the present offence.

Mitigating Circumstances

Drivers subject to 'totting up' can seek to reduce or avoid such disqualification by attending court and putting forward what are known as 'mitigating circumstances'. Unlike special reasons (above) these extend to personal circumstances rather than the offence itself. The doctor referred to above might not have been able to plead special reasons in respect of an excess alcohol offence, but *might,* if subject to totting up, be able successfully to plead mitigating circumstances so as to avoid or reduce the period of disqualification if a standard totting up disqualification (i.e. for six. 12 or 18 months) would cause him or her 'undue hardship', here presumably in relation to his or her working life, income and its consequent effect on his or her family. Similarly, the travelling salesperson but everything will depend on the facts and merits of each case and the view the court takes of his or her representations to it.

But the court expressly cannot take into account as 'mitigating circumstances':

- any offence-based mitigation (in the case of variable points this will already have been taken into account in fixing the points)
- any hardship other than 'exceptional hardship' thus, in the example of the doctor or travelling salesperson, it must be more than just inconvenience or cost; nor
- any similar mitigating circumstances accepted within the three years preceding the *conviction* for the present offence (an earlier court will, in such circumstances, have noted those circumstances very briefly on the counterpart of the driving licence). It is for the offender to show that any circumstances now being put forward are different in nature to earlier ones.

Interim Disqualification

As its name suggests, interim disqualification arises where the court has convicted an offender and has the power to disqualify him or her but is unable to proceed to sentence that day because, say, it needs a pre-sentence report (PSR) (*Chapter 7*), or is awaiting production of the defendant's driving licence by the offender.

Interim disqualification is a discretionary measure which arises most often in practice when the offence itself carries compulsory disqualification. In this way, offenders are removed from the road as soon as possible and they start working through their disqualification earlier than would otherwise have been the case (any interim period will be credited administratively by the DVLA against the length of the full and final disqualification).

Disqualification Until a Test is Passed

This form of disqualification reduces the offender to the status of a provisional licence holder, unless he or she is also at the same time or otherwise, fully disqualified in which case he or she cannot drive at all initially and becomes, in essence, a provisional licence holder when that full disqualification ceases.

Offenders made subject to this type of disqualification do not have to undergo a retest unless and until they wish to start driving again as a fully qualified driver (after the end of any full disqualification if relevant). However, should they drive in the meantime, any failure to comply with the requirements of a provisional licence (such as not displaying 'L-plates', not being unaccompanied in a car by the holder of a full driving licence, etc.) will result in a charge of driving whilst disqualified and not the lesser provisional licence-related offence.

The power to disqualify until the offender passes a driving test is discretionary on conviction for *any* endorsable offence and is to be used not as a punishment in itself but only in cases where inexperience, incompetence or infirmity (but not advanced age of itself) are indicated by the facts of the case. It might also be applied in addition when a lengthy disqualification is imposed as a form of 'deferred' road safety measure, so that a test will need to be taken before unaccompanied driving resumes. The order is said not to be appropriate, as say a 'straight punishment', or for offenders who simply ignore the rules.

In some more serious cases such as dangerous driving, ordering such a disqualification and retest is obligatory. There is a basic type of retest (as for all learner drivers) and also an extended version which applies where it was obligatory to order such a disqualification or where it accompanies 'totting up' (above).

Disqualification for Any Criminal Offence

This can be used in addition to the main sentence for an offence (i.e. as an ancillary order: *Chapter 7*) or as a penalty in its own right. It could apply, e.g. where a vehicle has been used to commit other offences but there are no limitations of this kind.

It can be a useful measure to prevent non-motoring offenders from moving about or as a straight punishment by way of placing a restriction on someone's liberty, in terms of their social life, where any fine might have to be small. But this power should not be used indiscriminately and matters such as the potential effect on the offender's working or personal life and overall proportionality will need to be considered.

Code		Points
AC10	Failing to stop after an accident	5-10
AC20	Failing to give particulars or to report an accident within 24 hours	5-10
BA10	Driving whilst disqualified by order of court	6
BA30	Attempting to drive while disqualified by order of court	6
CD10	Driving without due care and attention	3-9
CD20	Driving without reasonable consideration for other road users	3-9
CU10	Using a vehicle with defective brakes	3
CU30	Using a vehicle with defective tyre(s)	3
CU40	Using a vehicle with defective steering	3
CU50	Causing or likely to cause danger by reason of load or passengers	3
DD40	Dangerous driving	3-11*
DR10	Driving or attempting to drive with alcohol level above limit	3-11*
DR20	Driving or attempting to drive when unfit through drink	3-11*
DR30	Driving or attempting to drive then failing to supply a specimen for analysis	3-11*
DR40	In charge of a vehicle with alcohol level above limit	10
DR50	In charge of a vehicle with unfit through drink	10
DR70	Failing to provide specimen for breath test	4
DR80	Driving or attempting to drive when unfit through drugs	3-11 *
DR90	In charge of a vehicle when unfit through drugs	10

IN10	Using a vehicle uninsured against third party risks	6-8
LC20	Driving otherwise than in accordance with a licence	3-6
MS10	Leaving a vehicle in a dangerous position	3
MS90	Failure to give information as to identity of driver	6
MW10	Contravention of motorway regulations (excluding speed limits)	3
PC20	Contravention of Pedestrian Crossing Regulations with moving vehicle	3
PC30	Contravention of Pedestrian Crossing Regulations with stationary vehicle	3
SP10	Exceeding goods vehicle speed limits	3-6
SP20	Exceeding speed limit for type of vehicle (excluding goods or passenger vehicles)	3-6
SP30	Exceeding statutory speed limit on a public road	3-6
SP40	Exceeding passenger vehicle speed limit.	3-6
SP50	Exceeding speed limit on a motorway	3-6
SP60	Undefined speed limit offence	3-6
TS10	Failing to comply with traffic light signals	3
TS20	Failing to comply with double white lines	3
TS30	Failing to comply with "Stop" sign	3
TS40	Failing to comply with direction of a constable or traffic warden	3
TS60	Failing to comply with a school crossing patrol sign	3

The code TT99 signifies a disqualification under totting-up procedure (above)

* Penalty points only apply where 'special reasons' are found for not imposing a mandatory disqualification.

The 'Magistrates' Court Sentencing Guidelines' mentioned in *Chapter 7*, provide useful further information on road traffic offences: see sentencing-guidelines.co.uk

Figure 2: Common road traffic offences sentenced by magistrates' courts which carry endorsement and penalty points

DRIVING WHILE DISQUALIFIED

Offenders can be sent to prison for driving while disqualified. The offence arises if someone drives in contravention of any of the above types of disqualification.

The DVLA will not automatically return a licence to an offender after a disqualification has expired and offenders therefore have to make a specific application at the end of the disqualification period. If they drive again before any new licence is issued they are guilty of 'driving other than in accordance with a licence' and, if they are not then complying with the terms of a provisional licence they can be convicted of that offence. It means that by the time that they get their licence they will already have penalty points endorsed on it for the provisional licence offence.

'NEW DRIVERS'

Drivers who incur six or more penalty points in the two-year probationary period after passing their driving test automatically have their driving licences administratively revoked by the Secretary of State. If they wish to continue driving they need to reapply for a provisional licence and, effectively, start all over again with their driving career.

It is not unknown for offenders at risk of this measure to employ the tactic of asking the court to disqualify them instead of ordering penalty points (preferably for less than 56 days: above). A short period off the road might be seen as preferable to having to start all over again. Although this is within a court's power it does not, seemingly, accord with Parliament's original underlying intention.

CHAPTER TWELVE

Postscript

Magistrates' Courts (including youth courts and family courts) are creatures of statute as described in *Chapter 1* and effectively of the State in the sense that they only exist and exercise powers and jurisdiction due to legislation passed by Parliament. They are part of that arm of State known as the Judiciary and as such are both affected and protected by the doctrine of the separation of powers: *Chapter 5*. The powers they possess are extensive.

Without appearing to be 'melodramatic', they include those to:

- restrict, or otherwise interfere with an individual's general freedom and liberty, temporarily (as with bail conditions or a remand in custody) or for longer periods (as with a community sentence or imprisonment)
- take away an individual's money (e.g. a by way of a fine or compensation)
- confiscate an individual's property (e.g. under a distress or search warrant)
- impose 'enforced labour' (e.g. by unpaid work under a community sentence)
- restrict free speech (e.g. by stipulating or not 'lifting' reporting restrictions)
- interfere with family life (e.g. via bail conditions or under a contact order or emergency protection order with regard to a child, in the family proceedings court); or
- remove a child from a family unit (e.g. via a care order).

All of these powers and many more are noted within the preceding chapters. If someone were to look at them in their stark totality they might soon be protesting that here lie the makings of a 'totalitarian State', thus demanding the protection of the European Convention On Human Rights as invoked by the Human Rights Act 1998 (which of course does offer certain protections: *Chapter 5*).

Thankfully, not only is there a long tradition of judicial fairness in this country but nowadays both the Convention and the 1998 Act reaffirm and further enhance that proud tradition.

Above all in the context of this book, the magistracy, an institution going back for some six and a half centuries, is part of our democratic institutions just as much as the (more recently introduced) randomly selected jury of ordinary members of the public is in the Crown Court. They are at once a bastion against State oppression but have a duty to comply with the legitimate wishes of the Parliament by working within the legal trial and sentencing frameworks provided. This they must do by fair and proper means and by making independent judicial decisions rather than any that are capricious or unduly influenced by extra-judicial overtures.

Magistrates, like the people they deal with on a day-to-day basis, are also members of the public, not 'faceless bureaucrats' and their sheer numbers, diversity and inter-action with differently-minded judicial colleagues from a variety of backgrounds all act all help to underwrite a level of propriety, decency and integrity:

- they are selected by independent procedures against open and appropriate criteria
- they are trained using independent materials and trainers
- they have their own independently created competence criteria and independent measures to assess their development
- they receive robust independent advice from legal officers who enjoy a statutory protection when they are giving such advice as described in *Chapter 6*.
- they approach their decision-making in a consistent and structured manner
- they use independent national manuals and guidelines
- they cannot be removed from judicial office without just cause; and
- they have their own independent body, the Magistrates' Association, that represents their interests and supports their activities.

These are all matters covered in this work and they run like a golden thread through everything that magistrates do. Hopefully, the preceding chapters will have helped not only to explain the unique and reassuring nature of the magistracy, but will have conveyed the extent to which large parts of the justice system lie in the hands of ordinary members of the community.

Glossary of Words, Phrases, Acronyms and Abbreviations

AA (1) Alcoholics Anonymous; **(2)** appropriate adult (who should be present when, e.g. police interview a juvenile).

ABC acceptable behaviour 'contract', between a probation officer or member of a **YOT** and an offender (or someone at risk of offending) as a precondition to providing advice, support, access to services and so on

ABH actual bodily harm

abscond fail to surrender to bail, or leave a court police station, crime scene, etc. without permission or excuse

absolute discharge a sentence which can be used where the offence is deemed to be trivial or technical, and where punishment is considered to be 'inexpedient'. Contrast **conditional discharge** and see *Chapter 7*.

absolute right one by virtue of the European Convention On Human Rights, that cannot be departed from. Contrast **limited right**s and **qualified right** as noted in *Chapter 5*.

abuse of process improper or inappropriate use of laws, procedures, paperwork, etc

accomplice someone who assists in offence

accused (1) (used as a verb) 'accused of a criminal offence'; **(2)** (used as a noun) '[the] **accused person**'. Words such as accused, accusation (aka an allegation) and **suspect** emphasise the presumption of innocence (*Chapter 5*). The term **offender** is only used after conviction. But **prisoner** may be used neutrally whenever someone is in custody.

acquittal term used when someone is found 'not guilty' and **discharged**: see also **plea**

adjourn Put off a hearing to: **(1)** a new date fixed by the court when adjourning; **(2)** later the same day (aka **standing down**); or **(3)** indefinitely (aka an adjournment sine die) (rare in criminal proceedings). Cases are adjourned, defendants are **remanded**.

advance disclosure See **disclosure**

ACECOP Association of Chief Executives and Chief Officers of Probation

ACPO Association of Chief Police Officers

ACR (1) automatic conditional release from prison; **(2)** automated crime recording, i.e. by the police, using modern technology.

actus reus the physical act, omission or event involved in a criminal offence: as opposed to **mens rea** (below)

AD absolute discharge: see *Chapter 7*

Advisory Committee Advisory Committee on the Appointment of Magistrates: *Chapter 2*.

AEO attachment of earnings order to enforce a fine or other form of financial order: *Chapter 7*

affirmation As an alternative to swearing an **oath**, a witness is entitled to affirm, by stating:

'I do solemnly and sincerely declare and affirm that the evidence I shall give will be the truth, the whole truth and nothing but the truth'.

AFR automated fingerprint recognition

AG/A-G Attorney General/Attorney-General

agenda a term often used to describe: **(1)** the daily **list** of cases; **(2)** an agenda of business for a bench, committee, etc. meeting,

aggravating factor one which makes an offence more serious (as per **sentencing guidelines**). Contrast **mitigating factor**.

AJF Area Judicial Forum: *Chapter 2*

ancillary order one additional to a basic sentence, e.g. **disqualification, costs**: *Chapter 7*

ANPR automated [car, etc.] number plate recognition

antecedents see **character and antecedents**

appraisal a process via which magistrates', staff, etc. are assessed as to their progress against specific **competences**: see *Chapters 3, 4* and *6*

appointment (1) one for attendance at court by the **parties** re aspects of **case management**; or **(2)** to the bench: see *Chapters 3*.

Archbold *Archbold's Criminal Pleading and Practice.* The leading work on *evidence, practice* and *procedure* in the *Crown Court* (in particular); first published in 1825.

A&S allocation and sending, an embryonic procedure set to supersede **mode of trial** in respect of **either way offences**: see *Chapter 7*

ASB/O anti-social behaviour/order: *Chapter 10*

assessment assessment for a report, scheme, suitability, etc. A term widely used to signify the application of professional and expert opinion, advice or techniques to a problem or process, including assessment for a **PSR** (*Chapter 7*), re mental impairment or drug treatment. Offender assessments used by police or probation officers may be linked to **referral** to a specialist agency or service. Note in particular **ASSET, OASys** and **ONSET**.

ASSET A **YJB/YOT** assessment tool: *Chapter 8*

AUR automatic unconditional release from prison re lesser sentences of imprisonment

back duty unpaid vehicle excise duty which will normally be ordered to be paid if someone is convicted of having no vehicles excise licence (**VEL**): *Chapter 11*. The amount depends on the class of vehicle and time for which unpaid.

backed for bail a warrant on which has been endorsed an instruction by the issuing court that the person arrested under it is to be released on bail (originally 'on its back')

bailiff usually a private sector bailiff employed to enforce a fine by executing a distress warrant: see fine enforcement in *Chapter 7*. Hence **'sending in the bailiffs'** (who are also used by civil courts, e.g. to enforce orders re debts).

BCS *British Crime Survey*: A key source of data concerning public perceptions of and attitudes to crime. See homeoffice.gov.uk/rds

'being carried' being carried in or on a motor vehicle (or other conveyance) that has been taken without consent (aka **TWC; 'twocking'**)

bench a term used to signify: (1) the **judiciary** as a whole; (2) the judge, judges or magistrates sitting in court on a particular day; (3) the entire body of magistrates in a local justice area (**LJA**)*;* or (4) the raised dias or platform in a courtroom where judges or magistrates sit to dispense justice. Other common derivatives include: **bench warrant**; **bench chair**: the chairperson of a magistrates' court; **bench office**, i.e. at the police station dealing with court-related matters, now more commonly known as a Criminal Justice Unit (**CJU**).

best practice (or Best Practice) The finest way of dealing with a given matter, process, task, etc. as determined by senior management within an agency/service and/or experts and promulgated to managers, frontline practitioners, etc. Competing practices are considered to arrive at 'the best' method; sometimes after **multi-agency** consultation.

bill/Bill (1) a voluntary bill of indictment (in the Crown Court); **(2)** a bill of costs from a lawyer; **(3)** a Parliamentary Bill as part of the standard legislative process.

block listing the practice of **listing** (below) cases in groups or 'blocks' with a different broad time slot for each group, e.g. 10 am to 12 noon; 'not before 2 pm. Cases will then, so far as possible be heard at a time within that slot. This is intended to cause minimum inconvenience to all concerned as part of efficient and effective **case management**.

BME black or minority ethnic

bodies term often used as shorthand for prisoners in court cells or under **escort**.

breach failure to comply with a court order or release licence, e.g. breach of bail, a community sentence, parole or an anti-social behaviour order (**ASBO**). Breach is associated with **enforcement** to ensure that requirements, etc. are kept to. Note also breach of a **recognizance**.

breathalyser (1) the hand-held, roadside device use by policed to detect excess alcohol in someone's breath; or **(2)** the Intoximeter; or 'breath analyser' at a police station. An aspect of road traffic law: *Chapter 11*.

BTP British Transport Police

bye-law one made under powers delegated by **Act of Parliament**, often meaning by a local authority, railway authority, etc; and frequently creating (relatively minor) offences.

burden of proof See *Chapter 5*

CAFCASS Children and Family Court Advisory and Support Service: a nationwide service established in 2001 whose tasks include facilitating provision of information to family proceedings courts: *Chapter 9*.

case to answer a term used to signify that the evidence collected by the police or placed before a court by a prosecutor 'calls for an answer' from a **suspect/accused person**. In court it signifies that there is enough evidence for a court to convict, but whether it will do so depends an all the circumstances. An accused person does not have to provide 'an answer', but appropriate **inferences** can be drawn from silence: *Chapter 9*.

case stated Short for appeal by way of case stated.

case management umbrella term for the processes by which cases are managed from start to finish, whether in a purely administrative way or judicially by the court itself. Hence, e.g. a **Criminal Cases Management Framework (CCMF)** and **Youth Case Management Framework (YCMF)**. See in particular *Chapters 7, 8* and *9*.

caution (1) Even when an offence is discovered and a **suspect** identified, the police are not obliged to start criminal proceedings. They have a discretion whether or not to do so or refer the matter to the CPS with a view to a caution or prosecution. That decision is made by the CPS and the Code for Crown Prosecutors contains related guidance. Cautions are administered by a senior police officer, usually in uniform and at a police station. Cautions are cited in court if the offender commits a further offence and may affect the sentence for the new offence. Since 2003, requirements can be added to a **conditional caution** and the offender brought to court if these are not complied with (aka 'breach'). Re juveniles there is a system of warnings and reprimands (*Chapter 8*). Other uses of 'caution' include: **(2)** that by a **court legal adviser** re the accused person's rights concerning **mode of trial**/jury trial; and **(3)** a **police caution on arrest** (or before interview) re the 'right to silence' its implications.

CBO (1) civil behaviour order: *Chapter 10*; **(2)** community beat officer (police).

CCCCJS Cabinet Committee on Crime and the Criminal Justice System: see 'Partners in Crime' in *Chapter 2*.

CCRC Criminal Cases Review Commission

CCTV closed circuit television

CCU (1) Complex Crime Unit (usually meaning of the police, **CPS** or **SFO**); **(2)** Computer Crime Unit (of any agency/service).

CD (1) conditional discharge (below); **2)** criminal damage; **(3)** compact disc for storing data, evidence, records, etc.).

CDH criminal directions hearing

CDRP Crime and Disorder Reduction Partnership

CDS Criminal Defence Service. Nationwide agency providing defence services to those on legal aid: *Chapter 7* and see legalservices.gov.uk

CEO/M court enforcement officer/manager: a staff role re the pursuit of unpaid fines, etc.

CEOP Child Exploitation and Online Protection Centre: see ceop.gov.uk

certified extract a verified official copy of the outcome of court proceedings

charge and requisition a new way of commencing criminal proceedings that it is planned to phase in re public prosecutors: *Chapter 7*

child in a criminal context someone aged 10-13 inclusive: *Chapter 8*

CHIS covert human intelligence source (the statutory term for an 'informer')

CICB/S Criminal Injuries Compensation Board/Scheme

CID Criminal Investigations Department, i.e. in a local police area

circuit judge a regular judge of the Crown Court: see also and compare **recorder**

CJ (1) criminal justice; **(2)** community justice. Hence, e.g. **CJA** Criminal Justice Act; **CJB** Criminal Justice Board (**LCJB** = Local CJB); **NCJB** = National CJB); **CJCC** Criminal Justice Consultative Council; **CJS** Criminal Justice System; **CJSP** Criminal Justice Strategic Plan (of central government); **CJU** Criminal Justice Unit (**CPS**/police).

CJSSS Criminal Justice: Simple, Speedy, Summary: *Chapter 7*

CLS Community Legal Service

CO (1) community order; **(2)** custody officer (a police officer or a **civilian**); **(3)** Cabinet Office; **(4)** commanding officer: of military origin but also sometimes used by the police for someone in charge of an operation, etc.

comp compensation. Contrast **fully comp**, i.e. re comprehensive motor vehicle insurance

competence magistrates general levels of ability re aspects of their role are assessed by asking whether they have acquired certain competences, as set by **MNTI 2**, etc: *Chapter 4*

conditional discharge a court sentencing disposal whereby an offender can be discharged on condition that he or she does not commit another offence within three years: *Chapter 7*

construction and use i.e. of a motor vehicle. Hence **construction and use offences**: *Chapter 11*.

contempt contempt of court

conviction A central to **CJS** work signifying that: **(1)** magistrates or a jury have found someone guilty of a criminal offence following a trial;

or (**2**) that he or she has entered a guilty plea to a charge/indictment. A **previous conviction** is one incurred on an earlier occasion, i.e. before the present conviction or the date when some new offence was committed. A **list of previous convictions** (if any) is produced to the court by the prosecutor after conviction and before sentence. The rule that previous convictions were not admissible in evidence pre-conviction, i.e. to prove the present offence was relaxed by the Criminal Justice Act 2003; which also requires a court to consider previous convictions when sentencing. They may also show, e.g. that an offender is in breach of an earlier sentence.

cordon a police cordon (usually) at a crime scene. exclusion zone or 'no-go' area

costs (**1**) the costs of a criminal case that may be ordered to be paid by the offender (or to the offender from public funds) according to the outcome of a case. A **wasted costs** order can be made against a legal representative in certain circumstances. (**2**) The **costs of criminal justice**, sentences, etc. re which data is issued, e.g. by the **MOJ** from time-to-time.

CPA (**1**) crime pattern analysis. (**2**) Child Protection Agency.

CPF Correctional Policy Framework

CPO (**1**) chief probation officer; (**2**) crime prevention officer; (**3**) child protection officer;

CPS Crown Prosecution Service

CPRC Criminal Procedure Rule Committee

CPU Child Protection Unit (compare **MAPPA**; **VPU**)

CRA Constitutional Reform Act 2005

CRASBO criminal anti-social behaviour order; compare **ASBO**

'cracked trial' see *Chapter 7*

CRB (**1**) Criminal Records Bureau. (**2**) Crime Reporting Bureau.

CRO (**1**) Criminal Records Office. (**2**) crime reduction officer (police or local authority).

CRP crime reduction programme/partnership

CS (**1**) community sentence: *Chapter 7*; (**2**) criminal statistics; (**3**) crime scene (Hence also see **CSI** and **CSM** below); (**4**) CS gas; (**5**) custody sergeant who oversees **PACE** related matters of detention, etc. at a police station.

CSA Child support Agency: see csa.gov.uk

CSI/M crime scene investigation/crime scene manager

CSO (police) community support officer aka PCSO below

CSU (police/**CPS**) Court Support Unit

CTL custody time limit, i.e. where someone is in custody awaiting trail

CYPA Children and Young Persons Act: see especially *Chapters 8* and *9*

DAT (multi-agency) drug action team

DC (**1**) Divisional Court; (**2**) detective constable; (**3**) detention centre (nowadays usually an immigration detention centre or 'holding centre').

DCFS Department for Children, Schools and Families: see especially *Chapter 8*

DCI detective chief inspector

DCO defendant's **costs** order: one in favour of him or her following an **acquittal** or **discontinuance** of a case

declaration (**1**) a term used to describe a formal pronouncement or ruling, including one affecting the status of the law or 'compatability' with human rights, usually a **High Court declaration** (*Chapter 2*). (**2**) a **statutory declaration**, i.e. a 'solemn declaration' by someone who has been convicted of an offence that he or she never knew of the proceedings against him or her, which has the effect that the case is restarted.

default usually a reference to fine default

deferment postponement of sentence with some clear objective in mind: see *Chapter 7*

delegated legislation that made under delegated powers, e.g. by a Minister of State; aka **Statutory Instrument (SI)** or **regulations**

designated case worker a member of the **CPS** who is qualified and competent to deal with certain matters in court but not the full range of matters falling to a Crown prosecutor

detention (**1**) **police detention** (or that of other authorised law enforcement agencies) of suspects as per the Police and Criminal Evidence Act 1984 (PACE); aka detention without charge. **Further detention** can be authorised by a court up to a maximum of 96 hours by way of a **warrant of further detention**: *Chapter 7*. mission (SIAC) (see generally *immigration*). (**2**) **Detention at her majesty's pleasure** (aka **detention for life** can (in some cases must) be ordered by the Crown Court instead of life imprisonment); or re a young offender, someone unfit to plead or insane **(3) detention in a YOI. (4) Detention in a special hospital** (or other hospital): a Crown Court matter. **(5)** Other uses include **detention of foreign nationals** re border control; and **home detention curfew (HDC)** (a form of prison release licence using **EM**).

DG Director General. There are various such posts under the MOJ and its parts.

DI detective inspector

DIC (1) drunk in charge of a vehicle, child, etc; **(2)** driver improvement centre: *Chapter 11.*

disclosure (1) Revealing information, documents, reports etc. concerning aspects of a prosecution or defence case. Hence, e.g. **advance disclosure of the prosecution case** by the CPS to the defence before a decision is made concerning **mode of trial**. The Criminal Justice Act 2003 amended the Criminal Procedure and Investigations Act 1996 which contained certain pre-trial disclosure provisions relating to both **parties**; notably re **disclosure of the defence case** so that this now extends to the making and updating of a 'defence statement' re the nature of the defence, any specific defence, points of law, evidence, abuse of process and a list of defence witnesses (including experts). The Lord Chancellor can prescribe further matters. A court may draw **inferences** from shortcomings in such disclosure; but cannot convict solely on that basis. **(2) Disclosure of a pre-sentence report (PSR). (3) Disclosure of unused prosecution material.** Historically there were complaints that police or prosecutors withheld **unused material** which had it been disclosed may have assisted the defence. This featured in a number of miscarriage of justice cases. Since 2003 the prosecutor must disclose 'any prosecution material ... not previously ... disclosed to the accused person and which might reasonably be considered capable of undermining the case for the prosecution ... or of assisting the case for the accused'. **(4)** Since 2002, following the Police Act 1997, the **Criminal Records Bureau (CRB)** provides authorised access and disclosure of information via its **disclosure service**; allowing organizations in the public, private and voluntary sectors to make safer recruitment decisions. There are two levels of check depending upon the nature of the position, known as **standard disclosure** and **enhanced disclosure**: see crb.gov.uk **(5)** Note also **disclosure of information** under the Freedom of Information Act 2000.

discontinuance i.e. of a case by a Crown prosecutor where prosecution **threshold** or other tests are no longer met

distress warrant One to 'distrain' (i.e. cease) and sell a defaulter's goods, etc: see **bailiff**

DJ district judge. In a CJS context a district judge (magistrates' courts): see *Chapters 1* and *2*

DNA deoxyribonucleic acid

dock The (usually) wooden and/or glass structure where an accused person stands in court; sanctified by tradition and the needs of security rather than strict law. Use of the dock varies from place-to-place and a 'defendant's chair' is often used for lesser offences (see *Figure 1* on page xiii). The dock is usually used where defendants are produced by the police or **HMPS** from (and hence 'in') custody. It may be used for other **'imprisonable offences'** (below); or generally where there is an issue of security or control.

domestic (1) a domestic dispute; **(2)** national as opposed to international; **(3)** events within the confines of an agency/service, etc.

DPP Director of Public Prosecutions

DS (1) duty solicitor; **(2)** detective sergeant.

DSU (police) Divisional Support Unit

due care driving without due care and attention

DV (1) domestic violence; **(2)** developed vetting. Re both add **C** = coordinator; **L** = liaison; **O** = officer.

DVLA/C Driver and Vehicle Licensing Agency/Centre (aka **Swansea**)

EAH early administrative hearing before a judge or magistrate. Part of **case management**.

ECHR (1) European Convention on Human Rights; **(2)** European Court of Human Rights (but the latter is often written Eur. Ct. HR).

EDR (or sometimes **ERD**) earliest date of release, i.e. from prison

either way offence one that can be tried in either the magistrates' court or the Crown Court according to the outcome of the procedure known as mode of trial: *Chapter 7*

EM electronic monitoring

enforcement Generic term for **(1) law enforcement** in general; or **(2)** the 'chasing' offenders through **breach** proceedings or, e.g. **fine enforcement** (*Chapter 7*) to ensure that sentences are complied with. Both are modern-day **CJS** priorities.

equivocal plea One where the **accused person** admits the offence but gives an inconsistent explanation ('I stole the goods but intended to give them back'); which cannot be accepted. The case is **adjourned** for him or her to consider matters, take legal advice, etc. and, if necessary, for a trial to be held.

escort a prisoner escort, usually a security guard

estreat forfeit something such as a **recognizance**

EWO either way offence

excess alcohol the offence of driving with excess alcohol in the blood or urine: see road traffic

ex parte in the absence of the other **party**

expert someone whom a court accepts as sufficiently qualified to give **opinion** evidence rather than just evidence of fact. But the court will decide whether to accept that evidence.

extract a copy of that part of the court **register** applicable to a particular case, duly certified, for use, e.g. as evidence of a conviction

FBO football banning order: see *Chapter 10*

FDR fast delivery report, i.e. a short form of **PSR**

financial circumstances order one made in fine enforcement proceedings or at the sentencing stage for means to be disclosed.

first instance (court of first instance) the one which deals with trial and/or sentence, whether the magistrates' court or Crown Court, as opposed to an appeal (or 'appellate') court: see *Chapters 2* and *7* (page 92).

foreign court one elsewhere, not necessarily abroad

form previous form: a criminal record

FPN/D fixed penalty notice/for disorder

FSS/L Forensic Science Service/Laboratory

FTA fail to appear (at a police station or court, e.g. in answer to bail)

gatekeeping Keeping people out of the formal CJS, or away from more severe forms of punishment, including by 'alternatives' and 'diversion' schemes. A strategy often adopted

within the **YJS** in particular: *Chapter 8*.

GA Gamblers Anonymous

GATSO A variety of speed camera

GBH grievous bodily harm

'going equipped' i.e. for theft, deception, etc. (an offence in itself under the Theft Act 1968)

G&R grounds and reasons, i.e. for refusing to grant bail to someone: see *Chapter 7*.

grave crime one re which an older juvenile can or must be sent to the Crown Court for trial: *Chapter 8*.

guardian The person responsible for the care of a juvenile or other vulnerable person, such as someone suffering from mental impairment. But contrast independent guardian in relation to family proceedings: *Chapter 7*.

guidance advice or assistance pointing to how usefully or best to approach a task, decision or responsibility: of which countless examples exist across the courts and CJS

guideline usually a reference to those which have been considered, ratified or sanctioned, as per Sentencing Guidelines (see *Chapter 7*).

harm preventing harm is a general tenet re offences of violence and sexual offences in particular; whilst repairing or reducing harm is also a rationale of **restorative justice**

hate crime term used to describe a range of **hate-related offences** and/or those with a **hateful motive**, including, e.g. **incitement to racial, or religious, hatred**. CJS measures have targeted a growing range of such conduct, via police crackdowns and also the priorities of the CPS. Legislation means that all such offences are treated as generally more serious.

HDC home detention curfew (see **detention**)

HM Her Majesty's. Hence, e.g. **HMCI** HM Chief Inspector (including **HMICS**, i.e. of Court Services: but restricted to non-judicial matters); **HMPS** = Prison Service; **HMRC** (or **HMR&C**) = Revenue & Customs. Other examples include **HMP (1)** Her Majesty's Prison; **(2)** Her Majesty's pleasure.

holding charge One on which an offender can be held pending further investigations, usually meaning a less serious charge than that being pursued but nonetheless a criminal offence.

Howard League The Howard League for Penal Reform: see howardleague.org

hostile witness one not desirous of telling the

truth in the sense that he or she is departing from earlier testimony or an earlier statement due to bias; to whom special rules apply. Not necessarily 'hostile' in an aggressive sense.

HR/HRA human rights/Human Rights Act 1998

HSE Health and Safety Executive

IC intermittent custody (if and when in force)

ICVA Independent Custody Visitors Association (re police custody/detention): see icva.org.uk

ID identity/identification

IMB Independent Monitoring Board (locally at each prison: see imb.gov.uk)

'imprisonable offence' one which carries (or 'attracts') imprisonment, not necessarily one where that sentence will be used in a given case. Many powers are referable to whether an offence is imprisonable, such as that to pass a community sentence (since 2008) (*Chapter 7*). Hence a 'surreal' situation which arises in the youth court of asking whether an offence is imprisonable in order to determine whether youth court powers (which do not include imprisonment as such) apply: here meaning **'imprisonable in the case of an adult'**.

in camera in private, as when a court, exceptionally, sits 'behind closed doors'

indictable triable in the Crown Court 'on indictment'. Hence **'indictable only offence'** for those more serious matters that can only be tried there: *Chapter 7*. Contrast **summary offences** and **either way offences** (when the latter may be **indictable** depending on the procedure known as **mode of trial**).

information and summons the long standing method of commencing lesser (and some more serious) summary proceedings; that is scheduled to be replaced for public prosecutors by **charge and requisition**

ingredient offences are made up of ingredients, all of which must be made out by the prosecution evidence (normally: see *Chapters 5* and *7*) before there can be a conviction. For example, those for theft include: dishonesty, appropriation of property, the fact that it belongs to 'another', an intention to permanently deprive, and so on. Ingredients are contained in the legal definition of the offence in question. Ensuring that they all exist is integral to structured decision-making.

Intoximeter See **breathalyser**

intra vires within power. Courts, public officials, etc. must only act within their powers as handed down by Parliament or sanctioned by the Common Law: contrast **ultra vires**.

IOC interception of communications. Hence also **IOCA** = IOC Act.

IOM integrated offender management

IPCC Independent Police Complaints Commission

IPP imprisonment for public protection in the Crown Court (aka **ISPP**: indeterminate sentence for public protection, see *Chapter 2*)

IWF Internet Watch Foundation: see iwf.org.uk

J (1) 'Mr Justice' (i.e. a judge of the High Court), usually J in writing; **(2)** a Justice of the Supreme Court (when in being *Chapter 2*).

JAC Judicial Appointments Commission

JC (1) Judges Council; **(2)** justices' clerk.

JCS Justices' Clerks' Society

JCO Judicial Communications Office

JIG justices interests group: *Chapter 2*

JO Judicial Office (of the Lord Chief Justice)

JP justice of the peace

JR judicial review

JSB Judicial Studies Board

judicial appertaining to the **judiciary** and its **judicial decision-making** functions; and the pre-fix for each of several bodies to support the work of the judiciary, especially post-Constitutional Reform Act 2005.

judiciary generic term covering all judges and magistrates (and possibly tribunal members), but not jurors in the Crown Court.

justices' reasons those given **(1)** on request by a party for the purposes of judicial review: see the section on appeals in *Chapter 2;* or **(2)** **'ordinary reasons'** given at the end of (or sometimes during) a case in order to explain a decision (or what a court proposes so as to allow **representations** by the **parties**: *Chapter 5*).

KPI key performance indicator

LCJ Lord Chief Justice

LCJB Local Criminal Justice Board

liability order one in respect of council tax: allowing it to be enforced by magistrates

licence ('on licence') offenders released from prison may be subject to parole or other forms of release licence

lifer someone serving a sentence of life imprisonment. Hence, e.g. **mandatory lifer**,

discretionary lifer, two strikes lifer according to the exact provisions under which he or she was sentenced.

limited right See human rights in *Chapter 5*

list The daily list of cases in a particular court. Hence **listing officer** or **listing manager** and practices such as **block listing** (above)

LJA local justice area: *Chapter 2*

LO liaison officer: see also, e.g. **FLO** = family liaison officer, **VLO** = victim liaison officer

LSC Legal Services Commission

MA Magistrates' Association: *Chapter 2*

mags/mags court magistrates/magistrates' court. **Magistrates' court** is a description for: **(1)** the decision-making tribunal which sits as a court of law to deal with cases under statutory powers and to dispense summary justice; **(2)** the building in which the court sits and where accused people, barristers, solicitors (mostly), witnesses, etc, attend court hearings, aka the **courthouse**; and **(3)** technically speaking, all functions of JPs, in court or out, are discharged 'by a magistrates' court', e.g. when a **single justice** (below) signs a document.

mandatory obligatory/compulsory. Certain sentences or orders are mandatory, in the sense that the court has no further (or confined) discretion once some basic fact is established/exists. See, e.g. the various mandatory disqualifications noted in *Chapter 2* and football banning orders in *Chapter 10*.

MAPPA Multi-agency Public Protection Arrangements

MC magistrates' court. Hence, e.g. **MCA** = Magistrates Courts Act'.

mens rea guilty intention or mind, i.e. that required by the definition and ingredients of a criminal offence and which must be proved by the prosecutor in addition to the **actus reus** (above). Not all offences require mens rea, aka offences of strict liability, such as many lesser summary and regulatory matters. More serious offences invariably do demand it.

mentor Magistrates under training are allocated a mentor to act as a guide and sounding board: see *Chapters 3* and *4*. Mentors are also used with prisoners, other offenders and people at risk of offending (especially juveniles) within a range of programmes or schemes.

MHA Mental Health Act (various dates)

MID Motor Insurance Database (used by police)

miscarriage miscarriage of justice

mitigation a matter which makes an offence less serious than it might otherwise appear to be (**'offence mitigation'**) or which similarly goes to the offender's individual personal circumstances so as to suggest some degree of leniency (**'offender mitigation'**). Hence terms such as **plea in mitigation following conviction;** and **mitigating factors as opposed to aggravating factors (above).** Note also **mitigating circumstances** re **totting-up** in *Chapter 11*.

MNTI Magistrates National Training Initiative (now **MNTI 2**): see *Chapters 3* and *4*.

MO *modus operandi* (way of operating, re an offender or possibly **CJS** practitioners)

MOD Ministry of Defence; and hence **MODP** = Ministry of Defence Police

mode of trial the procedure for determining whether **either way offences** should be tried in the magistrates court or Crown Court: as described in *Chapter 7*

MODP Ministry of Defence/Police

MOJ Ministry of Justice.

MOT (1) Ministry of Transport (test certificate) **(2) mode of trial** (above).

MPS Metropolitan Police Service

MPSO money payment supervision order, i.e. to enforce a financial order

N general pre-fix for 'national'. Hence, e.g. **NI** = national interest; **NFIU** = (police) National Football Intelligence Unit; **NIM** = (police) National Intelligence Model; **NIS** National Identification Service (sometimes **NI Scheme**).

NA Narcotics Anonymous

Nacro Formerly the National Association for the Care and Resettlement of Offenders having since adopted this acronym; a leading crime reduction charity: see nacro.org.uk

NAFIS National Automated Fingerprint Identification System

NAI non-accidental injury. i.e. one that is unexplained and may well be suspicious

Napo National Association of Probation Officers

National Standards those issued nationwide within an agency/service, including in particular National Standards for the work of the **NPS** (which have a statutory basis)

NCJB National Criminal Justice Board

NDR normal date of release from prison

NEO no evidence offered, i.e. by a prosecutor, thereby inviting the court to dismiss the case

Newton hearing A 'trial within a trial', i.e. to determine the true facts in a situation where the accused enters a plea of guilty but then disagrees materially with some aspects of events as outlined by the prosecutor. From *R v Newton* (1983), *Criminal Law Review*, 198.

NFA (1) no further action (by the police, a court, etc), effectively where some matter is 'marked closed'; **(2)** no fixed abode/address.

NG not guilty

NIP notice of intended prosecution (as a prerequisite for the police re certain road traffic offences: see generally *Chapter 11*)

no case short **'no case to answer'**: *Chapter 7*

NOMS National Offender Management Service

non-police relating to a law enforcement agency other than the ordinary civil police; and hence terms such as 'non-police court': see *Chapter 7*

non-statutory not covered or provided for by **Act** of Parliament; whether a process, method or CJS agency. Hence the term **'non-statutory sector'** re parts of the 'wider criminal justice family': *Chapter 2.*

notes of evidence those taken so as to record evidence by a court legal adviser (or possibly individual magistrates in addition according to local practice) and that may be called for in the event of certain appeals.

NPIA National Policing Improvement Agency

NPS (1) National Probation Service; **(2)** National Policing Strategy.

NS (1) National Standards (above); **(2)** national security.

NSP no separate penalty, i.e. when a court passes sentence for several offences and views matters 'in the round'. It may then decide that re some lesser matters further punishment would be disproportionate in all the circumstances.

NSPCC National Society for the Prevention of Cruelty to Children (which may prosecute)

NW Neighbourhood Watch. Hence also, e.g. **BW** = Boat Watch/Business Watch, **CW** = Car Watch **FW** = Factory Watch/Farm Watch, **PW** = Pub Watch, **SW** = School Watch/Shop Watch.

OAPA (1) Offences Against the Person Act 1861

OAsys offender assessment system (as used by the **NPS**)

oath (1) that of a witness giving sworn testimony in the courtroom (or alternatively after making an affirmation). **(2)** For **oath of allegiance** and **judicial oath** see *Chapter 3.*

occasional court one held outside normal hours

OCJR Office for Criminal Justice Reform

offender Someone convicted of a criminal offence, i.e. as opposed to a (mere) **suspect** or **accused person**, both of whom are entitled to the presumption of innocence: *Chapter 5*

OJC Office for Judicial Complaints. Note that complaints re magistrates go initially to the **Advisory Committee** (*Chapter 2*).

ONSET A **YJB/YOT** assessment tool: *Chapter 8*

openness A virtue demanded of justice-related matters along with accountability, visibility and transparency. Hence, e.g. **open court** and further **'opening up of the courts'** as mentioned in *Chapters 8* and *9* in particular.

operational period that of a suspended sentence, i.e. the length of time for which it is suspended and the offender at risk of it being activated if he or she commits another offence

opinion the general rule is that evidence must be as to facts not opinions; but **experts** (above) can give opinion evidence once they have been accepted as such by the court. However, it is the court and not the expert who will then decide whether to accept the opinion offered (and there may be disagreements between experts for the opposing parties).

ordinary language legal requirements mean that various explanations must be given in 'ordinary language', i.e. avoiding technical, obscure or exclusive terms

OPSI Office for Public Sector Information: see opsi.gov.uk

original offence looking back, that which is the subject of current breach proceedings, enforcement, etc.

OSCT Office for Security and Counter-Terrorism

out-of-time beyond a legal time limit

PAC Penal Affairs Consortium

PACE Police and Criminal Evidence Act 1984. Hence also the **PACE codes** made under that Act relating to police **detention**, etc.

paperwork a term used in various situations where a case is conducted 'on the papers', as with written pleas of guilty (*Chapters 7*); and also when a court is 'clearing up paperwork' once cases with live participants are complete

parental responsibility/matters See *Chapters 8* and *9* re juveniles and children, respectively.

party the **party to a case**. In a criminal case the parties are the prosecutor and accused; although their lawyers and defence teams are sometimes loosely described using the same terminology. Those involved in other roles are often described as 'participants'.

PB (1) Parole Board; **(2)** Prisons Board. **(3)** Probation Board.

PBA Probation Boards Association

PBV plea before venue: *Chapters 7*

PC (1) police constable; **(2)** previous convictions; **(3)** Privy Council; **(4)** probation centre; **(5)** politically correct (general usage).

PCA Proceeds of Crime Act 2000

PCSO police community support officer (aka a **CSO**)

PDO potentially dangerous offender

penalty points those endorsed on a driving licence under the scheme for totting up in relation to road traffic (and certain other) offences: see *Chapter 11*

PF Police Federation

PGA Prison Governors Association

PII public interest immunity. It is possible for certain people who have participated in crimes to be granted PII: see specialist works

PIO (1) principal investigating officer; **(2)** Public Information Office (for its full title see **OPSI**)

plea the answer given by an **accused person** when asked by the court legal adviser how he or she pleads to a charge, either a **guilty plea** or a **plea of not guilty**. Note also **plea before venue** and **written plea of guilty** in *Chapter 7*.

PNC Police National Computer

PN/D See **FPN/D**

PO (1) public order; **(2)** probation officer. Hence also **CPO, PPO, SPO**.

POA (1) Public Order Act (various years); **(2)** Prison Officers Association

POTF Persistent Offender Task Force (multi-agency)

POU Public Order Unit (police)

PPO (1) principal probation officer; **(2)** Prisons and Probation Ombudsman.

preliminary hearing one at the start of a cse as part of case management: see *Chapters 7*.

prevalence the prevalence of an offence which may be a reason to impose a more severe

sentence than would otherwise have been the case: subject to **guidelines**

previous previous convictions aka **form**

prima facie on the face of it

printout usually a reference to a **DVLA** printout of a driver's record when a driving licence is not forthcoming

pronouncement pronouncement of a sentence, order or other decision; usually following forms of 'pronouncements' such as those recommended by the **JSB**: see jsboard.co.uk

PRT Prison Reform Trust: A leading penal reform group: see prison-reform-trust.org.uk

PSO probation service officer (who has lesser qualifications than a probation officer but who may carry out certain routine NPS tasks)

PSR pre-sentence report, usually meaning by the **NPS** or a **YOT**. See also **FDR** and **SDR**.

PTS pre-trial services

PYO persistent young offender: *Chapter 8*

QC Queen's Counsel (aka **'silk'**), i.e. a senior barrister who wears a silk gown

qualified right See human rights in *Chapter 5*

R Regina (or Rex), i.e. the Crown as in *R v. Smith and Jones*

RCC Rainer Crime Concern, a leading crime prevention charity: see raineronline.org

reasons reasons for a decision; including **grounds and reasons** for refusing bail, etc: *Chapters 11*. Reasons must nowadays be given in various specific situations and generally under human rights law. See also **justices' reasons** above.

recall to prison (which is an **MOJ/HMPS/NPS** function rather than that of a court)

reciprocal enforcement enforcement of orders across State boundaries on a *quid pro quo* basis

recognizance a formal promise to pay/forfeit a sum of money in the event of some future occurrence: as with a surety for bail (*Chapter 7*), **binding over** (*Chapter 10*), or to prosecute an appeal (*Chapter 2*) (when it would be forfeited in the event of an unreasonable failure to do so). Hence terms such as **taking a recognizance** for the process whereby the person concerned makes this promise to the Crown by signing a document, aka **'a recognizance'.**

recorder In a **judicial** context, a part-time circuit judge (but note that the Recorder of London is the senior circuit judge there). **Assistant recorder** is a description used pending any promotion to recorder. A **Practice Direction**

ets out the kinds of case with which each rank of Crown Court judge can normally deal.

rectification i.e. of mistakes: see *Chapter 2*

referral referral to agency or service, e.g. for assessment, treatment or an opinion. **Hence** also the **referral order** to a **YOP** of a juvenile by a youth court: *Chapter 10.*

Regina/Rex See **R**

register the official court record of outcomes

regulation usually one made under an **Act** and dealing with minutiae or detail not contained in or enacted at the time of the Act itself. However, regulations have increasingly included more significant content, including many new criminal offences.

remand whereas cases are **adjourned**, accused or convicted people are remanded (except in lesser cases when there can be a simple adjournment), either by way of a **remand in custody** or **remand on bail.** Hence also **remand centre** re young offenders (usually). Hence terms such as **remand wing** at a prison.

remit transfer a case or matter to another court (or in other senses to 'someone else'), as with remission of a juvenile case by the adult court to the youth court. Note also that fines can be remitted (meaning in this case wholly or partly 'written-off') in some circumstances: *Chapter 7*

re-open re-start a case, usually re **rectification**

reparation putting matters right or repairing harm, actually or metaphorically, vis-à-vis a victim re injury, loss or damage. Various reparation schemes exist, especially re juveniles.

representation usually a reference to **legal representation**, including **State funded legal representation**, aka legal aid: *Chapter 7*

reprimand normally a reference to the scheme of **reprimands and warnings** for juveniles: *Chapter 10*. But the term is also sometimes used to describe an admonishment by a bench when someone is sentenced, in effect a 'telling-off' and exhortation to future good conduct.

requirement usually that of a community sentence or release licence (or as attached to some other forms of sentence): *Chapter 7*

restorative justice (RJ) A form of justice which focuses on repairing harm rather than processes which enhance conflict, distress, pain, formality, etc. In a criminal justice context it does so by marking the seriousness of the offence (using punishment and/or shaming) linked to reparation, rehabilitation and reintegration into the community. It can be traced to the 12th century; and is often linked to 'sentencing circles' (especially those in New Zealand, Australia and the Middle-East. The **Restorative Justice Consortium (RJC)** is a nationwide collective of RJ-based organizations and a good starting point for information: see restorativejustice.org.uk

restraining order an order to prevent harassment under the Protection From Harassment Act 1997: *Chapter 10*

restriction A word with various CJS connotations: the lawful **restriction of liberty** of lawbreakers having existed since Roman times (at least). Since 1991 it has been a broad sentencing concept in England and Wales. Note also **restriction order**: one preventing given activities (but note that this term is also applied to certain civil court orders and also bankruptcy). Magistrate may impose **reporting restrictions** pending the outcome of a trial or concerning a juvenile; and there are certain standing reporting restrictions as noted in *Chapter 2*. The term is also to be found in contexts such as **legal restriction** or **physical restriction** aka 'restraint' (as per 'control and restraint' of a difficult prisoner).

review is the reappraisal or revisiting of events, usually by an independent and/or higher or specially appointed authority that may exercise related powers or make recommendations. Hence, e.g. the **Criminal Cases Review Commission**. Hence also **review by a Crown prosecutor** of a case file under a continuing duty; **review of police detention**; and **judicial review**: see *Chapter 2*. **Review of the Criminal Courts** refers to the *Auld Report* and **Review of the Sentencing Framework** the *Halliday Report*, prior to the Courts Act 2003 and Criminal Justice Act 2003, respectively.

retiring room the magistrates' own quarters attached to the courtroom where they can 'retire' by way of an **adjournment** to consider their verdict, sentence, etc. in private; and see *Chapter 6* where they need legal advice.

revocation cancellation of a sentence or order

RIC remand in custody

RIPA Regulation of Investigatory Powers Act

2000 (pronounced 'reaper')

RJ restorative justice See the explanation above

ROSH risk of serious harm

Royal Courts Royal Courts of Justice in (and hence aka) The Strand, Central London, where some of the higher courts are located: *Chapter 2.*

RSPCA Royal Society for the Prevention of Cruelty to Animals

RSPB Royal Society for the Protection of Birds

RT road traffic. Hence, e.g. **RTA** = Road Traffic Act or road traffic accident; **RTI** = road traffic incident; **RTO** = road traffic offence; **RTRA** = Road Traffic Regulations Act.

rule usually in a **CJS** context a reference to a statutory or Common Law rule

SAP Sentencing Advisory Panel

SAR (obligatory) suspicious activity report, i.e. by a bank, lawyer, business, etc. to various prosecuting authorities

scheduled listed somewhere, but usually meaning in an Act of Parliament, as with a **schedule of offences** to which a particular power, jurisdiction or provision applies. The term is also used to signify **scheduling** as it applies to court sittings (whereas 'listing' usually signifies the more precise allocation of cases to individual dates and courtrooms).

SDR standard delivery report, i.e. a full **PSR**

SE social exclusion. Hence **SEU** for Social Exclusion Unit (of government). Inclusive strategies are intended to reduce crime.

section The section of an Act of Parliament. Note **'being sectioned'** where someone is suffering from mental impairment, i.e. ordered into hospital: see specialist texts.

sending (1) part of **A&S** (pending); **(2)** but also the correct present description where an indictable only offence (*Chapter 7*) is committed to the Crown Court for trial.

sentencing guideline nowadays a reference to one issued by the **SGC**: *Chapter 7*

'serious enough' the threshold test for a community sentence: see *Chapter 7, Figure 1.*

SFO Serious Fraud Office

SGC Sentencing Guidelines Council

SI Statutory Instrument (a form of **delegated legislation**), often containing **regulations**

silk See **QC**

single justice certain matters can be dealt with by one JP sitting or acting alone, hence this

term is common shorthand re such situations

SOCA Serious Organized Crime Agency

social services usually a reference to the social services department of a local authority (now frequently combined with education duties)

SOCO scenes of crime officer; who, e.g. searches for forensic evidence, materials from which to take samples and conduct tests.

SOCPA Serious and Organized Crime and Police Act 2005

solemn usually a reference to one that the person concerned was unaware of the proceedings against him or her: *Chapter 2*

SOTP Sex Offender Treatment Programme (in prison or in the community)

source a police information or intelligence source, usually, possibly an informer

'so serious' the threshold test for a custodial sentence: see *Chapter 7, Figure 1.*

special reasons See endorsement in *Chapter 11*

specified activities, i.e. in a community sentence

SPO senior probation officer, usually

standard of proof See *Chapter 5*

starting point that within a **guideline**, especially a **starting point**

State funded representation legal aid

statement (1) A formal pronouncement, e.g. by a Minister of State (in the House of Commons or elsewhere and usually in public or in writing). **(2)** Similarly, by the head of an agency/service, etc. or by someone who has secured an acquittal. **(3)** A **statement of facts** is integral to procedures for a **written plea of guilty**: *Chapter 7*, or an appeal by way of case stated: *Chapter 2*. **(4)** According to the context, a **statement of reasons** may be made by a court, a police officer or other official as appropriate, or, e.g. by the **CCRC**. **(5)** A **witness statement** may be used in evidence subject to complying with certain procedures.

statutory instrument See **SI**

stereotyping Categorising someone (or something) by reference to a preconceived notion of their (its) supposed type; by reference to features unlikely to be all-embracing or universally applicable; such that the stereotype may be misleading, prejudicial, or in some instances offensive.

Stone *Stone's Justices' Manual* Leading work on proceedings in magistrates' courts first published in 1842 (now in three blue volumes)

structured decision-making See the explanations in *Chapters 3 , 4* and *7,* especially that on page 149.

submission a submission to the court, e.g. re a point of law or evidence or that there is **no case to answer**

subpoena a witness summons: this more informative term usually being used in criminal proceedings

summary (1) A word used in various contexts, most significantly re **summary justice**, usually meaning: in a technical sense, justice in the magistrates' court which can also be quite correctly described as a **court of summary jurisdiction**; hence also **summary offence** means one triable only in the magistrates' court and the **CJSSS** initiative: *Chapter 7.* **(2)** similarly in relation to military discipline in particular or that under the Prison Rules; **(3)** justice meted out speedily, simply and untrammelled by complex procedures or rules, whether in a court or, e.g. by way of a police **caution, FPN**, etc. but the term having been adopted in particular in modern times to describe 'justice' stemming directly from police or local authority action rather than the courts. **(4)** More loosely, any form of 'justice' which occurs speedily and whether officially (and lawfully) or not. Hence **summary trial** for trial before magistrates. **(5) summary of the prosecution case**: the outline given at the start of a trial or when making **disclosure** ; or **(6)** any synopsis or brief version of events.

sus 'suspicion'. Hence the **sus laws** allowing police to stop and search people 'on suspicion' of an offence (or generally re terrorism).

suspect someone suspected of a criminal offence and who may, e.g. be in police **detention**

surety a surety for bail: *Chapter 7*

suspended sentence suspended sentence of imprisonment: *Chapter 7*

Swansea See **DVLA**

tag an electronic tag as for **EM**

tampering (1) tampering with a motor vehicle, e.g. interfering with the operation of its brakes, steering or to gain entry to it. **(2) tampering with a jury. (3)** Informally, any similar offending behaviour involving 'interference', e.g. with children.

tariff (1) The going rate as per a **sentencing guideline**; or **(2)** one set by a Crown Court judge re a life sentence or certain other sentences, i.e. the time to be served before the offender can be considered for release.

testimony the oral evidence of a witness in the court room on **oath** or **affirmation**

TFO transfer of fine order, i.e. from one **LJA** to another for enforcement

'three strikes' An allusion to the USA rule of baseball whereby the batter is given out if he or she fails to strike the ball during three consecutive attempts. Hence the USA **three strikes law**, or in England and Wales in the Crown Court a **two strikes law** re various mainly serious offences. In the last Queen's Speech of 2008 an intention was announced to pass a **one strike law** re temporary withdrawal of benefits following a false claim.

threshold a hurdle to be surmounted before a particular power, right, etc. can be exercised, particularly a **sentencing threshold**: *Chapter 7*

TIC take(n) into consideration

ticket usually a reference to a **FPN/D**

time limit one restricting events to a given time frame, such as a custody **time limit** or limit for bringing **summary proceedings**

totting-up that under the penalty points system re endorsement and disqualification: *Chapter 11.* Hence defendants who are **'totters'**.

TV Licensing the agency responsible for the enforcement and prosecution of TV licence evasion: see tvlicensing.co.uk

TWC or sometimes (the verb) **'twocking'**: taking a motor vehicle without consent of the owner

UKAEC United Kingdom Atomic Energy Constabulary: see ukaea.org.uk

ultra vires beyond power

Unlock The National Association of Reformed Offenders: see unlock.org.uk

unrepresented usually meaning a defendant who does not have legal **representation**; when there is a duty on the court (discharged via the court legal adviser) to assist him or her

variable points See *Chapter 11*

variation alteration of a sentence or order where applicable/permissible

VASCAR Visual Average Speed Calculator (or Camera) and Recorder

VDR/S Vehicle Defect Rectification/ Scheme: run

by the police as an alternative to prosecution for road traffic offences: see *Chapter 11*

verdict the decision as to whether someone is guilty or not guilty made by magistrates (or a jury in the Crown Court) at the end of a criminal trial. The term is also used coroners' verdicts and more loosely to describe other findings. Criminal cases have two main stages, verdict and (if there is a conviction) sentence.

vexatious litigant one who abuses court process by seeking to bring baseless charges; and who can be deemed 'vexatious' by the High Court so that the magistrates' court does not then have to act on his or her applications

VFM value for money

VP vulnerable person/vulnerable prisoner

VEL vehicle excise licence. Hence the offence of having **no VEL**.

VODS vehicle online descriptive search (police)

VPS victim personal statement, made to a police officer (or possibly a probation officer) and produced in writing to a court for its information before sentence is passed.

VS (1) Victim Support; and hence **VSS** for Victim Support Scheme: *Chapter 7*. **(2)** voluntary sector. **(3)** voluntary service.

warrant usually a reference to court process issued by a magistrate or a judge allowing or requiring an arrest. See also **'backed for bail'**. Note also in particular **WFD** = warrant of further detention: see *Chapter 7*. Note also in particular the term **entry warrant**, i.e. one to enter premises, e.g. for the purposes of a search. In some instances the Home Secretary can issue warrants, e.g. re interception of communications (aka 'intercepts').

warning (1) any general warning by the police re a hazard or future conduct and sometimes re the latter by a court; but **(2)** specifically a reference to the system of **warnings and reprimands** for juveniles: *Chapter 8*.

welfare The CJS has long been associated with welfare aspects of offending, not least through the work and history of the Probation Service and rehabilitation. Many organizations operate in this field. For **welfare principles** and **welfare checklists**, see *Chapters 8* and *9*.

'winger' a magistrate who sits to one side of the bench chair in court. There are usually two wingers. The Initial Training of magistrates

(*Chapter 3*) is often dubbed 'winger training'.

written plea one under the paperwork procedures described in *Chapter 7*

written statement one made in writing by a witness and that may be admissible as evidence in criminal proceedings provided that related procedures have been followed

WS Witness Service

YC youth custody

YCAP (or **Y-cap**) youth crime action plan (national or local): *Chapter 8*

YJ youth justice. Hence also, e.g. **YJB** = Youth Justice Board; **YJS** = Youth Justice System; **YJT** = Youth Justice Team.

YO young offender: one aged 18 to 20 inclusive

YOI young offender institution

YOP youth offending panel (aka referral order panel): *Chapter 8*

YOT youth offending team

youth alternative term for a juvenile: *Chapter 8*

YP (1) young person (14-17 years): *Chapter 8*; **(2)** young prisoner (18-20 inclusive).

The *Pocket A-Z of Criminal Justice* (2009) contains 2000 entries and cross-references drawn from 'The Language of the Criminal Justice System'. It also includes a wide-ranging section on *Touchstones and Curiosities*, an extensive *Glossary* and a substantial *Timeline*.

To view extracts visit WatersidePress.co.uk

A Timeline of Summary Justice

1150	Keepers of the Peace emerge: the first traces of magistrates
1195	Richard I (1189-1199) appoints knights in various parts of the country swear-in men over 15 to act as Conservators of the Peace
1197	First Fleet Prison built in London
1215	Magna Carta: an enduring foundation for rights and liberties
1361	Justices of the Peace Act (containing a power to bind people over: *Chapter 10*). A lone justice is often local judge, 'policeman' and administrator.
1406	Each parish must erect a wooden stocks and pillory
1550s	Bail and committal statutes, including the **1555** 'Marian Committal Statute' which requires JPs to conduct speedy pre-trial examinations of defendants following their arrest. An era of corruption: magistrates gradually being dubbed 'basket justices' from the practice of carrying a basket for bribes to be placed in, or placing it in front of the bench. Bridewells (town and city gaols) foreshadow police cells and local prisons.
1572	Stricter punishments for beggars. Constables punished for ignoring them.
1615	Transportation begins as an alternative to capital punishment
1650	Prison expansion: then as now partly using the private sector
1660	Watchmen, aka 'bellmen' or 'Charleys' (after Charles II) paid to keep watch, especially at night. Magistrates get the power to call in the militia after reading the Riot Act.
1689	Glorious Revolution and Bill of Rights: Parliament free from the Crown (as are the judges gradually). The start of the separation of powers. Excessive bail, fines and cruel and unusual punishments are outlawed.
1701	Act of Settlement establishes a fragile form of judicial independence
1730	An Act for the Better Regulation of Juries is passed after MPs hear of 'evil practices', abuses and corruption
1739	Bow Street Magistrates' Court opens
1748	Sir Henry Fielding becomes stipendiary magistrate there
1749	Bow Street Runners
1774	Gaol Act passed after John Howard (1726-1729) highlights abuses and in **1777** his ground-breaking *The State of Prisons, etc.* is published
1780	The Old Bailey and Newgate Prison destroyed in the Gordon Riots
1789	French Revolution leads to repression across England and Ireland

1791	Barrister William Garrow establishes the presumption of innocence (in the trial of George Dingler at The Old Bailey on a charge of murder)
1794	Habeus corpus suspended (as at many later times of emergency)
1800	Increasing levels of imprisonment of offenders and the 'dispossessed'. Dirty prisons. A time of gaol fever.
1812	A Parliamentary Select Committee report leads to increased police powers. Magistrates get supervisory powers re the police.
1815	Society for Investigating the Causes of the Alarming Increase of Juvenile Delinquency in the Metropolis formed. Corn Law riots.
1822	Robert Peel becomes Home Secretary. Police wear 'blue lobster' uniforms, i.e. blue coats and red waistcoats.
1823	Gaol Act lets magistrates regulate prisons and prescribes a prison diet
1825	*Archbold's Criminal Pleading and Practice* first published
1826	Police reform. Magistrates' courts now commonly known as 'police courts'.
1829	Metropolitan Police Service (MPS) formed as 'The New Police'
1837	Vagrancy Act targets rogues, vagabonds and the 'idle and disorderly'. *Justice of the Peace* newspaper first published (since **2009** the *Criminal Law & Criminal Justice Weekly* incorporating *Justice of the Peace*).
1838	Horse Patrol removed from the jurisdiction of the chief magistrate
1839	Bow Street Runners disbanded. Justices' Clerks' Society formed
1842	*Stone's Justices' Manual* first published
1847	Juvenile Offenders Act gives magistrates power to sentence children aged 14 or under to a whipping.
1848	Summary Jurisdiction Act (aka Jervis's Act after Attorney General Sir John Jervis) greatly enlarges the judicial powers and duties of magistrates
1850	Juvenile Offenders Act
1855	Criminal Justice Act paves the way for a further expansion of the work of magistrates in the 19th and 20th centuries. They eventually deal with over 95 per cent of all criminal cases.
1861	Larceny Act. Offences Against the Person Act (the latter still in being).
1862	Whipping of Offenders Act restricts whipping to 12 strokes for juveniles
1865	Prison Act enables 'hard bed, hard board and hard fare'
1880	London Police Court Mission established as a philanthropic befriending service to provide help and support to offenders seeking to 'mend their ways': the origins of the Probation Service (see also **1907**)

1895	Herbert Gladstone's report on prisons recommends the abolition of the prison treadmill, less solitary confinement and a better diet for prisoners; and as many offenders as possible are to be kept out of prison altogether. Recidivism the report declares, is 'a growing stain on our civilisation'.
1904	Early road traffic laws in the wake of 'arrogant behaviour' by motorists
1907	Birth of the Probation Service and probation supervision as the Probation of Offenders Act allows courts to 'suspend' a sentence if the offender is placed under probation supervision
1908	Children Act (aka the 'Childrens Charter') deals with child protection; forbids the imprisonment of children; and establishes juvenile courts. Older juveniles can only be sent to prison if a court issues an 'unruly certificate'. Local authorities get power to keep poor children out of the workhouse and protect them from abuse (the genesis of social services). Children barred from dangerous trades and buying tobacco or alcohol. Prevention of Crime Act introduces borstal training based on an experimental scheme located in the village of Borstal in Kent.
1916	Another Larceny Act (the predecessor of the Theft Act **1968**)
1920	Magistrates' Association founded.
1922	Herbert Rowse Armstrong, justices' clerk for Hay-on-Wye, Powys is executed for murder at Gloucester Prison after poisoning his wife and attempting to do the same to a rival solicitor. He remains the only lawyer in modern times to undergo capital punishment (but historically there are several, including famously St Thomas More (1478-1535)).
1932	House of Lords case of *Woolmington v Director of Public Prosecutions* reaffirms the burden and standard of proof in all criminal cases: the prosecutor must prove his or her case beyond reasonable doubt (*Chapter 5*).
1933	Children and Young Persons Act establishes the 'welfare principle' which applies to children in all courts and still exists alongside other considerations whenever children are involved in court processes: *Chapters 8* and *9*
1948	European Convention On Human Rights and Fundamental Freedoms
1952	Magistrates' Courts Act creates a comprehensive framework. Prison Act.
1957	Magistrates' Courts Act introduces written pleas of guilty. Where 'MCA procedures' are adopted in lesser cases and the offender writes to the court pleading guilty there is no longer a need, as there was before, for the prosecutor to prove the case by calling evidence and/or the accused person to attend court. The start of more streamlined procedures.

1959	A 45 per cent rise in reported crime over a decade and a trebling of violence over the same period leads to police pay increases in the face of a 14% shortfall in officers
1960	Ingleby Report on Children and Young Persons in Custody. Prison(er) population reaches 25,000.
1961	Criminal Justice Act. Detention centre powers and regimes for juveniles and young offenders modified. Streatfield Report on the Business of the Criminal Courts.
1962	Magistrates' Association granted a Royal Charter
1964	Home Office publishes the *The Sentence of the Court*: see *Chapter 7*
1967	Road Safety Act introduces the breathalyser and a novel offence of 'excess alcohol' determined by sampling blood or urine. Criminal Law Act sees the birth of 'paper committals' to expedite the transfer of cases to (what is now) the Crown Court thereby saving the resources formerly devoted to recording live evidence in court known as taking 'depositions'
1968	Theft Act 'codifies' the law of theft, etc. in place of the Larceny Act 1916
1969	Children and Young Person's Act revises the powers of the juvenile court and introduces a twin-track system of care and criminal proceedings.
1970	Embryonic Magistrates' Association Sentencing Guidelines. Prison(er) population reaches 35,000.
1971	Beeching Report leads to the abolition of Assizes and Quarter Sessions and the creation of the Crown Court in their place. Criminal Damage Act 'codifies' such offences, including arson and aggravated offences.
1972	Criminal Justice Act introduces community service (now a requirement of 'unpaid work') and a power to defer sentence (see *Chapter 7*)
1973	Powers of Criminal Courts Act introduces the suspended sentence Family proceedings court created under the umbrella of the magistrates' court
1974	Community service begins (at first as 'an alternative to custody'). It later becomes the community punishment order and, in **2003**, a requirement of 'unpaid work' within a generic community sentence. Rehabilitation of Offenders Act introduces 'spent' convictions (on a graduated scale) which need not be disclosed, e.g. to employers but which are still made known to a criminal court when sentencing (but marked 'spent').
1976	Bail Act 'codifies' the general right to bail and gives a new impetus to the way in which remand applications are dealt with.

1977	Criminal Law Act increases the powers of the juvenile court (later the youth court) and introduces 'partly suspended' sentences of imprisonment (which prove unpopular with the judiciary and are quietly abandoned)
1978	Another Theft Act adds further offences of dishonesty, etc.
1980	Magistrates' Courts Act and subsequent Rules update those of **1952**
1981	Road Traffic Regulations Act. Contempt of Court Act. Criminal Attempts Act.
1982	Criminal Justice Act abolishes borstal, modifies detention centre orders and introduces youth custody. First Juvenile Justice Units (JJUs), the forerunners of youth offending teams (YOTs), become influential in taking 'initiatives' with young people and creating schemes to divert juveniles from custody. Juvenile custody falls dramatically, but later begins to rise again as the wider political mood changes.
1984	Police and Criminal Evidence Act (PACE) and PACE Codes in response to a number of high profile miscarriages of justice.
1985	Crown Prosecution Service (CPS) formed. Increasing diversity of benches.
1986	Public Order Act updates an earlier such statute of **1936**
1988	Home Office publishes *Punishment, Custody and the Community*. Criminal Justice Compensation Board created. An era of private sector involvement in the provision of CJS services begins, at first with private remand prisons and prisoner escort services.
1990	Home Office issues *Crime, Justice and Protecting the Public* as a prelude to major criminal justice reforms. Courts and Legal Services Act. *Victims Charter*. Victim Support (*Chapter 7*) develops: an independent charity which helps people cope with the effects of crime by providing free and confidential support and information. Prison(er) population 45,000.
1991	Criminal Justice Act introduces the first statutory sentencing framework, based on just deserts and proportionality. First directly CJS-related anti-discrimination provisions are introduced.
1992	First National Standards for probation work.
1993	Stephen Lawrence is murdered in Eltham, South-London and the Metropolitan Police Service is later found to be institutionally racist. Criminal Justice Act abolishes key parts of the **1991** Act (including 'unit fines' and a rule that previous convictions should not be taken into account when sentencing). The era of 'prison works'.

1994	Police and Magistrates' Courts Act severs funding links between the Home Office and magistrates' courts and transfers responsibility to the Lord Chancellor's Department (later to become the Department of Constitutional Affairs and eventually in **2007** the Ministry of Justice). Criminal Justice and Public Order Act. First inroads into the historic right to silence. Local justice areas (LJAs) replace petty sessional divisions.
1995	Home Office publishes *Protecting the Public*. Witness support schemes develop leading to the Witness Service: *Chapter 7*.
1997	Home Office publishes *No More Excuses: A New Approach to Tackling Youth Crime*. Justices of the Peace Act. Law Commission report on evidence in criminal proceedings.
1998	Crime and Disorder Act introduces the Youth Justice Board (YJB), youth offending teams (YOTS), a principle aim of youth justice (preventing offending) and the first anti-social behaviour order (ASBO) provisions. Human Rights Act makes the European Convention of **1948** part of English law. Magistrates' New Training Initiative (MINTI) begins.
1999	Access to Justice Act revises legal aid and legal services. Youth Justice and Criminal Evidence Act.
2000	Criminal Justice and Court Services Act creates the National Probation Service (NPS) and renames community sentences in terms of punishment and/or rehabilitation. An era of enhanced public protection begins: expansion of databases, increasing reliance on science and technology, identification procedures, surveillance and border controls, evidence-led policing, targeting of offenders and the proceeds of crime. Terrorism Acts passed regularly from now on. Prison(er) population reaches 65,000.
2001	Criminal Defence Service (CDS) established. Criminal Justice and Police Act. Halliday Report and Auld Report make recommendations concerning the sentencing framework and the structure of the criminal courts, respectively. Home Office publishes a series of White Papers, including *Criminal Justice: The Way Forward*. September 11 (USA) triggers an era of yet more heightened security.
2002	Child Exploitation and Online Protection Agency (CEOP) established. White Paper, *Justice For All*. Police Reform Act gives the Home Secretary stronger default powers re police forces, creates an Independent Police Complaints Commission (IPCC) and expands anti-social behaviour powers. allowing the police to issue fixed penalty notices for disorder (FPNDs). Bench Training and Development Committees (BTDCs) introduced.

2003	Carter Report proposes a National Offender Management Service (NOMS) and leads to a greater and more diverse range of service provision to the CJS by the private sector, voluntary sector and public sector 'in competition' (known as 'contestability'). Criminal Justice Act revises the sentencing framework; creates statutory purposes of sentencing for adults; new sentences (some not yet in force); and creates a Sentencing Guidelines Council (SGC). For all of these see *Chapter 7*. Introduction of the *Adult Court Bench Book* by the Judicial Studies Board (JSB).
2005	Serious Organized Crime and Police Act (SOCPA) creates the Serious Organized Crime Agency. London bombings ('July 7'). Home Office publishes *Rebuilding Lives: Supporting Victims of Crime*. Constitutional Reform Act transfers key judicial responsibilities to the Lord Chief Justice. Magistrates' New Training Initiative becomes MINTI2.
2006	Criminal Defence Service Act. Police and Justice Act. Violent Crime Reduction Act. Road Safety Act. Racial and religious hatred legislation.
2007	Bow Street Magistrates' Court closes. Ministry of Justice (MOJ) created. Home Office restructured after Home Secretary Dr. John Reid announces that it is 'not fit for purpose'. Prisons and probation join the courts under the umbrella of the MOJ (with judicial matters dealt with separately: see *Chapter 2*). Lord Chancellor becomes 'Justice Secretary and Lord Chancellor'. Department for Children Schools and Families (DCSF) assumes de facto responsibility for juveniles. Offender Management Act. Serious Crime Act creates the serious crime prevention order (or 'gangster ASBO': *Chapter 10*) and revises incitement and related offences. Enhanced diversity initiatives re the appointment of magistrates building on those from the 1980s onwards.
2008	MOJ issues 'HM Courts Service Framework'. Criminal Justice and Immigration Act makes wide-ranging provision, including re the police, offender management, criminal law, crime and disorder, international fine enforcement, immigration status in certain cases involving 'criminality', automatic deportation of offenders and the maintenance of public order. Sentencing Guidelines Council (SGC) publishes 'The Magistrates' Court Sentencing Guidelines' (*Chapter 7*). It is estimated that some 3,000 criminal offences have been added to the statute book since 1997. Prison(er) population exceeds 80,000.
2009	Youth justice reforms scheduled for the autumn: *Chapter 10*. Home Office announces plans to allow open searching by postcode linked to court results to discover 'who the criminals are in the neighbourhood'.

Index

Found this useful?

The Magistrates' Court is one of several titles in the Introductory Series:

The Criminal Justice System
An Introduction
by Bryan Gibson and Paul Cavadino, with the assistance of David Faulkner.

Youth Justice and The Youth Court
An Introduction
by Mike Watkins and Diane Johnson

Police and Policing
An Introduction
by Peter Villiers

The New Ministry of Justice
An Introduction
by Bryan Gibson

The New Home Office
An Introduction
by Bryan Gibson

A History of Criminal Justice
In England and Wales
by John Hostettler

The Pocket A-Z of Criminal Justice
by Bryan Gibson

Build your set at all good bookshops, online and **WatersidePress.co.uk**

� WATERSIDE PRESS
Putting justice into words

Printed by BoD™in Norderstedt, Germany